T0301568

Qualitative Comparative Analysis

Qualitative Comparative Analysis

Learning from Cases

Roel Rutten

Associate Professor, Department of Organization Studies, Tilburg University and Senior Research Consultant, European Regional Affairs Consultants (ERAC), the Netherlands

Edward Elgar
PUBLISHING

Cheltenham, UK • Northampton, MA, USA

Published by
Edward Elgar Publishing Limited
The Lypiatts
15 Lansdown Road
Cheltenham
Glos GL50 2JA
UK

Edward Elgar Publishing, Inc.
William Pratt House
9 Dewey Court
Northampton
Massachusetts 01060
USA

A catalogue record for this book
is available from the British Library

Library of Congress Control Number: 2024942860

This book is available electronically in the **Elgar**online
Economics subject collection
https://doi.org/10.4337/9781839104527

ISBN 978 1 83910 451 0 (cased)
ISBN 978 1 83910 452 7 (eBook)

Printed and bound in Great Britain by
TJ Books Limited, Padstow, Cornwall

Contents

Preface

RECLAIMING THE Q FOR QUALITATIVE IN QCA

The second AQCA meeting, the Annual QCA event of the Americas, held at the University of Southern California (USC) campus in Los Angeles, hosted 'A conversation with Charles Ragin'. During this conversation, which took place on Friday 17 March, 2023, Charles was asked whether large-N QCA should develop a logic of its own or follow the logic of small-N QCA. Without a moment's hesitation, Charles returned that it should follow the logic of small-N QCA. This logic, which he first laid down in 1987 in *The Comparative Method*, entails a commitment to intimate case knowledge and interpretation rather than parameters of fit.

I have always interpreted QCA as, what I think, Ragin designed it to be: a method for learning from cases by dialoguing knowledge of cases, context and concepts – a qualitative method. This is what I read in Ragin's original QCA book (1987 [2014]); in his brilliant essay on '"Casing" and the process of social inquiry' (1992); and his 'Reflections on casing and case-oriented research' (2009). These latter two book chapters, to me, capture the case-based methodological foundations on which Ragin developed QCA. The way I have always understood Ragin's work is that Boolean algebra in QCA serves to make cross-case comparison more rigorous and systematic than is the case in other comparative case study methods (e.g., Eisenhardt, 2021 and Gioia, Corley and Hamilton, 2013). However, Boolean expressions must not be mistaken for causal claims. Boolean expressions describe cross-case patterns and must be interpreted into causal claims based on what they mean, which follows from dialoguing knowledge of cases, context and concepts. In other words, QCA combines the analytical rigour of quantitative methods (from its use of Boolean algebra) with the interpretive strength of qualitative methods (by going back and forth between empirical and theoretical knowledge). There is a crucial difference between mathematical sufficiency and substantive sufficiency. The former identifies consistent subset relationships between explanatory conditions and outcomes. The latter is a plausible (substantive) explanation of the outcome that also draws from knowledge of cases, context and concepts. Finding consistent subset relationships does not amount to having a substantive explanation.

However, recent years have revealed an emphasis on quantification in both applications of QCA and in its methodological development. QCA studies published in scientific journals are increasingly large-N studies with little or no recourse to cases, and which, consequently, rely heavily on parameters of fit for causal inference. Such studies suggest QCA as a data-analytical technique not unlike regression analysis, where cases are reduced to rows in a spreadsheet, rather than understood holistically as events that happened in social reality. To me, this defeats the essence of a case-based method. QCA was developed, at least partially, in response to quantitative methods disassembling social reality into decontextualized variables. But reducing cases to rows in a database achieves just that. Drawing from knowledge of cases, context and concepts to interpret Boolean expressions becomes that much harder, and researchers may be tempted to conflate Boolean expressions with causal statements. I do not think that such studies qualify as QCA any longer. Not if we take Ragin's above comment seriously.

Methodological developments in QCA have facilitated this quantification, although I must stress that this was never the intention of any of my QCA colleagues developing parameters of fit and robustness tests. Such metrics were only ever meant to help researchers interpret set relationships. They were never intended as hard, empirical criteria and must never be applied mechanically. However, lacking recourse to cases, this is exactly what happens in many QCA studies. The increasing focus on parameters of fit in the QCA methods literature has legitimized this development. There are genuine concerns about QCA's case sensitivity, and parameters of fit reveal just how sensitive a particular solution is. But as QCA is not an empirical method in the sense that, for example, regression analysis is an empirical method, it is not at all obvious why a lack of robustness should be problematic. If researchers carefully define their case population and carefully calibrate their cases, then the solution they find is always the correct solution for that case population. Generalization in QCA is analytical to comparable cases, not empirical to a given population. The trouble starts when cases and case populations are not clearly defined and calibrations are poorly substantiated. But these are problems of poor practice that no amount of robustness testing will solve. Nor do higher consistencies of set relationships make for better descriptions of cross-case patterns. Given the heterogeneity of social reality, we cannot expect to find perfect set relationships and should not benchmark our empirical findings against them. Any consistency of 0.8 or higher suggests that the set relationship is empirically valid and may be causally interpreted. What matters is the plausibility of the interpretation, not the empirical robustness of the set relationship from which it is interpreted. In other words, the validity of case-based causal claims is a function of the quality of the underlying dialogue between knowledge of cases, context and concepts. This position echoes that of Amrhein, Greenland

and McShane (2019) in *Nature*, who argued that substantive arguments rather than *p*-values must decide what is a good explanation.

However, QCA seems to be moving away from its qualitative anchors to assume the appearance of a quantitative approach. Owing to generations of training in quantitative methods, the search for robust empirical patterns equals good practice for most social scientists. I am not disputing the merits of quantitative methods, but qualitatively oriented case-based methods follow a different logic – and QCA is one of those methods. In this book, I have set myself the task of reclaiming the Q for qualitative in QCA, to do justice to the interpretive nature of QCA that is so obvious in Ragin's work. Emphasizing QCA's quantitative elements at the expense of its qualitative elements does not amount to learning from cases. Lacking case-based knowledge to interpret Boolean expressions into causal claims, it is better to turn to other (set-theoretical) methods – for example, set coincidence analysis (Ragin and Fiss, 2017). Choosing QCA is to commit oneself to the logic first explained by Ragin in 1987, and which he so passionately defended in Los Angeles in March 2023. My aim is to demonstrate this logic and how it pervades every step of a QCA study. This, I feel, is underdeveloped in the otherwise excellent QCA handbooks currently available. It makes this book a handbook in the strict sense of the word. It explains QCA, emphasizing its qualitative logic. After reading this book, readers should feel comfortable about starting to use QCA. This book does not place QCA in a broader context nor discuss its relative strengths and weaknesses. Other handbooks (e.g., Mello, 2021; Schneider and Wagemann, 2012) have done that admirably and I have nothing to add to that. My aim is simply to explain how good QCA is done and I hope readers find this book a helpful resource.

Acknowledgements

While this book is my own, it benefitted tremendously from many years of wonderful conversations with my QCA colleagues. From my first participation in a QCA meeting, in Wuppertal, Germany, in 2018, I felt welcome in this diverse and intellectually open community. I am immensely grateful to the colleagues who organized the many QCA events that I visited over the years. To Johannes Meuer, Manuel Fischer, Sofia Pagliarin and Christian Rupietta for the many QCA meetings in Zürich, Switzerland. To Claude Rubinson, Peer Fiss, Gary Goertz and Jim Mahoney for AQCA, the Annual QCA meetings in the USA. To Bart Cambré, Peer Fiss and Johannes Meuer for the biannual QCA subtheme at the European Group for Organization Studies (EGOS) meetings. And to Benoît Rihoux and Bart Cambré for the QCA meetings in Antwerp, Belgium. They were inspiring platforms where I could learn and grow. During these events, I gradually felt that I had something to contribute to the ongoing debate on QCA, which fundamentally is to use critical realism as the science-philosophical foundation for QCA's interpretive approach. The comments and feedback I received on my work at the QCA events confirmed my belief and encouraged me to write this book.

In addition to the persons I have mentioned above, I am grateful for the wonderful exchanges I had with Giulia Bazzan, Adrian Duşa, Santi Furnari, Lasse Gerrits, Thomas Greckhamer, Federico Iannacci, Julia Leib, Nena Oana, Vallery Pattyn, Carsten Schneider and Eva Thomann. They and many others were sometimes enthusiastic and sometimes critical of my ideas, but always in a constructive and friendly way. It helped me tremendously to shape and polish my ideas, particularly where they depart from 'mainstream' QCA (if there is such a thing).

My departure from mainstream QCA is also my main contribution to QCA – my grounding the method in critical realist philosophy of science. Though I am not the first to make this connection, I do think I connect QCA and critical realism most comprehensively and systematically. Attending the International Association for Critical Realism (IACR) meeting in The Hague in 2022 was very helpful for getting the critical realist bit of my argument right. I am particularly grateful for constructive comments from Margaret Archer, Johnny Go, Phil Gorski and Leigh Price. I am also grateful to Huiwen Gong, Johannes Glückler and Arnoud Lagendijk for the discussions we had on QCA and critical realism in our mutual field of economic geography. And, of course, I am immensely grateful to Charles Ragin. I met him only for the few days of the QCA meeting in Zürich in 2019, but what a privilege it was to connect to the source of QCA. I re-read much of Charles's work preparing for this book and was again amazed by its depth and originality. At times I felt that in writing this book, I was merely reiterating Charles's arguments. And, of course, in many places of the book, I was.

I consider myself an unlikely methodologist. Before I started to engage with QCA in 2016, methodology sat at the very fringe of my research interests. Having been educated in a mainstream social science school, methods for me equalled correlations and statistics. And I have always thought of those as too stylized to talk about social reality. Ragin's work and its emphasis on learning from cases opened up a whole new world for me. Working with all the people I have mentioned, and all those I did not, helped me explore this world and make it my academic habitat. It is profoundly satisfying that I can now make a contribution to this world of QCA and case-based methods with this book. A very special thankyouverymuch to Peer Fiss and Claude Rubinson for their extremely helpful feedback on the manuscript. And to Claude also for the many hours we talked, on Zoom and in bars, about QCA, about life, and about the most important thing of all, family.

Roel Rutten
Tilburg, January 2024

1.   QCA: learning from cases

Qualitative comparative analysis (QCA) is the comparative case study method developed by Charles Ragin from 1987 onwards (Ragin [1987] 2014). It has since proliferated throughout the social sciences. QCA is a method by which to learn from cases by combining case-level (or singular) and cross-case (or general) causal evidence. The former kind of evidence identifies why or how an outcome happened on the case level. The latter kind of evidence identifies whether this explanation is relevant across cases (Goertz, 2017, p. 5). Being a comparative method, QCA emphasizes cross-case evidence more than case-level evidence; however, both are necessary to make valid causal claims (Rohlfing and Schneider, 2018). Furthermore, being a qualitative method, QCA conducts an ongoing dialogue between conceptual (theoretical) and case-based (empirical) knowledge (Ragin [1987] 2014, pp. 67–8). This dialogue, too, is what helps QCA researchers learn from cases. In other words, causal explanation in QCA goes beyond merely establishing robust cross-case patterns (Ragin, 1992). Establishing cross-case patterns is important for a comparative method, and QCA has developed 'parameters of fit' to evidence their robustness. However, developments in the past 15 years have increasingly emphasized these metrics and partially did so at the expense of the Q for qualitative in QCA (Finn, 2022; Pula, 2021). This book reclaims the qualitative in QCA, hence its subtitle: *Learning from Cases*. QCA's main task is to interpret cross-case patterns into causal claims by asking what they mean. This book highlights how every step in a QCA study is about interpreting meaning from cases and cross-case patterns.

Much of my theoretical and empirical work is in economic geography, and it is from this field that I draw my examples. However, I am confident that social scientists from other disciplines will find my book equally accessible. The present chapter develops the qualitative mindset that is required for learning from cases with QCA – a mindset very different from the quantitative one (Mahoney and Goertz, 2006). First, I explain how QCA combines case-level and cross-case causal evidence. Second, I ground QCA in critical realist philosophy of science (Bhaskar [1975] 2008). The critical realism provides a philosophical legitimization for Ragin's interpretive approach and an important heuristic for QCA researchers. It explains why we must move beyond empirical robustness if we are to make case-based causal claims. The chapter ends with an outline of the book.

1

SINGULAR AND GENERAL CAUSAL EVIDENCE

The principal challenge of case-based causal inference is to connect singular and general causal evidence (Beach and Pedersen, 2016, pp. 42–4; Goertz and Mahoney, 2012a, pp. 87–8). Singular causal evidence is developed from individual (i.e., single) cases. It suggests that, on the case level, an explanatory condition is causally related (or not) to an outcome. Singular causal evidence may be very compelling because it establishes why or how the explanatory condition 'produces' the outcome in a case (or several cases). However, for that very reason, singular causal evidence may be idiosyncratic – that is, highly case specific. Because all cases are unique, time- and place-contingent 'assemblages' of characteristics (explanatory conditions and outcomes), context (scope conditions) and human agents (those actually 'producing' the outcome), there is no reason why a causal relationship established in one case will also be present in another (Decoteau, 2018). Even when the same explanatory and scope conditions are present, different human agents may still achieve different outcomes in different cases (Bhaskar [1975] 2008, pp. 95–7; Delanda, 2016, p. 26). Singular (case-based) causal evidence is vital for case-based causal inference; however, being singular, it is notoriously difficult to generalize to other cases.

General causal evidence is of an entirely different nature. It follows from similarities across cases – that is, from cross-case patterns. General causal evidence comes in the form of constant conjunctions between an explanatory condition and an outcome across a population of cases. Strong and robust cross-case patterns suggest causality in terms of a tendency of the explanatory condition to 'produce' the outcome. However, this may not 'happen' in all cases, nor does it explain why or how it happens (Goertz, 2017, p. 42). The problem is, of course, that a cross-case pattern may be spurious. It may follow from measurement error or be an artefact of the data that does not mean anything, such as the constant conjunction between being a European monarchy and being a democratic country. The constant conjunction between the two is perfect but there is no causal relationship between them. General causal evidence is only meaningful when substantiated by case-level (singular) causal evidence (Rohlfing and Schneider, 2018). Consequently, case-based causal inference is an exercise in connecting singular (case-level) and general (cross-case) causal evidence. One without the other is meaningless; they are both individually necessary but only jointly sufficient to make valid causal claims.

Learning from cases means to develop both singular and general causal evidence from one's cases in order to develop a plausible explanation of an outcome. However, because singular and general causal evidence are very different kinds of evidence, connecting them requires a methodical approach – and that is what QCA delivers. Granted, QCA builds more on general than on singular causal evidence; however, absent a connection to singular causal evidence, all that QCA does is to describe differences and similarities across cases (Ragin [1987] 2014, p. 119). What makes patterns causal is their being connected to singular causal evidence – that is, to meaning. Just as general causal evidence gives relevance to singular causal evidence, singular causal evidence gives meaning to general causal evidence. QCA researchers need not have in-depth knowledge of all their cases, but they must have enough case-level knowledge to meaningfully interpret their cross-case patterns (Thomann and Maggetti, 2020). QCA helps researchers dialogue case-level and cross-case causal evidence via the truth table (see Chapters 2 and 10). Each truth table row contains cases that share the same characteristics (explanatory conditions); however, not all cases may have the same outcome. QCA researchers must resolve these contradictions, drawing from the singular causal evidence from the cases in a row. Thus, resolving contradictory singular causal evidence allows QCA researchers to interpret a row as general (cross-case) evidence for either the presence or the absence of the outcome (Ragin, 2008, pp. 124–30; Schneider and Wagemann, 2012, pp. 120–23). In other words, each truth table row is an (imperfect) cross-case pattern. Whether this cross-case pattern suggests a causal explanation depends not only on the strength of the regularity (i.e., how few 'exceptions' there are) but mostly on whether singular causal evidence from the cases in the row suggests that the pattern means anything.

Having thus established that each row does or does not explain the outcome, QCA then looks for similarities between rows that have the same outcome. Each row is a configuration of explanatory conditions that co-occurs with the presence or absence of the outcome. Looking across rows with the same outcome allows redundant explanatory conditions to be eliminated. Suppose one truth table row suggests that all regions that are wealthy, have a higher-educated population, and are urbanized are also green energy-producing regions. This does not mean that all regions (cases) in this row are green energy producers. Maybe one region is experiencing economic decline and, consequently, has not invested enough in green energy production to be considered a green energy-producing region. However, this 'negative' singular causal evidence does not refute the claim that being wealthy, having a higher-educated population, and being urbanized makes it possible to be a green energy-producing region (Ragin, 2023, p. 60). This is how contradictory singular causal evidence may be interpreted into a general causal claim on the level of a truth table row. Now suppose another truth table row suggests that all regions that are wealthy, have a higher-educated population, and are not urbanized are also green energy-producing regions. The two rows are identical but for the presence of being an urbanized region in the first row and its absence in the second row. Consequently, 'urbanized region' is a redundant condition; when regions are wealthy and have a higher-educated population, being or not being an urbanized region makes no difference to being a green energy-producing region (Ragin [1987] 2014, pp. 36–9). The two rows may thus be simplified to regions that are wealthy and have a higher-educated population are also green energy-producing regions. This cross-case pattern of two conditions is a more general causal claim; it covers more cases – viz., the cases in both rows. But does this more general bit of general causal evidence also suggest a causal explanation? That depends on singular causal evidence making such an explanation plausible (Ragin, 2000, p. 144). In this example, we may plausibly argue that a higher-educated population may push for more green energy, while regional wealth allows the region to invest substantially in green energy production. This is how simplified truth table rows – that is, general causal evidence – may be reconnected to singular causal evidence.

This, in a nutshell, is how QCA makes causal inferences; how QCA learns from cases by dialoguing between singular (case-level) and general (cross-case) causal evidence to develop plausible explanations of the outcome. While developing general causal evidence (identifying cross-case patterns) is a quantitative exercise, learning from cases as a whole is a qualitative exercise. QCA, as are all case-based methods, is a qualitative method because it takes cases seriously as analytically relevant units of analysis (Ragin, 1992, 2009). Instead, quantitative methods abstract from cases and disassemble social reality into decontextualized variables. This allows quantitative methods to identify robust empirical patterns (e.g., statistically significant co-variation between an independent and a dependent variable). However, absent plausible singular causal evidence, it remains unclear what such empirical patterns mean (Abbott, 1988, 1998). In aiming to learn from cases, it is critically important that QCA researchers connect general and singular causal evidence.

THE QUALITATIVE NATURE OF QCA

QCA develops general causal claims in a systematic way, using set analysis and Boolean algebra, and by verbalizing findings as statements of sufficiency and necessity. This systematic use of formal analytical tools and language has led some qualitative researchers to mistake QCA for a quantitative method. Profoundly, it is not. QCA merely makes explicit what remains hidden in other case-based methods (Ragin [1987] 2014, pp. 49–52), such as the Eisenhardt (2021) and Gioia (Gioia et al., 2013) methods. Like most qualitative methods, QCA is based on the logic of the 2 × 2 table, which is, effectively, a very basic truth table (Goertz, 2017, pp. 58–9). The 2 × 2 table assigns cases to a cell depending on their 'having' or 'not having' a condition (X) and an outcome (Y). QCA pursues this logic more rigorously and more systematically than other qualitative methods. However, QCA agrees with other qualitative methods that inferences from systematic comparison can only be made on the basis of intimate knowledge of cases, their context and the concepts used to study them. This is where QCA differs from quantitative methods (Ragin [1987] 2014, pp. 53–4) and from other set-analytical methods that do not require intimate case knowledge (e.g., Baumgartner, 2015; Ragin and Fiss, 2017). Quantitative analysis effectively stops after one has established robust empirical patterns (general causal evidence). Finding robust empirical patterns (e.g., statistically significant correlations) is an express aim of quantitative methods, and the strength and robustness of these patterns is a (causal) argument in itself. Not for QCA. Robust cross-case patterns are merely the starting point for causal inference in QCA. They must be interpreted into causal claims that are plausible in the light of knowledge of cases, context and concepts, where knowledge of cases pertains to both case-level and cross-case knowledge. Like other qualitative methods, QCA strongly relies on interpretation. The quality of the dialogue between knowledge of cases, context and concepts, and the substantive plausibility of the causal claims that follow from it, define the validity of a QCA study. The empirical strength of the cross-case patterns as such is not decisive (Finn, 2022; Pula, 2021). Set analysis and Boolean algebra mostly serve to ensure that the causal inference starts from empirically valid cross-case patterns.

However, QCA practice increasingly focuses on quantitatively oriented empirical rigour and moves away from the method's qualitative anchors (e.g., Oana and Schneider, 2024; Rohlfing, 2018). This reduces QCA increasingly to a technique in Boolean minimization wherein knowledge of cases, context and concepts plays a (much) diminished role. However, the aim of QCA is not to infer causality from maximally robust cross-case patterns. Instead, QCA aims to identify sufficiently robust patterns and *interpret* them into causal explanations. It may very well be that, in the light of knowledge of cases, context and concepts, a less robust cross-case pattern can be much better interpreted into a causal claim than a more robust pattern (Rutten, 2023). This book explains how QCA is a tool for learning from cases and not merely a tool for systematic cross-case comparisons.

Learning from cases pervades every step in a QCA study (Pagliarin, La Mendola and Vis, 2023). It begins with the definition of what is a case and selecting relevant cases into a case population. A QCA study always starts with two questions: what is a case and what is it a case of (Ragin, 1992, 2009)? Rather than simply performing QCA on a 'given' population, researchers learn from cases by going back and forth between their research question and their cases. Defining concepts and calibration – that is, describing cases in terms of the degree to which concepts apply to them – is also about learning from cases. In QCA, this is neither an inductive nor a deductive process but an abductive one – a going back and forth between conceptual knowledge and knowledge of cases (Ragin [1987] 2014, p. 164). Knowledge of cases helps define a concept – for example, what does it mean to be an attractive residential area? Knowledge of the concept helps identify relevant cases – for example, why does this neighbourhood (not) qualify as an attractive residential area? Identifying patterns is one thing, interpreting what they mean requires researchers to 'go back' to their cases to infer the 'logic' or explanation behind the pattern. Interpreting empirical patterns may lead researchers to reconsider their definition of a case and the calibration of their concepts (Ragin, 2000, p. 171). Put differently, learning from cases deliberately blurs the line between the 'theoretical moment' and the 'empirical moment' of a study. This line defines (most) quantitative studies where one develops hypotheses first (theoretical moment) and then tests them (empirical moment) to deliver a verdict on their validity (Mahoney and Goertz, 2006). Qualitative methods, like QCA, are not like that. In QCA, one 'updates' one's conceptual knowledge based on what one learns from the cases, and one 'updates' one's definition of a case based on one's ('updated') conceptual knowledge (Goertz and Mahoney, 2012a, pp. 41–2).

Of course, none of this is new for those familiar with Ragin's work. So why does it not feature more prominently in QCA practice? One answer is that social science is strongly dominated by the quantitative template. Even though, for example, Goertz and Mahoney (2012a) have clearly explained the differences between the variable-based quantitative and case-based qualitative traditions, the quantitative template continues to shape much (most, in many disciplines) social science practice (Abbott, 1988, 1998). Why then is the quantitative template so dominant? Perhaps because it is based on very straightforward (and, therefore, attractive) assumptions on the nature of social reality (ontology) and social science's knowledge about it (epistemology). However, these straightforward assumptions are deeply problematic.

LEARNING FROM CASES USING CRITICAL REALIST PHILOSOPHY OF SCIENCE

Informed by empiricism and (the Newtonian version of) the natural sciences, the quantitative format suggests that, if left undisturbed, the same cause will always 'produce' the same outcome (Beach and Pedersen, 2016, pp. 14–17; Bhaskar [1975] 2008, pp. 69–78; Mahoney and Acosta, 2022; Rohlfing and Zuber, 2021). The job of social scientists is to establish event regularities. Event regularities establish an empirical relationship between a cause and an outcome, and the more robust the empirical regularity, the stronger the causal claim that follows from it. This approach has given rise to ever more sophisticated empirical (mostly statistical) techniques to identify empirical regularities (general causal evidence). It also created a growing distance between social reality itself and the data-analytical techniques describing it. This, in turn, encouraged a tendency to reduce social reality to empirical co-variation between decontextualized variables (Gorski, 2018; Pula, 2021). In a nutshell, this is what Abbott (1988, 1998) refers to as 'general linear reality'. It is flawed for two main reasons. First, empirical knowledge and, thus, empirical patterns, are socially constructed. Unlike biologists looking at a virus through a microscope, social scientists are themselves part of the social reality they study (Bhaskar [1975] 2008, pp. 57–8; Rutten, 2023). Social scientists cannot but look at social reality through the lens of their concepts, theories and methods. And social science concepts are much more theory and value laden than those used in the natural sciences (Bhaskar [1979] 2015, pp. 1–4). Empirical patterns are as much a function of these concepts, theories and methods as they are a reflection of what is actually going on in social reality. Consequently, the robustness of empirical patterns is not a benchmark for causal inference. Empirical patterns can only be interpreted into causal claims based on a dialogue between empirical and theoretical knowledge. Put differently, statements about the nature of social reality (such as causal claims) cannot be reduced to empirical description (i.e., empirical patterns) of social reality. Second, there is no such thing as an independent variable in social reality. What statisticians call multicollinearity is the norm; causality in social reality is contingent (Decoteau, 2018; Ragin [1987] 2014, p. 20). Rather than causes having an analytically identifiable effect of their own, whether a cause contributes to an outcome is contingent on the presence and absence of other factors (causes). This means that, even under controlled circumstances, there is no reason the same cause would always produce the same outcome. Since every case is a unique time- and place-contingent 'assemblage' of characteristics, context and human agents, the same cause (treatment) may 'work' differently in different cases to, potentially, 'produce' different outcomes (Archer, 1995, p. 53; Delanda, 2016; Lawson, 2005; Ragin, 2023, p. 40).

Consequently, we need a metaphysical position on the nature of social reality and our knowledge of it – a position that both legitimizes Ragin's interpretivism and provides a heuristic for it, a metaphysics that recognizes that social reality is real and not merely a social construct, but also a metaphysics that does not conflate social reality (ontology) with our knowledge of it (epistemology) (Porpora, 2018). This is what regularity theories of causality do insofar as they infer causality from observed empirical regularities (e.g., cross-case patterns) (Baumgartner, 2015; Mahoney and Acosta, 2022). Instead, we need a metaphysics that recognizes Ragin's distinction between Boolean expressions describing cases and cross-case patterns (i.e., knowledge of cases) and causal claims (Ragin [1987] 2014, p. 84).

This distinction only makes sense when we assume a stratified reality, one where our knowledge of cases (epistemology) is but a partial and perspectival interpretation of actual reality (of events), which in turn is the outcome of human agents 'doing things' – that is, exercising a variety of causal powers that we cannot directly observe (ontology). Causal inference then becomes what Ragin suggests it is: interpreting epistemological knowledge of cases (events) into ontological claims about causal powers. Regularity theories of causality generally do not distinguish between ontology and epistemology (Bhaskar, 1986, pp. 27–8). Instead, they assume that empirically observed regularities more or less accurately capture causal relationships, such that the robustness of an empirical pattern becomes evidence for causality. However, this position is problematic for a number of reasons, particularly in the social sciences (Bhaskar [1979] 2015, p. 21). Social reality (events, cases) is an open system. There is no reason to assume that the same cause will always produce the same outcome, even under controlled circumstances (Porpora, 2018). Instead, causality is contingent and contextual. Empirical regularities are outcomes (of human agency) requiring an explanation, not invariances that suggest one. Regularity theories also risk ignoring that human agency is the effective cause of all outcomes in social reality (Groff, 2013, p. 101). Explanatory conditions or independent variables do not do, much less cause, anything. Causal explanation must focus on why it is possible for human agents to 'produce' or achieve the outcome when the cause is present (Rutten, 2023). This focuses causal explanation on the potentiality of causes, rather than on how they are (invariantly) connected to outcomes – for example, via paths, sequences or mechanisms. Such mechanisms, and so on, abstract from human agency (effective causes) (Porpora, 2018) and, because of social reality being an open system, they run the risk of producing idiosyncratic (case-specific) explanations (Groff, 2016, 2019). That is, we need a meta-physics that focuses not on causal mechanisms (linking causes to outcomes) but on generative mechanisms explaining why or how causal power emerges (Bhaskar [1975] 2008, pp. 82–3; Elder-Vass, 2005; Porpora, 2018), which dovetails with QCA's configurational causality where outcomes are explained from configurations of conditions – that is, where configurations capture an emerged causal power. The job of QCA researchers is to make it plausible that (1) causal power emerges from the explanatory conditions in a configuration; and that (2) exercising this causal power makes it possible for human agents to achieve the outcome of interest.

Critical realism (Bhaskar [1975] 2008) is a philosophy of science that assumes the above positions. It believes that social reality is ontologically real (ontological realism) but that our knowledge of it is partial and perspectival (epistemic relativism). Social science, therefore, must interpret empirical findings into statements about reality, drawing from empirical as well as conceptual knowledge on the basis of a systematic procedure (judgemental rationality) (Bhaskar, 1986, p. 24). Consequently, critical realists divide social reality into the domains of the Real – where unobservable causal powers reside. When exercised by human agents, these powers produce events in the domain of the Actual that scientists can study as cases. Scientists develop partial and perspectival knowledge of these cases in the domain of the Empirical, which they then interpret into claims about (the potentiality of) causal powers using their judgemental rationality. As this book demonstrates, ontological realism, epistemic relativism, judgemental rationality, the three domains of reality and the notion of causality as a power provide an important heuristic for QCA. It helps researchers use QCA as a method by which to learn from cases and prevents them from reducing it to an empiricist exercise of finding cross-case patterns, all completely in line with Ragin's interpretive logic. What follows is a brief and necessarily incomplete discussion of critical realism. I refer to the works of Archer (1995); Bhaskar (1986; [1979] 2008; [1979] 2015); Decoteau (2018); Elder-Vass (2010); Gorski (2018); Groff (2013, 2016, 2019); and Lawson (2005) for a full discussion of critical realism. The work of Groff in particular has been a great help for me to develop a theory of causality that dovetails with QCA (see Chapter 3).

ONTOLOGICAL REALISM

Critical realists argue that social reality is socially constructed, but that still makes it just as real as physical reality. 'Real' means that (social) reality is mind independent, that reality is not (merely) a product of the mind, and that reality is independent of how human beings perceive it (Bhaskar, 1986, pp. 121–9). Countries, places, organizations, networks, communities are all socially constructed. Yet, every citizen, every inhabitant, every member of an organization, network or community knows that these 'things' exist independently of what they think (or do not think) of them. These 'things' have, as it were, a life of their own (Decoteau, 2018; Gorski, 2018). They have dispositions or causal powers that enable and constrain the human agents 'populating' them. Countries, places, organizations, networks, communities and all other 'things' in social reality consist of social structures and social institutions. Social structures (i.e., linkages) and social institutions (i.e., rules, norms, values) enable and constrain (but do not determine) the human agents populating social structures and being governed by social institutions (Lawson, 2005). Structures and institutions may be formal or informal, weak or strong. They must be 'produced' or 'actualized' by human agency to be efficacious, but they are all independent of any one particular human agent (Elder-Vass, 2010, pp. 64–8; Groff, 2016). For example, social capital in a network is real; it exists because network members are connected (structure) and because particular norms and values (institutions) govern their interactions. However, this social capital must be exercised or actualized for it to 'work'. One network member may turn to another member for support, thereby actualizing the network relationship between them. The other one may then support the first one, thereby actualizing the social capital of the network. Alternatively, one may think of oneself as occupying a central position in a network and act accordingly, only to see one's efforts frustrated by the actual central network members. In this example, one tries to actualize a network structure that does not exist (viz., oneself as a central player). The action then leads the real central members to reconfirm the reality of the network.

Of course, structures and institutions also change because of human agency. This is called upward causation, while structures and institutions enabling and constraining human agency is downward causation (Archer, 1995, pp. 65–6; Delanda, 2016, p. 21). However, upward causation usually happens on a longer time scale, and for structures and institutions to change they must exist first. The dynamic between upward and downward causation is the subject of Archer's (1995) seminal work in the critical realist literature. For our purpose, it matters that 'things' in social reality have causal powers because of the way they are structured and because of the institutions governing them (Elder-Vass, 2010, pp. 43–7). Human agency may exercise these causal powers to 'produce' (or avoid) outcomes. An organization is an organization because it has the causal power to coordinate people and resources, otherwise we would not recognize it as an organization. This does not mean that causal powers of social entities are fixed or permanent features; they change, they develop – in other words, they are emergent (Archer, 1995, p. 14; Elder-Vass, 2005; Lawson, 2005). That is, critical realism commits itself to a weak form of 'essentialism'. The causal power of an organization to coordinate people and resources is an essence of organizations; however, the nature and the extent of this power is different from one organization to another and changes over time. Causal power is itself socially constructed and, therefore, may be socially reconstructed or deconstructed. However, such efforts will meet with resistance because the causal powers as they exist (the social structure and institutions from which they emerge) benefit those in a position to exercise the powers. They are resistant to change, which is what defines them as structures and institutions (Archer, 1995; Elder-Vass, 2010; Groff, 2016), as with the above real central members of a network. Strong essentialism is what defines physical reality. Once constructed, the essence of a chair, car or billiard ball is fixed.

Causality, then, is the power to do (Groff, 2013, pp. 76–81). Members of an organization have 'the power to do' because they occupy a position in their organization (the structure) and because of the authority (institutions) connected to it. A compliance officer has the power to suggest and implement corporate social responsibility (CSR) measures. Senior management has the power to overrule them. That is, causal power may be exercised, as in the compliance officer developing CSR measures; however, that does not mean the power is always efficacious (Rutten, 2023). Moreover, anticipating being overruled, the compliance officer may not even develop CSR measures – that is, not even exercise the causal power. This is important because social scientists can only observe an empirical pattern between a cause and an outcome if the causal power was exercised and efficacious. However, often, causal powers are (partially) negated or remain unexercised. Consequently, empirical patterns can only partially reveal causal powers. Researchers must interpret this incomplete picture and cannot infer causality from robust empirical patterns alone (Bhaskar, 1986, p. 24; [1975] 2008, p. 51).

Social reality is the outcome of human agency, of lots of human agents exercising lots of different powers at the same time. These powers then 'interact' to produce the events that we can observe and study as cases (Archer, 1995; Elder-Vass, 2010). A regional government agency may exercise its causal power to develop a wind turbine park to produce green energy. An environmental conservation group may exercise its causal powers to prevent the park from being constructed to protect a vulnerable natural area. A municipal government may exercise its causal powers to have the wind turbine park built at that exact location to minimize nuisance for local residence. How these powers interact decides whether and where the wind turbine park is built, and whether there will be a regional wind turbine park development event. Looking across multiple such cases, QCA researchers may establish that regional government agencies with certain characteristics are able to realize their plans. These characteristics form a configuration of explanatory conditions, a configuration that describes causal power that makes wind turbine park development possible.

EPISTEMIC RELATIVISM

Critical realists recognize that (scientific) knowledge about social reality can only be partial and perspectival (Bhaskar, 1986, pp. 72–3; [1975] 2008, pp. 36–8). It is relative to the theories, concepts and methods that we use to develop knowledge about social reality. The human mind understands the world in terms of the categories (concepts) that have come to us through socialization and that do not neatly overlap with 'things' in reality (Bhaskar, 1986, p. 284; Lakoff, 1987, pp. 130–35). Socialization in a particular discipline critically shapes the kind of questions a researcher will think relevant, and the concepts, theories and methods used to investigate them. In a discipline as fragmented as economic geography, this is all too obvious. The 'relational turn', the 'cultural turn', 'institutional economic geography', 'evolutionary economic geography' are all different epistemological perspectives from which to understand the reality of the regional economic landscape (Lagendijk, 2006). Nor is that a bad thing. Knowledge grows not so much through more and better observations (measurements) but through critical reflection on the plausibility of our explanations against counterarguments and counterclaims. The truth is not 'out there', waiting to be discovered, because in social reality, the truth is itself (largely) a social construction. Instead, social science aims to develop an as plausible as possible explanation of what we see in social reality. And what we see, of course, is contingent on our concepts, theories and methods (Bhaskar, 1986, p. 94; [1975] 2008, p. 178; Lakoff, 1987, p. 175; Lawson, 2005). For example, the 'learning region' (to which I dedicated much effort early on in my career) was a good tool to explain why some regions are more innovative than others. Learning region scholars like me explained regional innovation from regionally available resources (e.g., investments in research and development) and regional networks, and the fact that these resources and networks are unevenly distributed across regions. However insightful, it is also a limited perspective for understanding regions as bounded territories rather than relational spaces. Firms performing innovation are unconcerned with the regional boundaries that administrations or economic geographers draw on maps. Therefore, I now think of regional innovation in terms of an interaction between physical places and social places (Rutten, 2017). The characteristics of the physical places (the locations) where firms are located obviously affect their innovation efforts – as the learning region suggested. However, these innovation efforts happen in the social spaces of teams, organizations and networks that are multilocal. Social spaces 'connect' to multiple locations, allowing firms to benefit from resources and other endowments available in multiple places. This does not mean that the learning region was wrong; in fact, it got lots of things right. However, we (economic geographers) have developed better explanations by highlighting different aspects of social reality – for example, that for innovating firms, geography is a relational space rather than a bounded territory. But that does not invalidate the empirical work that I and many other colleagues have done on the learning region. The empirical patterns that we found in our data are still there.

The point is that empirical patterns are not so much observed but constructed. To no small degree, they are a function of the concepts, theories and methods used to investigate social reality (Gorski, 2018; Lawson, 2005). Most obviously, even changing the number of control variables in a regression analysis changes the correlation coefficients of the independent variables. However, that does not change anything about the underlying causality (social reality). Given that we can never include all relevant control variables in a regression analysis (even if we knew which they were), the search for the 'correct' net effect of an independent variable is a rather dubious affair. The effect (size) of an independent variable is contingent on the choices that a researcher makes concerning, among others, the number and kind of control variables. There is nothing wrong with this, as long as these choices are (theoretically and substantively) plausible. However, it does underline that empirical knowledge is relative – it demonstrates the notion of epistemic relativism. It is therefore best to think of empirical patterns as descriptive only (Bhaskar [1975] 2008, p. 125). For a critical realist, there is no such thing as a causal (data-analytical) technique. Describing the patterns in one's data (e.g., QCA's cross-case patterns) is a necessary first step, but causality only follows from interpreting what the pattern means. The robustness of empirical patterns is only relevant as a threshold – to distinguish between empirically valid descriptions of social reality (that can be causally interpreted) and invalid descriptions (that cannot be interpreted) (Pula, 2021; Rutten, 2023). To borrow again from statistical methods, any p-value ≤ 0.1 suggests that, probabilistically, the correlation is genuine rather than spurious. A model with a p-value of 0.01 does not necessarily suggest a better explanation than one with a p-value of 0.09 (Amrhein et al., 2019; Wasserstein, Schirm and Lazar, 2019). Which model one reports is the one that makes the most sense in the light of conceptual and contextual knowledge, not on how low its p-value is.

In sum, epistemic relativism suggests that causal statements cannot be reduced to empirical patterns; that to get from empirical patterns to causal claims requires interpretation. It requires social scientists to ask, what does this pattern mean? Interpretation follows from a dialogue between knowledge of cases, context and concepts and this is exactly Ragin's position (Ragin, 1992, 2009).

JUDGEMENTAL RATIONALITY

Because of ontological realism, knowledge is not merely a social construction; it reflects something about the nature of social reality. Because of epistemic relativism, knowledge is not just a fact; it is contingent on the concepts, theories and methods used to develop it (Bhaskar [1975] 2008, pp. 36–9; Elder-Vass, 2010, pp. 243–5). Consequently, for critical realists, knowledge is a judgement. Knowledge follows from interpreting epistemically relativist statements about what we know about social reality (e.g., from measurement and observation) into ontological statements about what we believe social reality to be like (Bhaskar, 1986, p. 24). Causal claims are a good example of ontological statements. They state what we believe is how social reality 'works' (Bhaskar [1975] 2008, pp. 132–5; Rutten, 2023). Causal statements elucidate the reasons, the workings and the powers behind the outcomes that 'happen' in social reality. To interpret statements about our knowledge of social reality into statements about (what we believe to be) the nature of social reality, social scientists draw on a vast body of theoretical and empirical knowledge, knowledge of context and experiences. No researcher is an island, and all research is embedded in a discipline or a field and builds on previous research. Interpretation (making judgements) 'happens' against this vast body of knowledge. This is why interpretation (making judgements) is rational; it proceeds in accordance with established procedures and good practice rules, and it engages with existing (scientific) knowledge (which also means that being rational does not automatically make it right or true) (Bhaskar, 1986, pp. 60–61).

Developing knowledge is thus a process of exercising judgemental rationality. The fact that knowledge is a judgement means that it is never final; it can (and should) always be updated, also within the context of a research project, such as a QCA study. Doing research (within and across projects) is to conduct an ongoing dialogue between data and theory, between the specific (e.g., cases) and the general (e.g., their context). Without having ever engaged with critical realism, Ragin's work shows a strong commitment to judgemental rationality – or substantive interpretation as it is more commonly known in the QCA literature (Ragin [1987] 2014, pp. 16–17; Rutten, 2023).

Critical realism, as a school of thought on how social science 'works', dovetails with how Ragin suggests QCA as a method to learn from cases. I have connected QCA to critical realism in my paper 'Uncertainty, possibility and causal power in QCA' (Rutten, 2023), and others, too, have made this connection (e.g., Gerrits and Pagliarin, 2021; Gerrits and Verweij, 2016; Pula, 2021). Most importantly, critical realism legitimizes why QCA distinguishes between empirical patterns on the one hand and causal statements on the other – and how getting from the former to the latter is a process of interpretation, of dialoguing knowledge of cases, context and concepts.

CASES, CROSS-CASE PATTERNS AND CAUSALITY

So how do we use the notions of ontological realism, epistemic relativism and judgemental rationality to learn from cases? For that, we need to look at how critical realism stratifies social reality in three domains: the Real, the Actual and the Empirical (Bhaskar [1975] 2008, pp. 12–14; Elder-Vass, 2010, p. 44). The domain of the Real is the domain where social structures and institutions reside. They are the (ontologically) real 'things' that exist in social reality. They are socially constructed but exist independently of any specific human agent or agents. They endure beyond individual social interactions and resist change (Elder-Vass, 2010, pp. 45–7; Groff, 2013, pp. 93–7). Causal powers emerge from structures and institutions and enable human agents to do things (and may constrain them from doing other things). Human agents themselves have a range of causal powers, such as their intellectual faculties and their physical strength, and these may well feature as explanatory conditions in a QCA study

(Archer, 1995, pp. 92–9; Groff, 2016). But social scientists are usually more interested in 'social' powers – powers that emerge from social structures and institutions, such as the above power of a compliance officer to develop CSR measures. However, these powers are not (readily) observable; the domain of the Real is largely unobservable (Bhaskar, 1986, p. 133). It is difficult enough to map linkages between, for example, organizations, but structures (e.g., networks) cannot be collapsed into linkages. We can observe the consequences of institutions (e.g., norms and values) but not the institutions themselves. 'Observing' causal powers emerging from structures and institutions, then, is (largely) impossible. When exercised, causal powers 'produce' events in the domain of the Actual – events that can be observed and studied as cases. That is, the domain of the Actual is the social reality in which we live and that we can see. But the events in the domain of the Actual are only a small proportion of all the events that could have happened (could have been actualized) (ibid., pp. 27–31). The CSR measures implementation event can happen in the organization because the causal powers of the (position of the) compliance officer allow it to happen (make it possible). However, it will not happen when the CEO exercises his (let's assume it is a he) causal powers (the causal powers connected to the CEO position) to overrule the compliance officer. That is, one can think of the domain of the Real as containing all possible events (possible given the causal powers that exist) and the domain of the Actual as containing only those events that have been actualized (by exercising causal powers) (Bhaskar, 1986, pp. 285–6; Elder-Vass, 2010, p. 130). That is, the domain of the Actual is a subset of the domain of the Real. Researchers develop knowledge of events (cases) in the domain of the Empirical. Epistemically relativist knowledge describes cases and cross-case patterns. Cases may be described by a great many characteristics; however, researchers must focus on those they consider analytically relevant. One can only observe and measure so many characteristics of a case in a study. That is, researchers' knowledge of cases is always partial. This makes the domain of the Empirical a subset of the domain of the Actual (Bhaskar [1975] 2008, pp. 18–20).

For example, the structures and institutions of a network enable (or constrain) knowledge creation in the network. These structures and institutions 'reside' in the domain of the Real, and from them emerges the causal power to create knowledge. Structures and institutions may be 'captured' by the characteristics describing a network. A researcher now needs to identify (select) suitable cases of a knowledge-creating network in the domain of the Actual from which data may be collected. One such case (network) may have a flat hierarchy, which means that the condition 'flat hierarchy' describes this case (network). The researcher's epistemological relativist description of hierarchy (domain of the Empirical) will 'capture' what the real structure of the network (domain of the Real) is like. The network may also be small (composed of only three partners) and geographically clustered (all three partners are located in the same place). This makes it a flat, small, clustered network – that is, the network is described in a complex way by three conditions. Suppose the network successfully developed an app that allows social workers to connect to vulnerable people, then the network created knowledge in the form of a new app. This means the network is also described as a knowledge-creating network. The analytical task of a QCA researcher now is to investigate why the configuration – flat, small, clustered network – makes it possible for the network to create new knowledge. For example, the small size of the network allows trustful relationships that encourage sharing competitively sensitive knowledge. The flat hierarchy allows creativity, while geographical clustering allows the efficient exchange of tacit knowledge through face-to-face communication. From all this emerges the causal power to create new knowledge. Judgemental rationality may thus interpret this configuration into the following explanation of knowledge creation: flat, small, clustered networks establish a trustful environment for creativity and tacit knowledge exchange.

Three kinds of uncertainty surround this critical realist take on causal inference (Rutten, 2023). First, ontological uncertainty suggests that we cannot definitively know what social reality (domain of the Real) is like because we can only have partial and perspectival knowledge of it. Because our knowledge of social reality is epistemically relativist, we can never be certain that it captures the true nature of social reality. Second, epistemic uncertainty means that all measurement and observation is fallible and prone to error. This is not specific to QCA, and researchers must deal with epistemic uncertainty by following the good practice rules of whatever data collection method or tool they use. Third, possibilistic uncertainty is the principal kind of uncertainty to be addressed in a QCA study. Causal powers make outcomes possible but do not determine or guarantee that they occur (Bhaskar [1975] 2008, pp. 51, 98; Elder-Vass, 2010, p. 123). The causal power of the flat, small, clustered network may not be efficacious because the money for the innovation project ran out. The causal power may not have been exercised because other priorities meant that the innovation project never started. But none of that takes anything away from the causal power of flat, small, clustered networks to create knowledge. That is, power-based causal claims say something about the potentiality of the cause (the causal power) rather than the actuality of the outcome. For the causal claim to be valid, the outcome does not have to occur, as long as (1) a plausible argument can be developed as to why the cause (causal power) makes the outcome possible; and (2) negative cases can be explained in terms of something else 'interfering' with the causal power, leaving the causal power unexercised or its efficacy mitigated (Bhaskar, 1986, pp. 27–9; Groff, 2016). But here is where possibilistic uncertainty comes in. Because of ontological and epistemic uncertainty, we can never conclusively know whether the causal power (which we argue our empirically observed configuration describes) really makes the outcome possible. Maybe some other (unobserved) factors (causal power) partially or fully explain the outcome. Therefore, the plausibility of the argument connecting cause to outcome must reduce possibilistic uncertainty. In other words, the validity of a causal claim is a function of the quality of the judgemental rationality that developed it – that is, the quality of the dialogue between knowledge of cases, context and concepts.

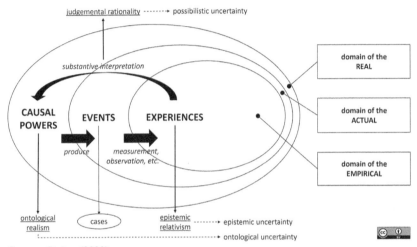

Source: Rutten (2023).

Figure 1.1   Critical realist causal explanation

Making causal claims about the potentiality of the cause rather than the actuality of the outcome means uncertainty is possibilistic rather than probabilistic (Rutten, 2023). Probabilistic uncertainty concerns the actuality of the outcome. Probabilistic claims are based on empirical regularities, on constant conjunctions between cause and outcome (on general causal evidence). The regularity must be genuine rather than spurious, which may be established on the basis of probabilistic criteria. But as constant conjunctions between cause and outcome (i.e., cross-case patterns) are only the starting point for causal inference in QCA, the principal uncertainty nagging QCA is possibilistic, not probabilistic. Is it possible for the cause to 'produce' the outcome? Can a plausible argument to that extent be developed via judgemental rationality (ibid.). Figure 1.1 summarizes the key argument of this chapter. It provides the principal heuristic for doing QCA. Assuming that social reality is stratified as Figure 1.1 suggests, Ragin's interpretive approach leads to valid and generalizable findings. I will refer to Figure 1.1 and its domains of reality throughout the book to explain how researchers can learn from cases with QCA.

OUTLINE OF THE BOOK

This chapter demonstrated how a commitment to ontological realism, epistemic relativism and judgemental rationality helps researchers interpret empirical knowledge (domain of the Empirical) of cases (domain of the Actual) into possibilistic causal claims (domain of the Real). Critical realism thus legitimizes Ragin's interpretive approach and provides the philosophical foundations on which to design and conduct a QCA study. How to actually do QCA is explained in the following chapters.

Chapter 2 introduces the logic of case-based methods and how it is very different from variable-based methods. The chapter also introduces the truth table, QCA's investigative heart, and how it dialogues case-level and cross-case causal evidence. Using truth tables for systematic cross-case comparison defines the 'Ragin revolution' in social science methods. It marries the analytical rigour of formal logic and the substantive interpretation of conventional qualitative methods. QCA uses a variety of causal tools, such as regularities, difference-making and INUS[1] conditions; however, Ragin never committed QCA to any one theory of causality. In Chapter 3, I explain how a causal powers approach naturally connects to QCA's configurational causality and how it is substantiated in critical realism.

Chapter 4 explains how 'casing' is a critical step in any QCA study. Casing defines what counts as a case in a particular study. QCA being a comparative method, cases must be comparable. Casing helps researchers construct a population of cases that is homogeneous on key scope conditions. Working with constructed populations rather than samples from given populations means that generalization in QCA is analytical rather than empirical, which underlines the importance of interpretation and reduces that of empirical robustness. Chapter 5 introduces the basics of Boolean algebra, which is all that the application of QCA requires. Boolean algebra is the formal language of QCA and users must learn how to 'speak' it. However, Boolean algebra merely describes cross-case patterns; it does not make causal statements. Chapter 6 discusses how causality in QCA is complex – that is, configurational, equifinal and asymmetrical. Relying on Boolean algebra, complex causality produces more sophisticated causal explanations compared to correlational (variable-based) methods. Chapter 7 familiarizes readers with the logic and practice of set analysis. Set analysis equips QCA with key parameters, such as consistency and coverage, that help interpret Boolean expressions into causal claims. The chapter explains how to calculate these parameters. Even if automated in QCA software,[2] it is important that researchers understand what is happening. Chapter 8 explains the key notion of calibration. QCA is a threshold method (Goertz, 2020, p. 182); it investigates whether being above or below a threshold on an explanatory condition makes a difference for being above or below a threshold on the outcome. Calibration is about finding a meaningful threshold and to assign cases (a degree of) membership in sets accordingly. The chapter explains different calibration methods and how calibration and aggregating measurements into concepts are closely related.

Even though fuzzy sets are now the default in QCA, for a variety of reasons, I prefer crisp sets. In Chapter 9, I discuss my reasons, and also how calibrating into categories accounts for the colourfulness of social reality without having to 'buy into' fuzzy set metrics. Chapter 10 explains how the truth table works, how it dialogues case-level and cross-case causal evidence, and how the truth table investigation is much more than an exercise in Boolean minimization. It is a tool with which to learn from cases. QCA software automates the Boolean minimization; it does not automate truth table investigation. For didactical purposes, I present a glossary of key concepts at the end of this chapter and Chapters 2–10. Chapters 11 and 12 discuss a large-N and a small-N example, respectively. Chapter 11 discusses calibration options for large-N studies (with more distance to cases) and how confounding conditions allow the admission of additional causally relevant conditions in a QCA study. Chapter 11 also explains how to work with Ragin's fsQCA software (Ragin et al., 2023). Chapter 12 demonstrates how to use qualitative data in a QCA study. Importantly, both chapters demonstrate how to dialogue knowledge of cases, context and concepts. Finally, Chapter 13 presents a critical realist heuristic for QCA. It summarizes the philosophical assumptions underlying QCA (see above) and how they inform every step of a QCA study. The chapter presents an adapted version of Figure 1.1 as a road map for learning from cases with QCA.

HOW TO READ THIS BOOK

This book presents a comprehensive introduction on how to do QCA. It consistently presents QCA as a qualitative method and demonstrates how QCA's qualitative logic pervades its every step. The book draws from critical realism to explain the logic and practice of QCA. Most notably, and in a departure from mainstream QCA (and mainstream social science more generally), the book suggests causality as an emergent power. I believe that this position dovetails with QCA's configurational causality so QCA researchers will have no problem relating to it. So while this book presents a critical realist take on QCA, it can unproblematically be read as 'just' a QCA handbook. The book discusses QCA in accordance to the method's good practice rules. Readers who are not particularly interested in critical realism can give Chapter 3 a cursory read. I also depart from mainstream QCA in favouring crisp rather than fuzzy sets and I explain my position in Chapter 9. Readers who are comfortable with QCA's default position on fuzzy sets can skip this chapter. All chapters build on one another, allowing readers to develop a cumulative understanding of the book's substance. Readers new to QCA are strongly encouraged to read the book from start to finish. The chapters can also be read individually and this is what more experienced users may want to do, to refresh or deepen their understanding of certain topics. Inevitably, this causes some overlaps between chapters.

GLOSSARY OF KEY CONCEPTS

Case	The object of study of case-based methods. Cases are holistically relevant; they have characteristics, context and human agents that cannot be considered in isolation
Causal powers	These emerge from social structures and social institutions in the domain of the Real. Human agency may (or may not) exercise causal powers to 'produce' events
Domain of the Actual	Contains events that human agency produced by exercising causal powers, which exist in the domain of the Real
Domain of the Empirical	Contains empirical knowledge developed from events, which exist in the domain of the Actual
Domain of the Real	Contains the social structures and social institutions that enable and constrain human agency
Epistemic relativism	The belief that knowledge of social reality is socially constructed; that social scientists cannot look at social reality but through the lens of their concepts, theories and methods
Epistemic uncertainty	Uncertainty about the validity of measurements and observations
Events	'Things' that happen in social reality and that social scientists can study as cases
General causal evidence	Causal evidence developed from cross-case patterns. This kind of evidence suggests that an explanatory condition tends to co-occur with an outcome
Judgemental rationality	Interpreting epistemically relativist statements about our knowledge of social reality into ontological statements about the nature of social reality
Learning from cases	Combining singular and general causal evidence to make plausible, generalizable causal claims from one's cases. Conducting a dialogue between knowledge of cases, context and concepts

Ontological realism	The belief that, although socially constructed, social reality exists independent of particular human agents and is resistant to their attempts to change it
Ontological uncertainty	The impossibility of knowing the true nature of social reality
Possibilistic causality	Pertains to the potentiality of the cause (causal power), not the actuality of the outcome. Causal powers (causes) make outcomes possible (when they are exercised) but do not determine or guarantee that the outcomes occur
Possibilistic uncertainty	Because of ontological and epistemic uncertainty, social scientists cannot know whether the causes they identified, or some other factor, make the outcome possible. Possibilistic uncertainty is mitigated by the plausibility of the argument connecting cause to outcome
Singular causal evidence	Causal evidence developed from single cases. This kind of evidence establishes why or how an explanatory condition 'produces' an outcome

NOTES

1. That is, insufficient but necessary conditions of an unnecessary but sufficient conjunction – see Chapter 5.
2. Visit https://compasss.org/software/ to find links to all available QCA software. The most commonly used QCA software is Charles Ragin's fsQCA programme (Ragin, Davey and Corcaci, 2023) and the R-packages for QCA developed by Adrian Duşa. The examples in this book (Chapter 11) are based on Ragin's fsQCA software, which is the software I always use. At the time of writing, all QCA software can be downloaded free of charge.

2. The Ragin revolution

When Ragin published *The Comparative Method* in 1987, he started a revolution in the social sciences (Vaisey, 2010). He challenged the dominant correlational (variable-based) approach (King, Keohane and Verba, 1994) and introduced a compelling alternative: the case-based approach and its set-analytical logic. The analytical strength of the variable-based approach is also its weakness – it is decontextualized (Brady, 2010; Mahoney and Goertz, 2006). It focuses on variables and correlations between them but loses sight of what actually happens in social reality, of people doing stuff.[1] People and the stuff they do are reduced to empirical regularities. Variable-based researchers ask themselves: 'What does this variable do?' What they mean is, how much of the variation in one variable correlates with the variation in another variable, and suggest this as a causal effect. This is a very stylized way of talking about social reality and causality. The only sensible answer to the above question is: 'Nothing'. Variables are (statistical) abstractions; they do not do anything, much less cause anything. With the case-based method, Ragin brought context back into causal explanation (Byrne, 2005). Cases 'consist' of real human agents in real situations doing real things. And this context matters greatly for the explanation of an outcome (Eisenhardt, 2021; Rohlfing and Schneider, 2018). It may very well be that the education level of the regional workforce has an effect on the level of regional income. However, this says nothing about what will happen to any one particular region when it increases the education level of its workforce. For all we know, its regional income may decrease. What will happen to that region's income depends on a range of other factors too. Empirical patterns (regularities) alone are meaningless when not substantiated by case-level evidence. However, cases are holistic. On the level of cases, all characteristic (explanatory conditions) are interconnected; they cannot be considered in isolation (Bhaskar, 1986, pp. 56–7; Ragin, 2009). The question is not what the net effect is of, for example, education on income. Instead, it is about the combinations (configurations) of conditions that explain regional income. Education may feature in some configurations explaining regional income but not in others. This is the complex nature of causality in the real world. Set-analytical methods, such as QCA, capture this complex causality much better than correlational methods. With QCA, Ragin developed a systematic and rigorous method to investigate complex causality. Therein lies the Ragin revolution. He developed a tool to make context count in causal explanations and to do so in an analytically rigorous way by connecting searching for regularities (cross-case patterns) to interpreting their meaning from case-level evidence. In QCA, Boolean-algebraic expressions capture the co-occurrence of configurations ('causes') and outcomes on both case and cross-case levels. This allows researchers to dialogue knowledge of cases, context and concepts into causal explanations. This chapter looks at what 'drives' the Ragin revolution. It first explains the case-based method, how it is different from variable-based methods, and how it better captures the complex nature of causality. It then introduces the truth table as a tool for learning from cases and investigating complex causality.

VARIABLE-BASED VERSUS CASE-BASED RESEARCH

QCA is a case-based method, which means that it follows a logic completely different from variable-based methods. Perhaps the strongest advocates of variable-based methods are King et al. (1994), who suggest this template also for case study research. Ragin ([1987] 2014) and Goertz and Mahoney (2012a) have laid out important limitations of variable-based methods and suggested case-based methods as an alternative. I sketch the key differences between both kinds of methods to express what QCA is about. But see the above works and, for example, Abbott (1988, 1998), and my paper (Rutten, 2020) for further details.

Variables and cases are both analytical constructs but of a very different nature. Variables describe the distribution of characteristics in a population. Variable-based research is correlational; it identifies co-variation between independent and dependent variables. A causal effect is the amount of variation in the dependent variable that can be attributed to the variation in the independent variable, holding everything else constant. The causal effect 'works' the same in all cases: the same increase in X 'produces' the same increase in Y regardless of context (Ragin [1987] 2014). Variable-based research is about variables and how they correlate. It abstracts from cases and theorizes in terms of one variable 'doing something' to another variable. Causal evidence is exclusively empirical; the robustness of a co-variation (its statistical significance) decides the strength of a causal argument. Variables are suggested as real; they capture genuine characteristics of social reality – namely, their distribution in a population. The causal effect of one variable on another – that is, the change that one variable causes in another – is measured as co-variation between them. Thus, variable-based methods collapse the Real and the Empirical and hence assume a 'unified empirical reality' (Lawson, 2005).

Case-based methods are very different. To begin with, cases are holistic; they are 'assemblages' of characteristics, context and the human agents populating them (Delanda, 2016; Ragin [1987] 2014). They invite researchers to understand the relationship between characteristics in the context of actual cases, not as decontextualized variables. While variable-based methods look for co-variation in a population, holding everything else constant, case-based methods look at invariance (co-occurrence of cause and outcome) in specific cases (Goertz and Mahoney, 2012a). 'By examining differences and similarities [between cases] in context it is possible to determine how different combinations of conditions [characteristics] have the same causal significance and how similar causal factors can operate in opposite directions' (Ragin [1987] 2014, p. 49). This is a world away from the average net effects on the level of a population and it allows case-based methods to account much better for the complex nature of causality (see Chapter 6). While variable-based methods are about co-variation between independent and dependent variables, case-based methods are about invariance. If particular characteristics (explanatory conditions) co-occur with the outcome of interest in specific cases, it suggests that, in this context, these conditions may causally explain the outcome. This at once suggests that case-based causal explanations are (1) developed on the level of configurations of explanatory conditions; and (2) are contextual for the specific cases where the co-occurrence happens. It also means that case-based methods must interpret why this configuration of explanatory conditions causally explains the outcome. The robustness of the co-occurrence (the empirical pattern) is not in itself a causal argument as it is in variable-based methods. Consequently, case-based methods conduct a much richer dialogue between ideas and evidence (ibid.) to interpret constant conjunctions into plausible causal explanations, which means that case-based methods commit to a stratified reality where empirical reality (empirical patterns) is distinct from causal claims (the nature of reality).

EXPLAINING CASE-BASED RESEARCH

One of the most fascinating hypotheses to emerge in economic geography this century is that regional socio-cultural diversity benefits regional innovation. In a nutshell, the argument is that new ideas bubble up in socio-culturally diverse environments and that, in those environments, the regional business community can develop these ideas into new products and services (Florida, 2002). The conventional way to investigate this hypothesis is to develop a scale for regional socio-cultural diversity and one for regional innovation, and then to correlate them. Suppose the two variables were correlated – what does that mean? Those used to variable-based theorizing would argue that it suggests that the more socio-culturally diverse a region is, the more innovative it will be. But that is only true on the level of a population of regions. It says nothing about whether a particular socio-culturally diverse regional will be innovative (Goertz and Mahoney, 2012a, pp. 43–4; Ragin [1987]

2014, p. 11). A population-level correlation coefficient is not a case-based probability. Correlational studies say something about effect sizes on the level of a population (Abbott, 1988, 1998). This is relevant for policymakers in government or the business community making decisions on where to invest resources for new product development. The above correlation suggests that such investments would more likely flourish in regions with higher levels of socio-cultural diversity, but it says nothing about whether investments will be successful in any one particular region, however socio-culturally diverse it may be. Correlations pertain to variables, not cases. If one wants to explain the causal relationship between socio-cultural diversity and innovation on the level of regions (i.e., cases), correlational (or variable-based) methods (searching for population-level empirical regularities) have two insurmountable problems, as follows.

First, there is no such thing as a net effect on the level of cases. Cases do not vary; they have or do not have certain characteristics (or have these characteristics in degree). They may change over time, but that is a different question; on the case level, the notion of co-variation is meaningless. Moreover, cases are holistic (Ragin [1987] 2014, p. 16). All characteristics 'happen' simultaneously (they all characterize the case at the same time) and they are all interrelated (Delanda, 2016). For example, the education level of a regional workforce is contingent on its industrial make-up. On the case level, it is not possible to isolate the effect of any one regional characteristic from that of the others.

Second, also on the case level, variables are not (readily) manipulable (Brady, 2010; Goertz and Mahoney, 2012a, pp. 10–11). A statistically significant correlation between socio-cultural diversity and innovation on the level of a population of regions is wonderful. However, a region cannot just increase its level of socio-cultural diversity in pursuit of innovation. Many of social science's key variables are not (readily) manipulable on the case level. Individuals cannot change their ethnicity to have a better prospect of finding a job. Nor can they change the education level of their parents if they want to climb the social ladder. Organizations cannot change the characteristics of their geographical location, and regions cannot (readily) change their industrial make-up. What we really want to know, when we talk about cases, is (1) in combination with what other factors does socio-cultural diversity explain regional innovation in order to understand what else needs to be 'in place' to benefit from socio-cultural diversity; and (2), in the absence of socio-cultural diversity, which combination(s) of characteristics also explain (lead to) regional innovation? Answering these questions requires a fundamentally different approach, one that centres on cases and the characteristics they have in common, not on variables and correlations (Goertz, 2017, pp. 58–9).

Chapter 1 described the nature of causality in QCA as possibilistic; QCA makes claims about the potentiality of the cause, not the actuality of the outcome (Bhaskar, 1986, p. 34; Rutten, 2023). Case-based researchers do this by detecting plausible causes of known outcomes (Mahoney and Goertz, 2006). Substantive interpretation, or exercising judgemental rationality, is about detecting (identifying) a plausible configuration of explanatory conditions to explain an outcome that we know has occurred (Bhaskar, 1986, p. 24; Byrne, 2005). In other words, causal explanation in case-based methods works backwards – from outcome to cause (Goertz and Mahoney, 2012a, p. 41). The uncertainty that this 'backward' causal explanation faces is possibilistic. However plausible an explanation, we do not know for certain whether having these characteristics or something else makes the outcome possible. Instead, causal inference in variable-based methods works forward. Researchers estimate the effect (sizes) of known causes. They aim to predict the effect (size) of an independent variable on a dependent variable. As argued, this requires robust empirical regularities – that is, constant conjunctions between cause and outcome. Probabilistic criteria decide whether the observed empirical regularity is genuine or spurious. Detecting causes versus predicting outcomes is a critical difference between case-based versus variable-based methods, one that has major implications for the analytical strategies that researchers must follow (Goertz and Mahoney, 2012a). As a case-based method, QCA detects causes in a systematic and rigorous way with the help of truth tables. Truth tables invite researchers to interpret the meaning of cross-case patterns by drawing from case-level evidence.

THE TRUTH TABLE: SYSTEMATIC CROSS-CASE COMPARISON

The best way to explain a truth table is to show one. The truth table in Table 2.1 explains why EU countries are high-income countries. This truth table has three explanatory conditions: being a cosmopolitan society, being a knowledge economy, and being a country with a good-quality government. The cases are EU countries, the data are fictional.

The first thing to notice about this truth table is that it has eight rows. Each condition may be present (1) or absent (0). Or rather, the statement, 'This country is a cosmopolitan society' may be true (1) or false (0). Of course, every country has a degree of cosmopolitanism, but we only recognize a country as a cosmopolitan society above a threshold of cosmopolitanism. Thus, the 1s and 0s in the truth table are logical statements, not empirical values. Getting from empirical values (data) to logical statements is a process of calibration (Ragin, 2000, pp. 7–9), which is the topic of Chapter 8. As each condition may be present (true, 1) or absent (false, 0), a truth table has 2^k rows, where k is the number of explanatory conditions. Three conditions thus produce a truth table of $2^3 = 8$ rows.

Second, cases are unevenly distributed across the rows. The vast majority (23 out of 28) cases are clustered in only three rows (Rows 1, 7 and 8), while two rows (Rows 4 and 6) have no cases. This is called limited diversity (Ragin [1987] 2014, pp. 13–14). Social reality is limitedly diverse, meaning that most logically possible configurations (i.e., truth table rows) have few or no cases. As argued in Chapter 1, what statisticians call multicollinearity is the norm in social reality. On the level of cases, all characteristics are interconnected because cases are holistic (Ragin, 1992, 2009). Of course, the education level of a region's workforce is contingent on its industrial make-up. This interconnectedness 'favours' some configurations, while others are much less obvious, or even impossible – for example, residential areas where residents have a low income, unhealthy lifestyles, low social capital but are higher educated do not exist. Higher education does not co-occur with the three other conditions. Evidently, empty truth table rows may also happen because of a lack of cases. The truth table is designed to capture limited diversity as a key feature of social reality – something that is very much harder to do with correlational (variable-based) methods.

Third, each row is itself logically true (1) or false (0) in that the configuration that the row describes co-occurs with the presence (1) or absence (0) of the outcome (high income). In the present example, all countries in a row have the same outcome. Their incomes are all high enough to be recognized as high-income countries (1), or too low to be recognized as such (0). In real-world studies, this will often not be the case. Chapter 10 explains how to deal with that. The point is that a truth table row abstracts from the cases in the row to develop a logical statement about the configuration that the row describes (Ragin [1987] 2014, p. 88). The 1 or 0 in the outcome column of a truth table row suggests that the statement, 'This row (configuration) is sufficient for (explains) the outcome', is true (1) or false (0). Whether the statement is true or false is inferred from the cases in the row but the statement itself abstracts from these cases. That is, it interprets singular (case-level) causation into a general (cross-case) causal claim.

Fourth, researchers can make counterfactual assumptions on empty truth table rows (Ragin, 2008, pp. 50–51). This is visualized in Table 2.1 with the (0) after the (?) in Rows 4 and 6. Knowledge of cases, context and concepts suggests that, if cases existed for these rows, they would not have the outcome. Empty rows are possible worlds (in the domain of the Real) that have not actually happened (in the domain of the Actual) and may never do so. In other words, empty rows represent counterfactual cases. Exercising judgemental rationality from knowledge of (actual) cases, context and concepts, we can make a plausible argument as to whether the outcome is possible in these

Table 2.1   *Truth table for high-income countries*

Row	Explanatory Conditions			Outcome	Cases
	Cosmopolitan society	Knowledge economy	Good-quality government	High-income countries	
1	1	1	1	1	BE, DE, DK, FI, LX, NL, SE
2	1	1	0	1	IT
3	1	0	1	1	FR, UK
4	1	0	0	? (0)	–
5	0	1	1	1	AT, IE
6	0	1	0	? (0)	–
7	0	0	1	0	CZ, EE, ES, HR, LT, LV, PT, SI
8	0	0	0	0	BG, CY, EL, HU, MT, PL, RO, SK

Note: AT (Austria); BE (Belgium); BG (Bulgaria); CY (Cyprus); CZ (Czech Republic); DE (Germany); DK (Denmark); EE (Estonia); EL (Greece); ES (Spain); FI (Finland); FR (France); HR (Croatia); HU (Hungary); IE (Ireland); IT (Italy); LT (Lithuania); LV (Latvia); LX (Luxembourg); MT (Malta); NL (Netherlands); PL (Poland); PT (Portugal); RO (Romania); SE (Sweden); SI (Slovenia); SK (Slovakia); UK (United Kingdom).

counterfactual cases. How to do this is the subject of Chapter 10. For now, it suffices to know that the truth table makes inferences on all actual and counterfactual cases in the case population.

Fifth, using formal, propositional logic, the eight logical statements that make up the truth table can be simplified to just (in this example) the following three:

(a)   [cosmopolitan society AND knowledge economy] is sufficient for [high income]

(b)   [good-quality government AND cosmopolitan society] is sufficient for [high income]

(c)   [good-quality government AND knowledge economy] is sufficient for [high income]

Chapter 10 explains how this simplification works. It must be done with software; however, the logic behind it is very straightforward. Look at Rows

1 and 2 in Table 2.1. Both rows are sufficient for the outcome (high income is 1 for both rows). In both rows, 'cosmopolitan society' and 'knowledge economy' are present (1). The rows only differ in that 'good-quality government' is present (1) in Row 1 but absent (0) in Row 2. This means that, when [cosmopolitan society AND knowledge economy] is present, the presence or absence of 'good-quality government' is logically redundant. The presence or absence of this condition makes no difference for the presence or absence of the outcome. Consequently, Rows 1 and 2 may be simplified to the above configuration (a).

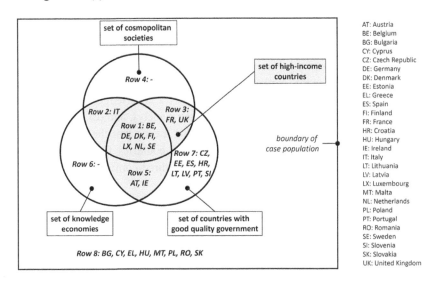

Note: AT (Austria); BE (Belgium); BG (Bulgaria); CY (Cyprus); CZ (Czech Republic); DE (Germany); DK (Denmark); EE (Estonia); EL (Greece); ES (Spain); FI (Finland); FR (France); HR (Croatia); HU (Hungary); IE (Ireland); IT (Italy); LT (Lithuania); LV (Latvia); LX (Luxembourg); MT (Malta); NL (Netherlands); PL (Poland); PT (Portugal); RO (Romania); SE (Sweden); SI (Slovenia); SK (Slovakia); UK (United Kingdom).

Figure 2.1   Venn diagram for the truth table of high-income countries

The outcome of the truth table minimization can also be visualized in a Venn diagram (Figure 2.1). Since QCA is a set-analytical method, it is helpful to introduce some of the basics of set analysis already here. In Figure 2.1, the set of countries that are cosmopolitan societies is represented as the upper circle. The left and right circles represent the set of countries that have a knowledge economy and the set of countries that have good-quality government, respectively. The sets (circles) partially overlap. For example, the overlap of the set of cosmopolitan societies and the set of knowledge economies defines the configuration [cosmopolitan society AND knowledge economy]. Only one country, Italy (IT) is described by this configuration, which corresponds to Row 2 in the above truth table. Italy thus is a member of both sets; it has both characteristics. Note also that Bulgaria (BG), Cyprus (CY) and six other countries do not have membership in any of the sets. They are placed outside the circles but still inside the area that represents the case population – that is, the population of 28 EU countries. This corresponds to Row 8, where all conditions are absent (0). Note further that the shaded area of the Venn diagram represents the countries that are members of the set of high-income countries (the outcome). This set coincides with Rows 1, 2, 3 and 5 of the truth table. From the Venn diagram, it is obvious that Row 1 (where all conditions are present) is not a separate explanation of the outcome because it is fully inside the overlaps of (a) [cosmopolitan society AND knowledge economy]; (b) [good-quality government AND cosmopolitan society]; and (c) [good-quality government AND knowledge economy]. This means that the cases in Row 1 are 'overdetermined'; they are high-income countries for three different reasons – the reasons suggested by the above three configurations (Goertz, 2017, pp. 78–81).

Sixth, the above three configurations that follow from simplifying the truth table must be interpreted into a causal explanation (Ragin [1987] 2014, pp. 168–71). The configurations are cross-case patterns observed in the domain of the Empirical. The patterns are inferred from the actual cases (in the domain of the Actual) and counterfactual cases (in the domain of the Real). What is still missing is an explanation of what these patterns (configurations) mean. This explanation should capture the causal powers (domain of the Real) that make the outcome possible. In this example, one could argue that configuration (a) [cosmopolitan society AND knowledge economy] suggests that 'high income' follows from innovation. Innovation requires a combination of ideas (cosmopolitan societies encourage idea generation) and knowledge (knowledge economies produce knowledge). This configuration thus captures the causal power of innovation to 'produce' high-income economies. Configurations (b) [good-quality government AND cosmopolitan society] and (c) [good-quality government AND knowledge economy] may be argued to be variations of the same causal power. Good-quality government creates a conducive environment for economic development and economic development may be driven by either ideas (cosmopolitan society) or knowledge (knowledge economy). That is, configurations (b) and (c) capture the causal power of stable government to 'produce' high-income economies – we have now interpreted that the causal powers of 'innovation' and 'stable government' exist in the domain of the Real and that these powers make it possible for countries to be high-income countries.

In sum, QCA uses truth tables for systematic cross-case comparison. The truth table is an analytical tool that helps QCA researchers navigate from the domain of the Actual (the cases) and the domain of the Empirical (the configurations) to the domain of the Real (the interpretation of the configurations). Doing so, the truth table dialogues between singular (i.e., case-level) and general (i.e., cross-case level) causal evidence. This makes the truth table the real unit of analysis of a QCA study (Ragin [1987] 2014, p. 88). It captures the whole of the constructed case population, both the actual and counterfactual cases, in a series of logical statements (the rows). Counterfactual cases are included in the truth table minimization by making assumptions on whether empty rows are sufficient for the outcome. Which makes QCA a logical rather than an empirical method because, obviously, researchers cannot have empirical data on counterfactual cases. The result of the truth table minimization is then interpreted into an explanation of the outcome. Ontological uncertainty concerns the thresholds between 1 and 0. Are the criteria that we use to distinguish between – for example, cosmopolitan societies and not-cosmopolitan societies valid? Do they truly capture what it means to be a cosmopolitan society? Epistemic uncertainty concerns the validity of the data that we use to judge whether a country is above or below the threshold for, for example, being a cosmopolitan society. Possibilistic uncertainty means that we cannot be certain that the above three configurations explain being a high-income country. These configurations may have too few or too many conditions, or the wrong conditions. What we can say (and that is very substantial) is that, on the basis of our knowledge of cases, context and conditions, the above three configurations are the most plausible explanations for the outcome.

CONCLUSION

The Ragin revolution takes cases seriously. It suggests case-based analysis as a fully fledged alternative to the variable-based (correlational) methods that dominate the social sciences. With QCA, Ragin developed a method that develops a deeper understanding of the complexity of causality, thereby departing from conventional quantitative methods. Using set analysis and truth tables, Ragin developed QCA into a method that allows systematic cross-case analysis and interpretation of empirical findings, thereby departing from conventional qualitative methods. Equally part of the Ragin revolution is the qualitative mindset required to learn from cases – to go beyond empirical regularities and interpret what they mean by dialoguing singular (case-level) and general (cross-case) causal evidence. Simply diving into explaining QCA risks focusing on its technicalities and its parameters of fit and losing sight of the Q for qualitative in QCA.

GLOSSARY OF KEY CONCEPTS

Case-based methods	Detect plausible causes of known outcomes, observed from cases. Case-based methods rely on set analysis to identify configurations of explanatory conditions that co-occur with the outcome on the level of cases. The co-occurrence of 'cause' and 'outcome' is the starting point for causal inference, for a dialogue between knowledge of cases, context and concepts
Complex causality	Causality on the level of cases is complex. On the level of cases, explanatory conditions are not independent but always interconnected. Complex causality is expressed as configurations of conditions that are sufficient for (i.e., explain) the outcome
General causal evidence	Causal evidence in the form of cross-case patterns
Limited diversity	Because explanatory conditions are interconnected on the level of cases, some configurations are very common while most others 'happen' much less often in social reality, or are simply not possible. Limited diversity manifests itself as cases clustering in a few truth table rows while other rows are sparsely populated or empty
Singular causal evidence	Causal evidence observed on the level of cases
Truth table	An analytical tool to detect configurations of explanatory conditions that co-occur with the outcome. The truth table is a series of logical propositions that are either true (1) or false (0). Truth tables allow making causal inferences on both actual and counterfactual cases – that is, on the empty rows in the truth table. The use of truth tables defines QCA as a method
Variable-based methods	Search for co-variation between independent and dependent variables. Variable-based methods are decontextualized. They search for correlations on the level of populations and abstract from cases. Variable-based methods 'predict' causal effects – that is, the size of the effect on the outcome

NOTE

1. My colleague and friend Paul Benneworth (1974–2020) often said that 'social science is about people doing stuff'. What he meant was that social science should not be stylized into variables and correlations. I'm always happy to borrow this quote because it is a catchy phrase that evidences Paul's (and my) commitment to learning from cases.

3.   A theory of causality for QCA

With QCA, Ragin developed an approach and a technique for case-based causal inference. He did not commit QCA to any philosophy or theory of causality. Except, of course, that he suggested causal inference as a process of interpretation (Ragin [1987] 2014, pp. 16–17). Boolean-algebraic expressions (configurations) that follow from the truth table minimization are not causal statements; they merely describe cross-case patterns (ibid., pp. 168–70). Suggesting causal inference as interpretation, Ragin distanced QCA from the (neo-)positivist and empiricist positions on causality that dominate variable-based methods (Ragin, 2000, pp. 311–16). In these methods, the robustness of empirical regularities between cause and outcome is the cornerstone of causal inference (Mahoney and Goertz, 2006). However, following Ragin, causal explanation requires interpretation of what empirical patterns mean. Ragin emphasized interpretation for yet another reason. In case-based research, causality 'happens' on the level of cases (i.e., the level of singular causality); however, causal claims are made on the level of configurations (i.e., the level of general causality) (Goertz, 2017, pp. 1–3). Getting from singular to general causality requires a dialogue between singular and general causal evidence – and that is what happens in the truth table (Ragin [1987] 2014, pp. 115–18). This chapter develops a theory of causality for QCA that explains how researchers dialogue between singular and general causality. It explains what a cause is in a QCA context and how different causal tools help identify configurations that may be causally interpreted. The chapter also explains how a powers approach to causality implies a commitment to activist (agent-based causality) rather than passivist (mechanism-based causality) (Groff, 2016, 2019). The theory of causality developed in this chapter informs the practice of causal inference in QCA; it aims to guide QCA researchers making causal inferences based on critical realist philosophy of science (Bhaskar [1975] 2008). I must emphasize that Ragin never committed himself (or QCA) to critical realism and that different philosophies of causality feature in the QCA methodological literature (see Mello, 2021, pp. 62–9 for a brief discussion). However, I believe that critical realism most accurately connects to Ragin suggesting QCA as a dialogue between knowledge of cases, context and concepts (see Chapter 1).

SINGULAR VERSUS GENERAL CAUSALITY

Case-based methods like QCA observe causality on the level of cases. This is where the outcome occurs, or fails to do so, and where explanations can be developed (Goertz and Mahoney, 2012a; Mahoney, 2008; Rohlfing and Schneider, 2018). Case-level causality is singular causality (also referred to as token causality). Cross-case patterns present causal general causal evidence, also referred to as type causality (Beach and Pedersen, 2016, pp. 42–5). In QCA, cross-case patterns come in the form of configurations that are consistent subsets of the outcome (Ragin [1987] 2014). However, as argued earlier, interpreting such cross-case patterns into (general) causal statements requires a dialogue between knowledge of cases, context and concepts. It requires researchers to 'go back' to their cases – that is, to draw from singular causal evidence (Ragin, 2008, p. 173). The step from singular to general causality happens on the level of a truth table row. In the (fictional) example of Chapter 2, which explored the explanatory conditions for high-income EU countries, all countries (cases) in a row had the same outcome. This will not usually happen with real-world data, particularly not with larger numbers of cases. This results in 'contradictory rows'; the singular causal evidence in the row is contradictory because not all cases in the row have the same outcome. This makes it difficult to suggest the row (i.e., the configuration) as a general causal claim, and to suggest that the row (the configuration) is sufficient for the outcome. How to resolve contradictory rows is explained in Chapter 10; however, it requires researchers to 'go back' to the cases, to dialogue between singular and general causal evidence. If the researcher believes the row to be sufficient for the outcome, the researcher must argue that the outcome is also possible in the negative cases. In other words, the researcher must make it plausible that 'something' interfered with the configuration (i.e., the cause) in the negative cases, rather than their not having the outcome evidencing that the row (configuration) does not make the outcome possible (Ragin [1987] 2014, pp. 113–18).

Once the (in)sufficiency of each truth table row has been established, QCA uses three tools to minimize the truth table:

- *Difference-making.* Principally, the truth table is a difference-making tool. Using formal, propositional logic, the truth table minimization investigates whether the presence or absence of a condition makes a difference for the presence or absence of the outcome (Ragin, 2008, pp. 135–8).
- *Counterfactual analysis.* The truth table makes causal assumptions on empty rows – that is, on counterfactual cases. Based on substantive knowledge (of cases, context and concepts), researchers decide whether the presence or absence of a condition contributes to the presence of the

outcome. This information allows the QCA algorithm to make counterfactual assumptions on empty rows being (in)sufficient for the outcome (ibid., pp. 163–73).

- *Regularity.* The robustness of the constant conjunction between cause (configuration) and outcome is expressed as the consistency of the subset relationship. Higher consistencies suggest that, in the case population, the outcome almost always co-occurs with the configurations, which helps establish general causal evidence (Goertz, 2017, pp. 66–8; Ragin, 2008, pp. 44–50).

These three tools draw from a regularity theory of causality (Mahoney and Acosta, 2022) and suggest causality in terms of the actuality of the outcome. All three tools establish a constant conjunction between cause and outcome. In other words, they contribute to developing general causal evidence. However, this does not suggest QCA as a difference-making, counterfactual or regularity method. After performing the truth table minimization, QCA 'goes back' to the cases to (re)connect general to singular causal evidence. To interpret configurations (i.e., cross-case patterns) into general causal statements, a QCA researcher must make it plausible that the explanatory conditions of the configuration make the outcome possible on a case level (Mahoney, 2008; Ragin [1987] 2014; Rohlfing and Schneider, 2018).

In sum, QCA uses various tools that suggest causality in terms of the actuality of the outcome. It uses these tools as part of a dialogue between singular and general causal evidence. QCA makes general causal claims about configurations; however, the plausibility of these claims is a function of the strength of both singular (case-level) and general (cross-case level) causal evidence. Patterns are established on a cross-case level (general causal evidence). What they mean is inferred with the help of case-level (singular) causal evidence. The truth table is a tool to dialogue singular and general causal evidence. It goes from singular to general causality on the level of truth table rows and, after the truth table minimization, connects general and singular causal evidence on the level of configurations in the solution to produce plausible general causal claims.

WHAT IS A CAUSE?

Ragin never unambiguously answered the question: what is a cause? This has led to considerable confusion (see Duşa, 2022) because the question allows different answers. If [lively pubs AND good public transportation] is sufficient for a neighbourhood to be an attractive residential area, then 'lively pubs' is a cause of 'attractive residential area' (Baumgartner, 2015). However, the presence of a lively pub does not cause a neighbourhood to be an attractive residential area. The set of neighbourhoods with lively pubs is not a consistent subset of the set of attractive residential areas. Only in conjunction with good public transportation (in this example) do we have a (an effective) cause for being an attractive residential area. In other words, configurational causality is 'holistic'; it suggests configurations as causes, not conditions (Ragin [1987] 2014, pp. 23–4). The notion of configurational causality implies that outcomes are 'caused' by configurations (of explanatory conditions). QCA is chiefly concerned with causality as sufficiency, and individual conditions are not (usually) sufficient for the outcome. They do not cause the outcome in the way that QCA understands causation (Rutten, 2023).

This is also Dușa's (2022) argument. His notion of robust sufficiency suggests that we can only identify a configuration as sufficient if we (can reasonably) know that it effectively explains the outcome; that together the conditions make the outcome possible. There is a crucial difference between mathematical and substantive sufficiency (see Chapter 7) (Pula, 2021). Mathematical sufficiency means that the configuration is a consistent subset of the outcome (where QCA usually considers a subset consistency of 0.8 as sufficient) (Greckhamer et al., 2018). However, a configuration is only substantively sufficient if we have good reasons to believe that it makes the outcome possible (Ragin, 2000, p. 87). Only then can a configuration be interpreted into a causal explanation. The point is that a mathematically sufficient configuration may not be substantially (or robustly) sufficient because it misses a substantively important condition – even if this condition is mathematically redundant (Rutten, 2023). Critical realism supports this holistic or configurational notion of causality, and, hence, of causality as substantive sufficiency. Critical realism suggests causality as an emergent power (Elder-Vass, 2010; Groff, 2016, 2019), which is easiest explained with an example from the natural world, viz. water. Water is a chemical configuration of hydrogen and oxygen (H_2O), which has the causal power to extinguish fire. However, the conditions hydrogen and oxygen separately do not have this causal power. In fact, hydrogen and oxygen fuel fire. Therefore, the causal power of water to extinguish fire is emergent; it emerges from merging hydrogen and oxygen into water. Or, in critical realist speak, the causal power of water is non-reducible to its component elements. Emergence 'produces' something (a causal power that makes the outcome possible) that did not previously exist (Archer, 1995, pp. 174–5; Elder-Vass, 2010, pp. 16–18).

In fact, critical realism takes the argument a step further. The configuration (H_2O or [lively pubs AND good public transportation]) only describes a causal power; it is not itself the causal power (Bhaskar [1975] 2008, p. 184). After all, the configuration 'sits' in the domain of the Empirical, while the causal power it captures 'resides' in the domain of the Real. Ergo, configurations are not causes either. Instead, they capture the conditions from which the causal power emerges (Pula, 2021). What actually causes outcomes in social reality is human agents exercising causal powers (Groff, 2016, 2019). This dovetails with the above distinction between mathematical and substantive sufficiency (Duşa, 2022; Rutten, 2023). For example, [lively pubs AND good public transportation] describes a causal power that emerges from a neighbourhood offering opportunities for leisure AND from the neighbourhood being easily accessible. Together they make it possible for people to think of the neighbourhood as an attractive residential area. Mathematical sufficiency makes an epistemological statement; it says something about cross-case patterns in the domain of the Empirical. Substantive sufficiency makes an ontological statement that says something about a causal power that we believe to exist in the domain of the Real (Bhaskar, 1986, pp. 23–5). As argued earlier, this makes causal explanation a matter of conducting a dialogue between knowledge of cases, context and concepts, which means that identifying the 'correct' configuration is not an exclusively empirical task (Ragin, 2000, pp. 144–5).

If a configuration must correctly describe the conditions from which a causal power emerges, it may be wrong in two ways. It may be too parsimonious – that is, it misses one or more conditions. Or it may be too complex – that is, it contains one or more redundant conditions.[1] Note first that any configuration that is a consistent subset of the outcome is mathematically correct. The question is: is it possible for the causal power to emerge from the conditions in a mathematically sufficient configuration? The answer to this question follows from a dialogue between knowledge of cases, context and concepts. Causal explanation in QCA is a logical not an empirical exercise. In other words, the 'correctness' of a configuration is about possibilistic uncertainty (see Chapter 1), not about the consistency of a subset relationship (as long as it is ≥ 0.8) (Finn, 2022; Rutten, 2023). From the perspective of possibilistic uncertainty, missing conditions are unacceptable while redundant conditions are largely unproblematic. Having lively pubs does not explain being an attractive residential area; the required causal power does not emerge from this condition alone. Equally, the causal power to extinguish fire does not emerge from hydrogen alone. The configuration [lively pubs AND good public transportation AND streets paved with red asphalt] contains all conditions for the causal power to emerge, even though having 'streets paved with red asphalt' may contribute nothing to how people think about the neighbourhood. Therefore, 'streets paved with red asphalt' is not a cause of 'attractive residential area'. Consequently, one may argue, the configuration including 'streets paved with red asphalt' cannot be a cause of the outcome either (Baumgartner, 2015). However, from a set-analytical perspective, redundant conditions merely unnecessarily limit the explanation (to neighbourhoods with red asphalt streets). Substantively, the explanation is unproblematic and given our current knowledge of cases, context and concepts, we may not even know that red asphalt is redundant (Duşa, 2022; Rutten, 2023). Our substantive knowledge thus leads us to conclude that the causal power emerges from this configuration – because we have no way of knowing that 'streets paved with red asphalt' is a redundant condition. More poignantly, suppose one wants to buy an item that costs £32.50. The power to purchase that item nicely emerges from the following configuration of banknotes: [£20 AND £10 AND £5] – even though it overshoots the target by £2.50. However, any configuration of just two of those three banknotes fails to do the job.

Put differently, more complex configurations have a lower possibilistic uncertainty because they emphasize singular causal evidence. However, this weakens their general causal validity. In other words, too complex configurations do not successfully make the step from singular to general causality. Too parsimonious configurations, as long as they are mathematically sufficient, suggest general causal evidence that is not substantiated by what 'happens' in cases – that is, by singular causal evidence (Ragin, 2000, p. 107). In other words, identifying the 'correct' configurations (i.e., the correct 'cause') is about dialoguing singular and general causal evidence. It underlines that causal inference in QCA cannot be reduced to the minimization of truth tables but, instead, is always a dialogue between knowledge of cases, context and concepts (Rohlfing and Schneider, 2018). Where knowledge of cases pertains to both singular causal evidence (knowledge of what 'happens' on the case level) and general causal evidence (knowledge of cross-case patterns) (Goertz, 2017, pp. 2–3).

PASSIVIST VERSUS ACTIVIST CAUSATION

Suggesting causality as an emergent power, as 'the power to do', raises the question: 'Who does the doing?' There are two possible answers to this question. One may believe in mechanism-based, or passivist causation and one may believe in agent-based, or activist causation (Groff, 2016, 2019). Mechanism-based, or passivist causation has by far the most followers. Mechanism is the most popular metaphor with which to talk about causation in the social sciences (Beach and Pedersen, 2016, pp. 31–3; Goertz, 2017, pp. 29–30; Hedström and Ylikoski, 2010; Mahoney, 2001); however, it does have a number of problems. There is a plethora of definitions of causal mechanisms, many of which have contradictory elements – one of the most contentious being whether causal mechanisms are empirically observable chains, sequences or paths, or more stylized, abstract and unobservable processes (Hedström and Ylikoski, 2010). This makes me weary of the mechanism metaphor. If a mechanism can be many things, how can we develop generalizable knowledge of it? More urgently, the question is what a causal mechanism is in a QCA context. It could be the 'thing' connecting a configuration to an outcome (Haesebrouck and Thomann, 2022). However, if a causal mechanism (the 'thing') is an observable chain, sequence or path that 'happens' on case level, it may well be idiosyncratic (Decoteau, 2018). Because every case is a unique time- and place-contingent 'assemblage' of characteristics, context and human agents (Delanda, 2016), different chains, sequences or paths may connect the same cause to the same outcome in different cases. This kind of mechanism captures singular causation. If, on the other hand, a mechanism (the 'thing') is a stylized process, it becomes conceptually almost synonymous with a causal power (Groff, 2016). Except there is a problem. Configurations are not mechanisms; mechanistic causal evidence is very different from configurational causal evidence. One may argue that the configuration [*A* AND *B*] 'covers' three very different mechanisms. Since configurations are time agnostic, [*A* AND *B*] may suggest that (1) *A* 'happens' before *B*; (2) *B* 'happens' before *A*; and (3) *A* and *B* 'happen' simultaneously. So neither singular nor general mechanisms connect very well to configurations. Instead, one may suggest mechanisms as connecting conditions to the outcome (Álamos-Concha et al., 2022). However, conditions are not causes in the way that QCA thinks of causes; they do not themselves cause the outcome, so these mechanisms would not be causal. Moreover, such mechanisms are equally vulnerable to the allegation of idiosyncrasy, while a stylized mechanism, again, is conceptually almost equivalent to a power.

Another problem is that, on the case level, cause and outcome often emerge synchronically (Gerrits and Pagliarin, 2021). Suppose that [having a flat hierarchy AND having trustful relationships] is sufficient for knowledge creation in a regional network. The flat hierarchy of the network exists in the domain of the Real but it must be actualized in the domain of the Actual to contribute to knowledge creation. The flat hierarchy does not actualize itself and then wait outside the meeting room where human agents (e.g., engineers and other experts) are about to exchange knowledge. It must be actualized by these human agents during the meeting. They do so via communication and other forms of social interaction that do not follow strict procedures (to actualize a *flat* hierarchy). The same goes for trust. For trust to contribute to knowledge creation, it must be actualized – for example, by human agents sharing competitively sensitive knowledge, again through communication. Knowledge creation, the outcome, also 'happens' via communication. So while human agents actualize the causal power of [flat hierarchy AND trust], they also create knowledge. Cause and outcome thus emerge simultaneously during the communication (social interaction); there is no meaningful before and after. This sits uncomfortably with mechanisms often being suggested as the 'thing' connecting cause and outcome (Hedström and Ylikoski, 2010; Mahoney, 2001); as that what must be triggered to 'produce' the outcome. Mechanisms are suggested to exist separately from the cause and outcome they connect.

Put differently, mechanisms suggest something horizontal – for example, an arrow connecting cause and outcome. Instead, causal powers suggest something vertical. When causal power is actualized, it emerges from its conditions synchronically with the outcome.

Finally, a mechanism suggests that social reality operates as 'fixed things working in fixed ways', at least on some level of social reality (Groff, 2016). Otherwise, mechanism, the machine metaphor, does not make a lot of sense. This does not suggest that mechanisms will always (mechanistically) 'produce' the outcome, but that its parts are always the same, and that these parts always work together in the same way (Beach and Pedersen, 2016; Haesebrouck and Thomann, 2022). I do not find this plausible. Fixed patterns in the domain of the Empirical are socially constructed. Suggesting them as causal mechanisms is to commit the epistemic fallacy (see Chapter 2). The domain of the Actual is characterized by idiosyncrasy, and by the diversity, contingency and heterogeneity that characterizes events. All events (cases) are unique time- and place-contingent assemblages of characteristics, context and human agents and, therefore, on a cross-case level, we will not find fixed things working in fixed ways (Abbott, 1992; Delanda, 2016). Fixed things working in fixed ways may exist in the domain of the Real. This would suggest a form of ontological determinism where, if left to themselves, the same cause would always produce the same outcome in the same way (Beach and Pedersen, 2016, pp. 44–5). However, ontological determinism is incompatible with critical realism's emergent view of social reality (Bhaskar [1975] 2008, pp. 107–8), which suggests social reality as an open system (ibid., pp. 33–5). Moreover, it risks denying the role of human agency in producing social reality (Groff, 2016, 2019).

From my critical realist perspective, this is the biggest problem of causal mechanisms; they commit to passivist causation (ibid.). If mechanisms are real, if they exist in the domain of the Real, then they 'do the doing'. Then mechanisms rather than human agents 'produce' the outcome (Groff, 2013, pp. 76–81). Human agents may trigger a mechanism; however, once triggered, the mechanism decides what happens and human agents are obliged to follow the mechanism's script if the outcome is to 'happen'. Of course, triggering a mechanism no more guarantees or determines the occurrence of the outcome than does exercising causal power (Archer, 1995, p. 55; Elder-Vass, 2010, pp. 42–7). However, contrary to causal powers, causal mechanisms explain the actuality of the outcome. Not only that, they also specify (prescribe) how the outcome is (to be) achieved – viz., via the mechanism (Beach and Pedersen, 2016; Hedström and Ylikoski, 2010). This reduces human agency to passively 'undergo' causation. Obviously, this sits uncomfortably with the nature of human agency as being intentional, non-determined and capable of spontaneity (Archer, 1995, p. 133; Groff, 2016, 2019) (which neither suggests human agency as rational nor denies unintended outcomes). Power-based causality is a form of activist causation. A causal powers approach says something about the potentiality of the cause and leaves it up to human agents how to actualize causal power and how to use it to (try to) achieve the outcome (Elder-Vass, 2005; Groff, 2019). This allows the idiosyncrasy we observe on the case level (domain of the Actual) – that is, on the level of singular causality – while still developing patterns (general causal evidence) across (actual and counterfactual) cases.

There may well be a mechanism connecting cause to outcome in any one case. One can always trace a path, process or sequence on the case level. But as all cases are unique, a different (unique) mechanism may 'work' in different cases. Stylizing such singular causal mechanisms into a general causal mechanism, therefore, is very problematic. If causal mechanisms confess to ontological determinism, a general causal mechanism imposes on human agents (at case level) a script they must follow to achieve the outcome. Instead, activist causality identifies human agency as the producer of social reality and it allows human agents every discretion as to how they do that (Groff, 2013, pp. 77–8). Importantly, powers-based causality is not a form of individual reductionism. The powers that human agents exercise exist independently of them. They emerge from social structures and institutions that are beyond the control of individual human agents (Archer, 1995, pp. 165–70) and that QCA captures in configurations (i.e., Boolean expressions).

Activist causal explanation always involves human agency exercising causal power. This means that QCA researchers must identify the human agents populating their cases (case knowledge). After the truth table minimization (see Chapter 10) they must answer two questions. First, why or how does causal power emerge from the conditions in a configuration? The answer to the question results in a name or label for the configuration that captures the nature of the causal power it describes. Second, why or how does exercising this causal power make it possible for human agents to achieve or 'produce' the outcome?

For example, if [lively pubs AND good public transportation] is sufficient for being an attractive neighbourhood, then residents are the human agents. The configuration (causal power) may be labelled the easy-going configuration because leisure time in a pub and easy access via public transportation figuratively and literally provide for 'easy-goingness'. Note that labelling a configuration requires a good understanding of cases, context and concepts as well as some creativity on the part of the researcher. This easy-goingness makes it possible for residents to think of their neighbourhood as an attractive residential area. If they do, they exercise this causal power (disposition) of their neighbourhood. If [flat hierarchy AND trustful relationships] is sufficient for knowledge creation in teams, then team members are the human agents.

The configuration (causal power) may be labelled the social proximity configuration because that is what flat hierarchy and trust imply. As argued, by communicating in an informal way and sharing sensitive knowledge, team members (human agents) exercise the causal power of social proximity. Doing so makes it possible for new knowledge to emerge in their communication. If [cosmopolitan society AND knowledge economy] is sufficient for being a high-income country (see Chapter 2), then knowledge workers are the human agents. Economies or countries do not create a high income, but firms and, more particularly, the people working in these firms, do. If one labels this configuration (causal power) the innovation configuration, it is obvious that engineers, scientists and other knowledge workers are the relevant human agents. In a cosmopolitan society, knowledge workers benefit from more ideas bubbling up and crossing over because such societies are open to things new. Knowledge economies create lots of new knowledge, while innovation may be understood as connecting knowledge and ideas. Innovations, in turn, contribute to a country being a high-income country (Asheim and Coenen, 2005; Florida, 2002; Rutten, 2019).

CONCLUSION

QCA is compatible with multiple theories of causality, and many researchers (implicitly) follow a regularity theory (Mahoney and Acosta, 2022), no doubt encouraged by the regularity tools employed in the truth table minimization. However, the minimization is a purely mechanical process that only results in a more parsimonious description of the case population than the one provided by the truth table. Minimization is not a causal analysis nor does it produce causal statements. Per Ragin, causal statements in QCA follow from interpreting Boolean expressions into causal claims. This commits QCA to a stratified reality, which connects to critical realism. Furthermore, the ontological determinism of regularity theories of causality sits uncomfortably with the idiosyncratic nature of cases (singular causal evidence). Particularly in combination with mechanismic causal explanations, regularity theories of causality reduce human agents to observers rather than creators of social reality. However, social reality is a living world of human agents, not a dead world of mechanisms.

A critical realist causal powers approach dovetails with QCA's configurational causality and its interpretive approach to causal explanation. Configurations capture causal powers that emerge from their constituent conditions. This precludes suggesting conditions as causes or causal; they merely describe cases and configurations describe cases in complex ways. Critical realism legitimizes the distinction between mathematical sufficiency (empirical statements in the domain of the Empirical) and substantive sufficiency (statements about causal powers in the domain of the Real) and the need to interpret the former into the latter following a dialogue between ideas and evidence. Conducting the dialogue in terms of human agents exercising causal power (i.e., of people doing stuff) helps to dialogue singular and general causal evidence. It explains why exercising the causal power makes it possible to achieve the outcome without specifying (in a mechanismic way) how this is done. It also explains why the outcome did not occur in terms of other causal powers interfering. This permits QCA to work with less than perfect cross-case patterns (general causal evidence). Theorizing in terms of human agents exercising causal powers focuses causal explanation on human agents doing something rather than on conditions doing something – as in one variable having an effect on another variable in correlational methods. Activist causal explanation explicitly connects to cases, to the human agents 'populating' a case, and the context within which they aim to achieve the outcome.

In sum, while critical realism is not the only basis on which to do QCA, its metaphysical position and its powers notion of causality provide a valuable heuristic for QCA. Critical realism, in fact, legitimizes much of QCA's good practice rules that follow from its distinguishing between mathematical and substantive sufficiency.

GLOSSARY OF KEY CONCEPTS

Activist causation	Agent-based causation, causation where human agents produce outcomes by exercising causal power
Cause	In QCA, neither conditions nor configurations are (effective) causes. The conditions in a configuration describe a causal power that, when exercised, makes the outcome possible. Mathematically sufficient configurations may be interpreted into causal powers
Contradictory row	A row in the truth table with contradictory singular causal evidence. Not all cases in the row have the same outcome
Counterfactual causality	A key tool for truth table minimization. It allows making assumptions on empty truth table rows (counterfactuals) that are (in)sufficient for the outcome
Difference-making	The principal tool to minimize the truth table. It investigates whether the presence or absence of a condition makes a difference for the presence or absence of the outcome
Emergence	Causal power is emergent. It emerges from the conditions in a configuration but it is not reducible to them

General causality	Causal claims that pertain to groups of similar cases. General causal evidence often comes in the form of cross-case patterns that are ignorant of substantive case-level (singular) causal evidence
Mathematical sufficiency	Configurations that are consistent subsets of the outcome are mathematically sufficient for the outcome. They may be interpreted into causal explanations (substantive sufficiency)
Passivist causation	Mechanism-based causation; causation where mechanisms produce the outcome
Regularity	Another tool for truth table minimization that establishes the consistency of a subset relationship
Singular causality	Causality that happens on case level. Singular causal evidence is often compelling but likely to be idiosyncratic (case specific)
Substantive sufficiency	A substantively plausible explanation of the outcome that suggests why the causal powers (that the configuration 'captures') makes the outcome possible

NOTE

1. The correctness of a configuration is not established against some sort of 'true causal structure' that is external to the case population (as Baumgartner, 2015, suggests). Even if it existed (in the domain of the Real), we would not know it. In fact, if scope conditions are properly defined, if cases are carefully selected according to the scope conditions, and if they are carefully calibrated on the basis of substantive or external criteria, then the 'causal structure' that follows from the truth table minimization is always the correct causal structure. It is the causal structure that 'belongs' to the case population as defined by the scope conditions and calibrations. Instead, the correctness of a configuration is benchmarked against the substantive plausibility of the causal claim that is interpreted from it.

4. Cases, case populations and generalization

Any case study must begin with defining what is a case, and what it is a case of. As obvious as this may seem, it is often ignored in QCA studies that inattentively use (samples from) given populations. This is usually not a very good idea because (samples of) given populations are often characterized by a good deal of heterogeneity (Ragin, 2000, pp. 62–3). However, to make meaningful cross-case comparisons, cases must be homogeneous; they must be comparable on key scope conditions. Defining what is a case, what it is a case of, and selecting a population of comparable cases on which to perform QCA is the process of casing (Ragin, 1992). Without carefully taking this first step, one cannot learn from cases. This chapter takes readers through the process of casing. It further explains how analytical generalizations may be made from constructed case populations and how this is very different from empirical generalization from samples.

CASES AND CASING

Suppose one wants to explain knowledge creation in regional inter-firm project teams. Suppose such project teams consist of two to five partners, which may be small firms, big firms, engineering bureaus and knowledge centres (e.g., a university). Suppose one could collect data on such project teams from a variety of regions, such as urban, suburban and rural regions, more innovative regions and less innovative regions. And suppose these regions are from different countries in Europe. That would result in a very heterogeneous population of inter-firm project teams, as is to be expected given the colourfulness of social reality.

Now enter QCA. QCA is a comparative case study method; it compares cases. However, one can only meaningfully compare cases that are comparable (Ragin [1987] 2014, pp. 49–52). One learns nothing from comparing apples and oranges. Consequently, QCA researchers need to homogenize their case population. The first step in that direction is to define what is a case, and what it is a case of (Mahoney, 2008; Ragin, 2009). For example, explaining the competitiveness of regions means that regions are cases. Explaining the role of proximity in inter-firm knowledge creation presents inter-firm dyads as cases.

In the above example, cases are regional inter-firm project teams working on knowledge creation. This precise definition of what are cases (regional inter-firm project teams) and what they are cases of (knowledge creation) is important in selecting comparable cases, in homogenizing the case population (Beach and Pedersen, 2018). Regional inter-firm project teams come in different shapes and sizes. They may be composed of big firms, small firms, or both. They may or may not include engineering bureaus and knowledge centres. The question is, does it matter? This is where contextual and conceptual knowledge come in. Scientific research is cumulative (Bhaskar [1975] 2008, p. 190); it always builds on the findings of previous studies. In addition, experiences from practitioners (in this case, from firms working on knowledge creation in inter-firm project teams) may provide relevant contextual information. This specifies the above question to, does conceptual and contextual knowledge suggest that firms' size matters for how knowledge creation in inter-firm project teams happens? The relevant literature clearly suggests it does. Consequently, it is not meaningful to compare knowledge creation in inter-firm project teams of big firms with those composed of small firms. The differences one finds may be a function of the differences in firm size rather than the presence or absence of one's explanatory conditions.

This makes firm size and project team composition important scope conditions. Scope conditions are the constraints under which an explanation 'holds' (Goertz, 2017, pp. 66–8). Consider Grillitsch et al.'s (2023) study on regional path development. An important scope condition of this study is the fact that it is performed on Nordic regions. Consequently, one must be cautious about generalizing its findings to regions in, say, Southeast Europe, or South America, because their institutional make-up is very different. This makes 'Nordic institutional context' the principal scope condition of this study. Similar considerations allowed me to focus my study 'Openness values and regional innovation' (Rutten, 2019) on regions in Northwest Europe. Going back to the above example on regional inter-firm project teams, one must narrow the definition of a case. A case could be a regional inter-firm project team working on knowledge creation that is composed of small firms and does not include engineering bureaus or knowledge centres. Only regional inter-firm project teams that meet this definition now count as cases in this example. One could do separate QCA studies on, for example, big firm and small firm project teams and compare the findings. That would demonstrate whether, and if so, how, firm size matters.

Put differently, one does not find cases in the world 'out there'. One must also be critical of the idea of 'given populations'. Of course, there is a given population of manufacturing firms and of EU regions. However, the members of these populations are very heterogeneous on multiple dimensions and this likely disqualifies them as comparable cases. What happens in social reality are events – for example, knowledge-creation events in project teams (where team members [attempted to] create knowledge); election events in countries (where countries [attempted to] organize(d) elections); and poverty events in households (where households [unsuccessfully] tried to make ends meet). Events happen in the domain of the Actual (see Chapter 1); this is what is actually going on in social reality. However, events are not neatly delineated in time and place, in the organizations involved, the human agents populating them, and so on (Ragin, 2000, pp. 53–7). Casing is the process of 'converting' events into analytically relevant cases (Bhaskar [1975] 2008, p. 119; Ragin, 2000, p. 45). For example, casing converts knowledge-creation events in projects teams into cases of knowledge creation in project teams. To do so, researchers must (1) define what a project team is; and (2) define what knowledge creation is. These are conceptual, not empirical questions. A project team can be many things (inter- or intra-firm, big or small, temporary or permanent, etc.), but which project teams count as cases of project teams is a matter of definition – that is, of casing. The same goes for knowledge creation. Researchers can identify relevant events that match these definitions for inclusion in their case population. However, this is not a mechanical exercise. All events are unique because they happened in different times and places and were populated by different human agents. No event will ever perfectly match the definitions. Casing is a dialogue between definitions (conceptual knowledge) and events (empirical knowledge). Qualifying an event as a case is to make a judgement (judgemental rationality) that may be updated or revised throughout a QCA study. Learning from events may change the definition of what is a case. Learning from concepts may change which events are included or excluded from the case population (Ragin [1987] 2014, p. 165).

One may have set the threshold for small firms at 50 employees, but find that definition too restrictive and change it to 100 employees. One may decide that subdivisions of big firms count as separate small firms. Changes to the definition of what is a case are unproblematic as long as they are plausible in light of knowledge of cases, context and concepts. One may further find that, in one particular small firm project team, a new CEO substantially changed the way the project team worked and, consequently, one decides to remove this case from one's population – for example, because the outcome of this case is a function of CEO intervention rather than the explanatory conditions of the study. The point is, as a case-based method, QCA is all about learning from cases. It is therefore acceptable, even recommendable, to continuously 'update' one's definition of what is a case as one learns more about one's cases during the research process – and to remove and select cases accordingly. Casing is important for all types of QCA studies, whether small-N studies from original data or large-N studies from secondary data in databases. Almost by definition, cases in databases are too heterogeneous for a meaningful comparison, and one needs to define scope conditions to select analytically comparable cases from the database. As casing is an ongoing process, one may end up collecting data from a case that one later removes from the case population. This is not a waste of time and effort because, by carefully considering the case, one has clarified the scope condition(s) under which the explanation holds and thus strengthened the validity of the study. The key point is not to settle too easily on a given population of cases. At one point, the UK had 12 Regional Development Agencies (RDAs), one for each of the nine English macro-regions and one for each of the three devolved nations (Scotland, Wales and Northern Ireland). However, considerable differences existed between how the RDAs worked and how they were organized. Therefore, this given population of 12 RDAs is not necessarily a population of 12 comparable cases. The same is true for secondary data in databases. CrossRoads 2 was an EU Interreg project (2016–20) of the Netherlands and Flanders. Amongst others, CrossRoads 2 funded 75 innovation projects – that is, cross-border collaborations between Flemish and Dutch small and medium-sized enterprises (SMEs) on new product development. This is a given population of 75 cases; however, casing must decide which of these cases are comparable and may be selected into the case population.

Casing homogenizes the case population on relevant scope conditions to allow meaningful cross-case comparison. Like explanatory and outcome conditions, scope conditions must also be calibrated (see Chapter 8). One can then select only those cases that are qualitatively the same on a scope condition. Both explanatory and scope conditions are causally relevant, and one researcher's scope conditions are another's explanatory conditions. As 'things' that exist 'out there', each case is unique. This means that cases (as units of analysis) differ from one another on a (near) infinite number of characteristics (Abbott, 1992; Ragin, 2009, p. 526). It is therefore impossible to have a fully homogeneous case population. Nor is that necessary, because not all differences will be causally relevant. Identifying scope conditions is about identifying conditions that are known to be, or expected to be, causally relevant in the context of a particular research question. This means that casing is a dialogue between one's knowledge of the cases and contextual and conceptual knowledge (Ragin, 1992). That is why casing is a necessary first step of all case-based research. Put differently, the explanatory power of a QCA study does not depend on the size of N but on whether casing has produced a sufficiently homogeneous case population to make meaningful cross-case comparisons (Collier, Brady and Seawright, 2010). Casing is a crucial part of a QCA study, albeit an often neglected one. Most of the casing happens at the start of a QCA study, before the analyses of sufficiency and necessity. However, casing may continue throughout a QCA study (Ragin, 1992, p. 225).

Importantly, the definition of what is a case covers actual as well as counter-factual cases. Counterfactual cases are 'possible worlds'. Such cases 'reside' in the domain of the Real and could 'happen' in the domain of the Actual. Although researchers cannot collect data from (have empirical knowledge of) counterfactual cases, they are relevant cases in comparative studies. Making assumptions on empty truth table rows is the principal way in which QCA makes inferences on counterfactual cases.

CASE POPULATION AND GENERALIZATION

A case population is the population of comparable cases (homogenized on scope conditions) on which QCA is performed. A case population, thus, is something very different from a sample. Samples must be representative of the (given) population from which they are drawn (Rutten and Rubinson, 2022). They must replicate the heterogeneity of the (given) population. If a sample is representative, empirical patterns (such as correlations between independent and dependent variables) in the sample may be empirically generalized to the (given) population (Mahoney and Goertz, 2006). Control variables deal with heterogeneity in correlational (variable-based) studies by controlling the variation of these variables with the dependent variable. However, heteroge-neity compromises the ability to make meaningful cross-case comparisons; they require a homogeneous case population. Selecting cases on key scope conditions – that is, homogenizing the case population – 'neutralizes' irrele-vant factors in case-based research by keeping these factors constant as scope conditions. As a result, case populations are not necessarily representative of a given population (e.g., the above population of regional inter-firm project teams) (Ragin, 2009). Moreover, case populations include both actual and counterfactual cases, which sharply distinguishes them from given popula-tions and samples that include only actual cases. The cross-case comparison that QCA makes, therefore, is a logical rather than an empirical exercise, and this makes generalization analytical rather than empirical (Abbott, 1992). Analytical generalization pertains to the causal explanation that is interpreted from cross-case (i.e., empirical patterns). It generalizes the (substantive) expla-nation rather than the empirical pattern from which it is interpreted (Beach and Pedersen, 2018).

For example, in my study 'Openness values and regional innovation' (Rutten, 2019), one of the configurations (cross-case patterns) explaining regional innovation is [economic diversity AND melting pot]. Economic diversity captures the presence of a diversity of economic activities and, hence, a diversity of knowledge. This is because, for example, manufacturing firms rely on and create different kinds of knowledge than, for example, financial service firms. Melting pot captures a region's socio-cultural diversity and its tolerance for this diversity. The idea is that the presence of melting pot (socio-cultural diversity and tolerance of it) makes it possible for knowledge and ideas to bubble up in a region and crossing over between communities. This configuration [economic diversity AND melting pot] is the diversity configuration. It explains regional innovation as follows: ideas for new products and other innovations emerge at the intersection of economic sectors and socio-cultural communities. Because of a diverse economy, a region is able to develop these ideas into new products and, being a melting pot region, regional consumers are open to these innovations. Put differently, economic diversity and melting pot reinforce each other (form a causal power), which enables the emergence of ideas and their 'translation' into new products.

This explanation may be generalized analytically to cases described by the same scope conditions. The robustness of the cross-case pattern is not particularly relevant. Nor does it matter that the empirical pattern was present in only 36 of the 89 innovative regions in this study. The pattern and the explanation inferred from it suggest that it is possible for a region to be innovative if it is an [economic diversity AND melting pot] region. Analytical generalization of this explanation may be made to cases within and beyond the case population. Analytical generalization generalizes the explanation, not the empirical pattern from which it is interpreted. The configuration [economic diversity AND melting pot] explains innovation in the regions of Northwest Europe, with their strong economies and institutions. Analytical generalization suggests that the same explanation of why regional innovation happens also holds in similar regions in, for example, North America and Australia. The more these regions conform to the definition of a case and the scope conditions of the original study, the more plausible it is that the study's explanation holds for these cases also.

Empirical generalization is what one does from samples. Working with samples, the 'true causal structure' belongs to the (given) population from which the sample is drawn (Baumgartner and Thiem, 2020; Oana and Schneider, 2024). Every sample from that population must reproduce the same causal structure – that is, the same solution in the case of QCA. Different solutions across different samples from the same population may suggest a validity issue. If a sample is representative of the population, the empirical patterns identified in the sample may be generalized to the population – because empirical generalization is based on the assumption of a unified empirical reality (see Chapter 1). The problem with sampling in QCA is that, being a case-based method, QCA is designed to be case sensitive (Rutten, 2022; Skaaning, 2011). Even in large-N studies, many truth table rows are populated by only a few, a single case or no cases. It is easy to see how a different sample could produce a different truth table, where an empty truth table row now becomes a populated row, and vice versa. These truth tables would produce (somewhat) different solutions. QCA's lack of robustness makes empirical generalization problematic. However, this empirical weakness becomes an analytical strength when one constructs a case population on the basis of scope conditions. If a researcher has carefully defined what is a case, has carefully defined scope conditions, and has carefully selected cases accordingly, then the solution that one finds is the solution that belongs to the case population described by these scope conditions. In other words, if casing and calibration have been done correctly, the solution that one finds is always the correct solution – for the case population defined by those scope conditions and these calibrations. Adding or removing cases changes the scope conditions and thus the case population. Changing the calibration changes the definition of what is a case and thus the case population. Consequently, one would expect to find a different solution. That is, for a case-based method like QCA, case sensitivity is an analytical strength.

In sum, variable-based (quantitative) methods rely on sampling and empirical generalization (King et al., 1994). Empirical patterns, mostly co-variation between independent and dependent variables, observed in a sample are empirically generalized to the (given) population from which the sample is drawn – following the assumption of a unified empirical reality. Case-based (qualitative) methods, such as QCA, rely on analytical generalization (Mahoney and Goertz, 2006). Because given populations (insofar as they exist), are too heterogeneous for meaningful cross-case comparisons, case-based (qualitative) methods construct populations of comparable cases. Case populations are not necessarily representative of a given population; instead, they are an analytically relevant population of actual and counterfactual cases. Analytical generalization assumes a stratified reality where causal explanations are not collapsed into empirical patterns. Substantive explanation of why explanatory conditions make an outcome possible are analytically generalized to cases defined by the same scope conditions. Substantive explanations suggest causal powers (described as configurations of explanatory conditions) in the domain of the Real that make the outcome possible in the domain of the Actual. Since the domain of the Real is not directly observable, knowledge of causal powers is substantive rather than empirical, which allows substantive rather than empirical generalization. Consequently, cross-case patterns (described in QCA by Boolean expressions) are not themselves causal statements. They merely describe empirical patterns and they are the point of departure for developing a causal explanation – one that answers the question: why is it possible for the outcome to occur when this configuration (of explanatory conditions) is present? This explanation may be analytically generalized.

GLOSSARY OF KEY CONCEPTS

Actual case
A case that exists in social reality. Data can be collected from actual cases

Analytical generalization
Generalizes the substantive explanation of why an outcome is possible, not the empirical pattern from which the explanation is inferred

Case
Events that are abstracted (cased) into analytically relevant units of analysis

Case population
The population of cases on which a QCA study is performed. Case populations are constructed by selecting cases based on (1) the definition of what is a case; and (2) relevant scope conditions. The case population is not (necessarily) representative of a given population and they are certainly not samples. Case populations include all actual and counterfactual cases that conform to the definition of a case

Casing
An ongoing dialogue between knowledge of cases, context and concepts. Casing decides which events in social reality qualify as analytically relevant cases and what are relevant scope conditions. Casing constructs a population of comparable cases. It is not confined to the early stage of a QCA study but may be ongoing throughout it

Control variables
Correlational researchers 'correct' for the effects of non-relevant factors by introducing them as control variables in their studies. Control variables allow correlational researchers to deal with the heterogeneity in their samples. Case-based research does not have control variables. Instead, it homogenizes case populations on relevant scope conditions

Counterfactual case
A case that could exist (a possible world) and from which inferences can be made in a cross-case analysis

Empirical generalization
Generalization of an empirical pattern from the sample to the given population. Empirical generalization equates empirical patterns with causal explanation (following a unified empirical reality) to a much greater extent than QCA, where Boolean expressions are (merely) the starting point for causal explanation (as substantive interpretation) (assuming a stratified reality)

Events
'Things' that happen in social reality

Given population
A population of similar 'things' that exists in social reality. Given populations are characterized by a good deal of heterogeneity. Although similar, members of a given population often differ on many characteristics. Because of their heterogeneity, given populations should not uncritically be used as case populations in a comparative case study

Sample   Populations of research units (cases) that are drawn from
                        a given population. Samples aim to reflect the heterogeneity of
                        the population from which they are drawn. Therefore, sampling
                        is not a very good way of obtaining a research population for
                        comparative methods like QCA

Scope condition   A causally relevant condition that is not an explanatory
                        condition in the truth table. For meaningful cross-case
                        comparison, the case population must be homogenized on key
                        scope conditions. In QCA, case populations are best constructed
                        by selecting cases on scope conditions, rather than by sampling

Substantive   Causal explanation in QCA is a logical rather than an empirical
explanation   exercise. Cross-case (empirical) patterns, captured as Boolean
                        expressions, are the starting point for a dialogue between
                        knowledge of cases, context and concepts. This dialogue
                        answers why the explanatory conditions make the outcome
                        possible

5. Boolean algebra

Boolean algebra is the formal language of set analysis. It formalizes set relations into mathematical expressions (Schneider and Wagemann, 2012). Boolean algebra is a very different mathematical language from statistics. Doing QCA requires an understanding of Boolean algebra, which this chapter provides. While Boolean algebra is perhaps the most conspicuous part of QCA, it is important to stress that QCA is a qualitative method (Ragin [1987] 2014; 2000). The Boolean algebra only serves to formally describe set relations. Boolean expressions are not causal statements (Rutten, 2023). In QCA, causality is interpreted from answering the question: why does the presence of (a configuration of) explanatory conditions explain the occurrence of the outcome? The answer to this 'why' question is QCA's causal claim. That is, in QCA, Boolean algebra is a mostly descriptive tool. It is a means (formalizing cross-case comparisons) to an end (developing causal explanations). Mathematical sufficiency (i.e., a consistent subset relationship) does not necessarily imply substantive sufficiency (i.e., a plausible causal explanation) – on the assumption of a stratified reality (see Chapter 1). This makes 'empirical' analysis in QCA very different from empirical analysis in correlational methods. The latter emphasize empirical robustness as the basis for causal explanation because it assumes a unified empirical reality (Chapter 1). Instead, QCA emphasizes the plausibility of the explanation in the light of knowledge of cases, context and concepts (Ragin [1987] 2014). With that important disclaimer in mind, let's now turn to the technicalities of Boolean algebra and set analysis.

SETS AND THEIR COMPLEMENT

Suppose one investigates less-favoured regions. This suggests that there are also regions that are not less favoured, which does not necessarily mean they are affluent regions – more on that below. In the context of EU regional development policy, an important criterion to define less-favoured regions is a gross domestic product (GDP) per capita of no more than 75 per cent of the EU's GDP per capita. Regions are defined loosely in the context of EU regional policy; however, the NUTS[1] 2 level (mid-size subnational units) is the usual level on which the EU provides regional statistics (a US equivalent to NUTS 2 regions would be a level in between counties and states). In 2020, the EU

counted 242 NUTS 2 regions, and 84 of them had a GDP per capita of no more
than 75 per cent of the EU's GDP per capita. That is, the set of less-favoured
EU regions comprises 84 cases. The remaining 158 regions are in the set of
not-less-favoured regions. Together these two sets form the universal set of EU
regions. If one studies less-favoured regions, then the set of not-less-favoured
regions is the complement of the set of less-favoured regions (Figure 5.1).
The complement of a set is usually referred to as the negation of the set, or
not-the-set, as in the set of not-less-favoured regions. In Boolean algebra,
negation is identified with a tilde (~). Boolean-algebraic notation abbreviates
the names of conditions such that less-favoured regions may become LFRs and
the negation of this set becomes ~LFRs.

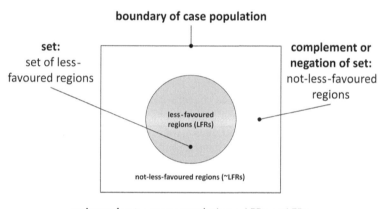

Figure 5.1   Set, complement (negation) and universal set

As argued, the negation of a set is not the same as its (semantical) opposite.
The negation of the set of less-favoured regions is the set of not-less-favoured
regions, not the set of affluent regions. This is because of the asymmetry of
sets, which results in QCA's asymmetrical causality (see Chapter 6). Although
the EU does not have a definition of affluent regions, it is plausible to argue
that regions with a GDP per capita of at least 125 per cent of the EU's GDP
per capita are affluent regions. Based on this definition, the set of affluent
regions has 40 cases. The negation of the set of affluent regions is the set
of not-affluent regions, and this set has 242 – 40 = 202 regions. This leaves
a substantial number of regions (118 to be precise [242 – (40 + 84) = 118];
remember that 84 regions were less-favoured regions) in the middle that are
neither less favoured nor affluent. The asymmetry suggests that different
factors explain being and not-being a less-favoured region than the factors

explaining being and not-being an affluent region. This is juxtaposed to correlational methods where the same factors explain both high and low levels of the outcome (e.g., affluent [high GDP] and less-favoured [low GDP] regions) (Rutten, 2020). Asymmetrical causality explains a problem of EU regional development policy. Even though many less-favoured regions become more affluent in absolute terms, the relative gap with the affluent regions does not narrow. Many regions that were less-favoured regions in 2000 now have a GDP per capita that is higher than 75 per cent of the GDP per capita of the EU in 2000. However, as not-less-favoured regions also grew their GDP per capita, the less-favoured regions of 2000 still have a GDP per capita below 75 per cent of the EU's current GDP per capita. In fact, GDP per capita of many affluent regions increased more than that of many less-favoured regions. This suggests that *becoming* more affluent (growing the regional GDP per capita beyond an absolute value) is explained by different factors than *being* an affluent region (having a GDP of ≥ 125 per cent of EU average). Different causal process are at work in regions that become more affluent than in regions that are affluent and create wealth even faster. Constructing different sets (less-favoured regions and affluent regions) from the same data (regional GDP per capita) allows QCA to investigate this kind of asymmetric causality in a way that is beyond the reach of correlational methods.

SUPERSET AND SUBSET RELATIONSHIPS

Look at the left pane of Figure 5.2. It shows how the set of regions with a higher-educated workforce is a superset of the set of affluent regions. This means that all affluent regions are also regions with a higher-educated workforce, but that not all regions with a higher-educated workforce are also affluent regions. Put differently, there are more cases in the set of regions with a higher-educated workforce (X) than there are cases in the set of affluent regions (Y). In Boolean algebra, this is written as $X \supset Y$, or the set of X is a superset of the set of Y. All of the set of Y is contained within the set of X, meaning that $X > Y$. Substantively, it means that X is a necessary condition for Y; to be in the set of Y, it is necessary to also be in the set of X.

The right pane of Figure 5.2 shows how the set of R&D-performing regions is a subset of the set of affluent regions. This means that all regions in the set of R&D-performing regions are also in the set of affluent regions, but that not all affluent regions are also R&D-performing regions. Put differently, there are fewer cases in the set of R&D-performing regions (X) than there are in the set of affluent regions (Y). In Boolean algebra, this is written as $X \subset Y$, or the set of X is a subset of the set of Y. All of the set of X is contained within the set of Y, meaning that $X < Y$. Substantively, it means that X is a sufficient condition for Y; to be in the set of Y, it is sufficient to also be in the set of X.

Qualitative comparative analysis

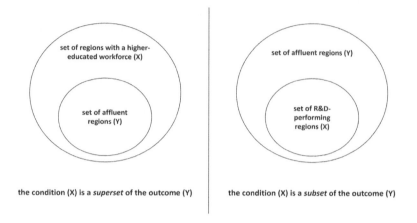

Figure 5.2   Superset and subset relationships

INTERSECTIONS AND UNIONS

Cases are holistic; they are characterized by multiple characteristics simultaneously and these characteristics are often interconnected (Ragin [1987] 2014, p. 15). Regions where firms spend a lot of money on R&D are mostly also regions with a higher-educated workforce because these higher-educated workers are employed in R&D. Furthermore, higher-educated workers tend to hold more open and less conservative values because, generally, that is the effect of higher education. This interconnectedness of characteristics defines the nature or essence of cases (ibid.).

Look at Silicon Valley. It is a large, diverse, high-tech regional cluster. That is, Silicon Valley is a case of a regional cluster (a group of interrelated and co-located firms) that is large (numbering many firms), diverse (these firms are in a variety of industrial sectors), and high-tech (these firms invest lots of resources in R&D) (Silicon Valley has plenty more relevant characteristics but, as an example, I will just focus on these three). In fact, Silicon Valley is the archetypical large, diverse, high-tech regional cluster. There are plenty more such regional clusters around the world. Many more regions have tried to copy Silicon Valley by investing in regional R&D (to become high-tech), encouraging business start-ups and acquiring firms (to become large), specializing in multiple fields of technology (to become diverse), and encouraging regional inter-firm collaborations (to become a cluster). Many regions that managed to become a cluster (i.e., become a case of a regional cluster) still became failed Silicon Valley wannabees because they did not acquire the other characteristics. Regional clusters may be high-tech, they may be large, they may be diverse, and they may have a combination of any two of these three characteristics, but none of these makes them into cases of Silicon Valley-like regional clusters. Only when regions have all three characteristics are they Silicon Valley-like regional clusters. In other words, Silicon Valley-like regional clusters are members of the set of large regional clusters AND members of the set of diverse regional clusters, AND members of the set of high-tech regional clusters. They occupy the intersection of these three sets.

This gives us the notion of an intersection or a conjunction. The left pane of Figure 5.3 visualizes the intersection of two sets, A and B. The intersection of the set of A and the set of B is the shaded area where the circles of A and B overlap. The intersection of A and B establishes a new set that includes only cases that are in both set A and set B. That is, intersections combine sets with a logical AND. The Boolean-algebraic symbol for intersection is ∩, but • and * are also often used to mean intersection. In QCA, it is customary to write A • B for the intersection of the set of A and the set of B. Written out in the body of a text, one would say a [diverse AND large AND high-tech] regional cluster (use [ ] to clearly identify the intersection in the sentence).

Let's consider the above two strategies for becoming a large regional cluster. Regions can either encourage business start-ups or acquire firms from elsewhere and have them (re-)locate to their region. If the outcome is merely becoming a large regional cluster, both strategies are logically equivalent. Following either strategy leads to growing the number of firms in the regional cluster. It may be that one strategy grows the number of firms quicker than the other and that combining the two strategies grows the largest regional clusters; however, that is not the issue here. Both strategies are sufficient for becoming a larger regional cluster, one with more firms. This means that the set of growing regional clusters is the union or the disjunction of the set of start-up-encouraging regions and the set of firm-acquiring regions. In other words, to be in the set of growing regional clusters, it is enough to be either in the set of start-up-encouraging regional clusters OR in the set of firm-acquiring regional clusters. A logical OR thus describes the union (or disjunction) of two sets. In Boolean algebra, the symbol for union is ∪ or +. In QCA, it is customary to write $A + B$ for the union of set A and set B. The right pane of Figure 5.3 visualizes the union of A and B. The circles for A and B are both shaded because to be in the union of $A + B$ one can be a case of A OR a case of B.

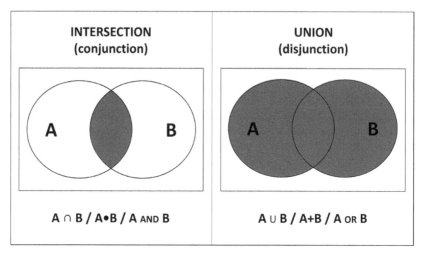

Figure 5.3   *Intersections (conjunctions) and unions (disjunctions)*

NOTATION

Intersections and unions are both configurations. Configurations combine sets with, a logical AND, a logical OR, or both. For example, we can say that $A \cdot B$ and $A \cdot C$ are both sufficient for outcome Y. This can be written as:

$$(A \text{ AND } B) \text{ OR } (A \text{ AND } C) \rightarrow Y \tag{5.1}$$

This means that $[A \text{ AND } B]$ is sufficient for outcome Y and that $[A \text{ AND } C]$ is also sufficient for outcome Y. The equation literally says: if $[A \text{ AND } B]$ OR $[A \text{ AND } C]$ then Y.

This Boolean expression may be simplified to:

$$A \text{ AND } (B \text{ OR } C) \rightarrow Y \tag{5.2}$$

which says if A AND $[B \text{ OR } C]$ then Y. If this is the whole solution, meaning that no other configurations explain outcome Y, then condition A is a necessary condition. Outcome Y cannot occur if condition A is not present. This is written as:

$$A \leftarrow Y \tag{5.3}$$

It says that if and only if (i.e., iff) A, then Y. There is no path to the outcome that does not include A.

It is also clear that *A* itself is not sufficient for outcome *Y*. Only in combination with *B* OR *C* does *A* explain the occurrence of outcome *Y*. This means that *A* is an INUS condition. INUS conditions are insufficient but **n**ecessary conditions of an **u**nnecessary but sufficient *conjunction*. Note that I am using the term INUS condition in a strictly Boolean way and not to suggest INUS causation (Mackie, 1965).

However, *B* and *C* are not INUS conditions. Neither *B* nor *C* is individually necessary for the occurrence of outcome *Y*. The presence of either one will do. [*A* AND (*B* OR *C*)] means that *B* and *C* are **s**ufficient but **u**nnecessary conditions of an **i**nsufficient but **n**ecessary *disjunction*. *B* and *C* are SUIN conditions. The disjunction (*B* OR *C*) is necessary for the occurrence of outcome *Y* but itself not sufficient. Only in conjunction with *A* does the disjunction (*B* OR *C*) explain the occurrence of outcome *Y*.

Let's consider a more complex Boolean expression to be absolutely clear on the differences between necessary, INUS and SUIN conditions. Let's say that:

$$A \text{ AND } (B \text{ OR } C) \text{ OR } (D \text{ AND } E) \rightarrow Y \tag{5.4}$$

This example has three configurations that are sufficient for the outcome: (1) [*A* AND *B*]; (2) [*A* AND *C*]; and (3) [*D* AND *E*]. This means that *A* is no longer a necessary condition because there is a path to the outcome (3) that does not include *A*. *A* is now merely an INUS condition. It is individually necessary but only sufficient in combination with [*B* OR *C*]. Consequently, *B* and *C* are still SUIN conditions. In conjunction with *A*, *B* and *C* are each sufficient but not necessary to 'produce' the outcome. Conditions *D* and *E* are both INUS conditions – they are individually necessary but only jointly sufficient for the outcome.

Correctly understanding the meaning of intersections (conjunctions) and unions (disjunctions), INUS and SUIN conditions, sufficiency and necessity is important in QCA because it directly relates to QCA's configurational theorizing. As argued, configurational theorizing suggests that configurations of explanatory conditions rather than single factors explain the occurrence of the outcome. However, to theorize accurately, it is still important to understand the particular role of each explanatory condition (Furnari et al., 2021; Greckhamer et al., 2018). A necessary condition has a higher theoretical relevance than an explanatory condition that is 'merely' an INUS condition. Finding that two conditions are logically equivalent, that they are SUIN conditions, requires a more complex (or perhaps more refined or nuanced) theoretical explanation. It requires a researcher to explain (to theorize) this logical equivalence in relation to the outcome. In other words, conditions describe cases, and configurations describe cases in complex ways. Configurations may be conjunctions, disjunctions and a combination of a disjunction and a conjunction. Different kinds of configurations require different theoretical explanations of why the outcome occurs (Rutten, 2020).

MEMBERSHIP IN SETS

When we say that Silicon Valley is a large regional cluster, it means that Silicon Valley is a member of the set of large regional clusters. It is a case in the set of large regional clusters. How one decides whether a case is a member of a particular set is an exercise called calibration. Next to defining and selecting cases (i.e., casing), calibration is the most critical step in a QCA study (Ragin, 2000, pp. 161–2; 2008, pp. 71–4) and I will discuss it at length in Chapter 8. For now, let's assume that we know that cases are members (or not-members) of a set. Membership in a set can be crisp or fuzzy, or rather, one can define (calibrate) crisp or fuzzy sets. Every human being has a degree of narcissism. This is because the apes that pottered along on the savannah believing that every other ape was a perfectly benign being that would also look after their interests – well, those apes never became our ancestors. Every human being genetically inherited a degree of narcissism from our ape-like ancestors in the remote past of the human story. However, we only recognize people as narcissists beyond a degree of narcissism, beyond the point where their narcissism starts to negatively affect their social relationships with other people. That is, all human beings score somewhere on the scale of narcissism but only beyond a point on this scale do people qualify as narcissists. This is the semantical threshold – the point where people have enough of the empirical characteristics of a narcissist to semantically qualify as a narcissist. In QCA, the semantical threshold is more commonly referred to as the crossover point (Schneider and Wagemann, 2012, pp. 26–8); however, I prefer the label semantical threshold. A semantical threshold is explicitly about meaning and (thus about) definition. It is not merely an empirical value, as the label crossover point may suggest (Rutten and Rubinson, 2022).

If a person is narcissist to a degree that exceeds the semantical threshold, that person qualifies as a narcissist. Consequently, that person is a member of the set of narcissist persons. This means that the statement, 'This person is a narcissist', is true, which calibrates that this person is a member (1) of the set of narcissist people. For a person whose degree of narcissism falls short of the semantical threshold, the above statement is false. Consequently, this person is not a member (0) of the set of narcissist people. The semantical threshold thus distinguishes between qualitatively different cases. Those cases are logically identified as members (1) and not-members (0) of the set. 1 and 0 are logical statements (true or false); they are not empirical values. Keeping to 1s and 0s defines crisp sets. Crisps sets do not suggest that social reality is dichotomous; instead, they highlight that semantical thresholds are very important and very common in social reality. A firm either makes a profit or it does not, and this has critical consequences for its survival. Almost making a profit still means the firm is in the red, which is (usually) sufficient for that firm going out of business. A student either passes or fails their exam. Also narrowly passing the exam is sufficient for getting a degree. QCA is a threshold method (Goertz, 2020, p. 182); it investigates whether the presence or absence of an explanatory condition is sufficient for the presence or absence of the outcome. Presence and absence are logical statements that mean above and below the semantical threshold (or crossover point). Crisp sets are all that is required for a method based on formal logic like QCA.

However, partially as a response to criticism from correlational methods, QCA is now commonly performed on fuzzy sets (Ragin, 2008, p. 82; Smithson and Verkuilen, 2006, pp. 1–3). In fuzzy sets, cases can have a degree of membership in the set that ranges from 0 to 1. Having 0 membership in a fuzzy set means that the case has none of the characteristics of the set. Having 1 membership in a fuzzy set means that the case has all the characteristics of the set. Suppose we define the fuzzy set of metropolitan regions. Whatever definition (meaning, semantics) we use to describe metropolitan regions, it is obvious that regions like London, Jakarta, Rio de Janeiro and Johannesburg qualify as metropolitan regions. Their membership in this set would be 1. It is equally obvious that the picturesque villages of Alsace and the rural farming communities of Indonesia (known as *desas*) do not qualify as metropolitan regions. Their membership in this set would be 0. But what about Newcastle-upon-Tyne in England or Memphis, Tennessee in the US? They are clearly big cities but not big enough to qualify as metropolitan regions of the London kind. And what about places like Durham in England and Tupelo, Mississippi? They are considerably smaller than even Newcastle and Memphis but not so small as to be on a par with an Alsatian village or Indonesian *desas*. That is, Memphis, Newcastle, Tupelo and Durham have a degree of membership in the set of metropolitan regions somewhere between 0 and 1, which means we can now calibrate the fuzzy set of metropolitan regions. In addition, fuzzy sets have a semantical threshold or crossover point. This threshold is set at 0.5 – that is, halfway between 1 (full member) and 0 (not-member). Clearly, Newcastle and Memphis would be above this semantical threshold as they are mostly or largely (but not fully) metropolitan regions. Sticking a fuzzy set value on them, Newcastle and Memphis may have 0.7 or 0.8 membership in the set of metropolitan regions. Durham and Tupelo are below the semantical threshold as they are somewhat or moderately metropolitan regions (but not not-metropolitan regions). Sticking a fuzzy set value on them, Durham and Tupelo may have 0.3 or 0.4 membership in the set of metropolitan regions.

Fuzzy sets thus explicitly acknowledge that social reality is more colourful than the 1s and 0s of crisp sets might suggest (Smithson, 1987, pp. 1–5).

However, for the set analysis in QCA, this is not particularly important because fuzzy set analysis is also about semantical thresholds. In QCA's truth table analysis, all fuzzy set values below 0.5 are interpreted as 0 (logically false) and those above 0.5 are interpreted as 1 (logically true). Fundamentally, QCA is a threshold method and it is easiest explained using the propositional logic of crisp sets. There are some differences in how subset and superset relationships are identified between crisp and fuzzy sets (which I will discuss in Chapter 7). In Chapter 9, I will discuss my reservations about fuzzy sets in QCA in detail. However, one obvious reservation is that fuzzy set values are a (ratio) scale (Ragin, 2000, pp. 154–8). While many social science concepts do not 'behave' as scales (Lakoff, 1987, pp. 141–8; 2014).

MEMBERSHIP IN NEGATIONS, INTERSECTIONS AND UNIONS

Calculating a case's membership in a negation of a set and in intersections and unions of sets is straightforward enough. Consider the eight fictional neighbourhoods in Figure 5.4. A primary school is located in five of these neighbourhoods. That is, in this example, the set of neighbourhoods with a primary school has five members. A supermarket is located in four neighbourhoods. That is, the set of neighbourhoods with a supermarket has four members. The table in Figure 5.4 identifies members of a set with a 1 and not-members with a 0. The 1 for Elizabeth Road in the column 'primary school' means that the statement, 'A primary school is present in Elizabeth Road', is true. Consequently, the statement, 'A primary school is not present in Elizabeth Road', must be false. In Boolean notation, this is written as, primary school = 1 and ~primary school = 0. It follows that membership of a case in the negation of a set is 1 minus its membership in the set. Or:

$$\sim A = 1 - A \tag{5.5}$$

Membership in crisp sets can only be 1 or 0 and, consequently, also membership in the negation of a crisp set is only 0 or 1. If membership in 'primary schools' = 1, then membership in '~primary schools' = $1 - 1 = 0$. Membership in the negation of a fuzzy sets is calculated with the same formula as for crisp sets; however, now values can range between 0 and 1. For example, if a neighbourhood is mostly (but not fully) a member of the set of affluent neighbourhoods, it will also have a degree of membership in the set of not-affluent neighbourhoods. A mostly affluent neighbourhood will also be somewhat a not-affluent neighbourhood. Suppose being a mostly affluent neighbourhood corresponds to a membership of 0.8 in the set of affluent neighbourhoods, then this neighbourhood's membership in the set of not-affluent neighbourhoods is $1 - 0.8 = 0.2$.

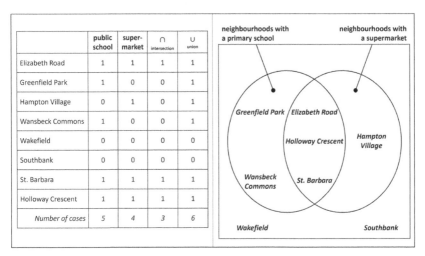

	public school	super-market	∩ intersection	∪ union
Elizabeth Road	1	1	1	1
Greenfield Park	1	0	0	1
Hampton Village	0	1	0	1
Wansbeck Commons	1	0	0	1
Wakefield	0	0	0	0
Southbank	0	0	0	0
St. Barbara	1	1	1	1
Holloway Crescent	1	1	1	1
Number of cases	*5*	*4*	*3*	*6*

Figure 5.4   Set membership in intersection and union

Let's return to the primary schools and supermarkets in Figure 5.4. The column 'intersection' identifies neighbourhoods that have a primary school AND a supermarket. Neighbourhoods for which the statement, 'A primary school AND a supermarket are present', is true, have a membership of 1 in the set defined by the intersection of the set of neighbourhoods with a primary school AND the set of neighbourhoods with a supermarket. There are three such neighbourhoods in this example: Elizabeth Road, Holloway Crescent and St. Barbara. All other neighbourhoods have 0 membership in this intersection. For them, the above statement is false on at least one count. That is, cases' membership in a conjunction (intersection) is equal to the minimum set membership in the individual terms of the conjunction:

$$A \cap B = \text{minimum } A, B \qquad (5.6)$$

This is the same in fuzzy sets. Suppose Elizabeth Road has 0.8 membership in the set of neighbourhoods with a primary school and 0.7 membership in the set of neighbourhoods with a supermarket, then the membership of Elizabeth Road in the intersection of these sets is the minimum of 0.8 and 0.7 = 0.7.

The minimum is used for set membership in an intersection because no amount of supermarkets can compensate for the absence of a primary school. Set membership in an intersection thus follows a weakest-link argument

(Goertz and Mahoney, 2012b). If no primary school is present in a neighbour-hood, that neighbourhood cannot be a member of any conjunction that includes the set of neighbourhoods with a primary school. Consequently, the number of cases in an intersection is (almost) always smaller than the aggregated number of cases in the sets composing the intersection.

Membership in the union (disjunction) of [primary school OR supermarket] is represented in the last column of the table in Figure 5.4. To have membership in this union, the statement, 'A primary school OR a supermarket is present in the neighbourhood', must be true on at least one count. In other words, either a primary school or a supermarket must be present in the neighbourhood. This is true for six neighbourhoods. Only Wakefield and Southbank are not members of this union because these neighbourhoods have neither a primary school nor a supermarket. This means that membership in a union is equal to the maximum set membership in the individual terms of the disjunction:

$$A \cup B = \text{maximum } A, B \tag{5.7}$$

This is the same in fuzzy sets. Suppose Wansbeck Commons has 0.7 member-ship in the set of neighbourhoods with a primary school and 0.4 membership in the set of neighbourhoods with a supermarket. Its membership in the union of these two sets, then, is the maximum of 0.7 and 0.4 = 0.7. Membership in a union thus follows a compensation argument (ibid.). To be a member of a union, it is sufficient to be a member of any one of the union's constituent sets, regardless of the number of constituent sets.

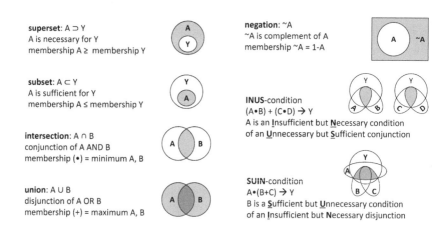

Figure 5.5   Set relationships and Boolean operators

In sum, the technicalities of Boolean algebra as they are used in QCA are fairly straightforward. Figure 5.5 provides a complete overview of set relationships and Boolean operators. While there is more to Boolean algebra than discussed here, QCA really only uses what makes up the content of this chapter. Ultimately, this is because QCA is a qualitative method and the function of Boolean algebra is mostly confined to describing cases and cross-case patterns (Ragin, 2000, p. 202). Turning these patterns into causal explanations is a matter of interpretation, not calculation.

GLOSSARY OF KEY CONCEPTS

~	Tilde. This identifies the negation of a set
$\sim A = 1 - A$	A case's membership in the negation of a set is 1 minus that case's membership in the set
∩	The Boolean symbol for conjunction (intersection)
∪	The Boolean symbol for disjunction (union)
$A \leftarrow B$	If and only if A then B (iff A then B). The presence of A is a necessary condition for the presence of B
$A \rightarrow B$	If A then B. The presence of A is a sufficient condition for the presence of B
$A \cap B = \text{minimum } A, B$	Membership in a conjunction is equal to the minimum (lowest) membership value in the component sets of the conjunction
$A \cup B = \text{maximum } A, B$	Membership in a disjunction is equal to the maximum (highest) membership value in the component sets of the disjunction
$A \subset B$	A is a subset of B; all cases in A are also in B. A subset relationship between A and B suggests that A is a sufficient condition for B
$A \supset B$	A is a superset of B; all cases in B are also in A. A superset relationship between A and B suggests that A is a necessary condition for B
AND; *; •	The Boolean operator for a conjunction
Conjunction	The Boolean-algebraic term for an intersection
Crisp set	A set where cases are either members (1) or not-members (0) of the set. 1 and 0 are logical statements (true or false), not empirical values. Crisp sets do not dichotomize social reality but distinguish between qualitatively different cases on the basis of a semantical threshold (or crossover point)

Crossover point	QCA more commonly speaks of the crossover point rather than the semantical threshold. However, to underline QCA's qualitative nature, I prefer to speak of a semantical threshold
Disjunction	The Boolean-algebraic term for union
Fuzzy set	A set where cases can have a degree of membership that ranges between 0 and 1. The semantical threshold (crossover point) in fuzzy sets is identified with the set membership value 0.5
Intersection	Combines two or more sets with a logical AND. A case can only be a member of an intersection if it is also a member of every set forming the intersection
INUS	An insufficient but necessary condition that is part of an unnecessary but sufficient *conjunction*. The conjunction, of which the condition is a necessary part, is sufficient but not necessary for the outcome
Negation or complement	The set of cases that are not-members of the focal set. These cases do not have the characteristic(s) of the focal set. Note that the negation of a set is something very different from its semantical opposite. The set of deprived neighbourhoods is a very different set from the set of not-affluent neighbourhoods. Many (if not most) neighbourhoods will be neither affluent nor deprived. They are members of the set of not-affluent neighbourhoods but they are not members of the set of deprived neighbourhoods
OR; +	The Boolean operator for a disjunction
Semantical threshold	The point where a case has enough of the characteristics of a condition (a set) to qualify the case as an example (an instance) of the condition (to be a member of the set). That is, the semantical threshold distinguishes between qualitatively different cases (*A* cases and ~*A* cases). Defining the semantical threshold is about meaning and definition and then connecting semantical meaning to an empirical value. Social reality is full of thresholds. For example, income may vary in a population of households; however, any one household either makes ends meet at the end of the month, or it does not. Being above or below this threshold has very meaningful consequences for how the members of the household live their lives
SUIN	A sufficient but unnecessary condition that is part of an insufficient but necessary *disjunction*. The disjunction, of which the condition is a sufficient part, is an insufficient but necessary part of a conjunction to make that conjunction sufficient for the outcome

Union	Combines two or more sets with a logical OR. A case is a member of a union when it is a member of at least one of the sets forming the union
Universal set	The union of the set and its complement. In a QCA study, the universal set is the set of all cases that meet the definition of a case of that particular study. That is, the universal set denotes the case population on which the QCA study is performed. Note that in QCA, the universal set includes both actual and counterfactual cases, as does any set

NOTE

1.   Nomenclature des Unités Territoriales Statistiques.

6.   The case-based causal logic

Case-based researchers think in terms of cases and sets of cases. Cases are holistic; their characteristics are not independent of each other and context matters (Abbott, 1992; Ragin [1987] 2014). Instead, variable-based researchers, aiming to isolate the 'net effect' of individual factors, disassemble social reality into decontextualized variables (Goertz and Mahoney, 2012a; King et al., 1994). Independent variables are independent; the effect of one independent variable on a dependent variable is unconnected to that of another. The case-based causal logic is complex and builds on the set relationships and Boolean algebra introduced in the previous chapter. Complex causality is configurational, because cases' characteristics cannot be understood in isolation (Abbott, 1992; Bhaskar, 1986, pp. 108–9; Ragin [1987] 2014). Complex causality is equifinal, because different cases achieve the same outcome for different reasons. And complex causality is asymmetrical, as the reasons for case failures differ from reasons for case successes. Instead, the formal language of correlational (variable-based) methods – that is, statistics – is designed to isolate net effects of individual factors and cannot capture complex causality. The language of necessity and sufficiency is crucial for case-based causal inference for yet another reason. Statements of sufficiency and necessity are if-then statements, viz. if X, then Y for sufficiency and if and only if (i.e., iff) X, then Y for necessity. This language connects singular (case-level) and general (cross-case) causal evidence because if-then statements describe causal relationship on both levels (Goertz, 2017). Instead, variable-based causal inference only produces general causal evidence, in the form of correlations between variables that are observed on the level of a population (Ragin [1987] 2014). Connecting singular (case-level) and general (cross-case) causal evidence allows learning from cases. Therein lies the true strength of the case-based causal logic (Ragin, 2008).

NECESSITY AND SUFFICIENCY

Suppose we say that innovative regions have strong institutions regulating economic life. We could interpret this as the strength of regional institutions having an effect on regional innovation. But that is not what the statement suggests. It says that innovative regions also have strong institutions. In other words, regions that are in the set of innovative regions are also in the set of regions with strong institutions. The statement does not suggest that regions in the set of regions with strong institutions are also in the set of innovative regions. The set of regions with strong institutions thus is a superset of the set of innovative regions. Therefore, a region cannot be innovative if it does not also have strong institutions. It means that strong regional institutions is a necessary condition for being an innovative region. However, having strong institutions is not sufficient for being an innovative region, because it alone does not explain being an innovative region. This superset relationship is visualized in the left pane of Figure 6.1.

Now suppose we say that regions that have a higher-educated workforce and that perform R&D are innovative regions. Again, we could interpret this as the level of education of the regional workforce having an effect on the level of regional innovation, and the level of R&D performance having an effect on the level of regional innovation, and that the interaction between level of education and level of R&D performance also has an effect on regional innovation. However, the above is not a correlational statement. Instead, it says that regions that are in the set of regions with a higher-educated workforce and that are in the set of R&D-performing regions, are also in the set of innovative regions. It suggests that neither having a higher-educated workforce nor R&D performance by themselves explain being an innovative region. However, regions that have both characteristics are innovative regions. That is, the intersection of the set of regions with a higher-educated workforce and the set of R&D-performing regions is a subset of the set of innovative regions. The statement thus says that being a region with a higher-educated workforce AND being an R&D-performing region is sufficient for being an innovative region – sufficient but not necessary because there are multiple ways for regions to be innovative. For example, socio-culturally diverse regions that also have many new start-ups can be innovative regions. New start-ups may benefit from ideas bubbling up and crossing over between different communities and develop them into innovations (new products and services). This would be a different kind of innovation from the one suggested by the combination of a higher-educated workforce and R&D performance, which suggests a more technology-driven innovation. The subset relationship (sufficiency) is visualized in the right pane of Figure 6.1.

Statements of necessity and sufficiency say something about cases, or regions in this example. There may very well be a correlation between the level of education of the regional workforce and the level of regional innovation, but this does not say anything about what will happen to innovation in any one particular region if it increases the education level of its regional workforce. Its innovation level may actually decrease. It is simply wrong to do a correlational study and to conclude that, for example, adding one year to the education of a regional workforce adds 10 per cent to the number of regional innovations

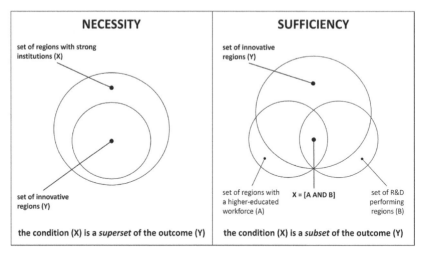

Figure 6.1   Necessity (superset relationship) and sufficiency (subset relationship)

(Abbott, 1988). This suggests a correlation coefficient of 0.1 but it cannot be mistaken for a case-based probability. The correlation is relevant knowledge for, for example, policymakers. It tells them that if they increase the education level of the workforce in their country (i.e., in all regions), they may expect to see an average increase (of about 0.1) in the level of innovation across the regions in their country. But it does not tell them in which regions innovation will increase or decrease. Moreover, variables may not be manipulable on the case level (Brady, 2010; Delanda, 2016). Having a non-western ethnicity may well decrease one's chances of finding a job in a western country, but one cannot suggest that non-western job-seekers change their ethnicity. Intrinsic motivation increases students' study performance, but one cannot suggest to students who want to pass their exam that they increase their level of intrinsic motivation. Moreover, in many countries, regions (as political subdivisions) do not have the means or resources to increase the education level of their workforce. What one wants to know instead is how can a job-seeker with a non-western ethnicity find a job? How can a not intrinsically motivated student pass their exams? And how can a region with a not higher-educated workforce become an innovative region? These questions can be answered with case-based methods and using set theory.

Set theory, the language of necessity and sufficiency, is a different causal language than the correlational language of net effects or causal effects of variable-based methods (Rutten, 2020). A more elaborate discussion of the differences between variable-based and case-based methods can be found in

Ragin ([1987] 2014) and particularly in Goertz and Mahoney (2012a), but the essence is easily explained. Suppose we want to explain innovation in inter-firm dyads. Economic geography theory tells us that embeddedness in regional networks is conducive to the exchange of knowledge and ideas that fuel innovation. The management of innovation literature suggests that having slack resources encourages creativity that drives innovation. This literature also suggests that project management skills are important to manage (inter-firm) innovation projects. In a variable-based, or correlational, study, these would be three independent variables: the level of slack resources (*SLA*), the level project management skills (*MGT*) and the level of regional embeddedness (*EMB*). A researcher would identify co-variation (correlations) between these three independent variables and the dependent variable – that is, the level of innovation (*INN*). The main purpose of a variable-based analysis is to isolate the contribution of each independent variable on the dependent variable, as well as the contribution of interaction terms of the independent variables. This net-effects thinking is visualized as boxes-connected-by-arrows causality (Abbott, 1988). The left pane of Figure 6.2 shows the conceptual model for the present example explaining knowledge creation. For aesthetic reasons, inter-action effects are not visualized. If one ran a regression analysis and included all two-way interactions, the full model would look like this:

$$INN = \beta SLA + \beta MGT + \beta EMB + \beta(SLA * MGT)$$
$$+ \beta(SLA * EMB) + \beta(MGT * EMB) \qquad (6.1)$$

The principal assumption behind correlational (variable-based) causality is that independent variables are indeed independent. Their effect on the dependent variable is independent of the effects of other variables and can be isolated from those effects. This makes sense if one disassembles social reality into variables. Correlational analysis abstracts from cases and context to only consider co-variation on population level. This is very problematic for case-based researchers, and for qualitative researchers more generally, who believe that cases are holistically relevant units of analysis and that context matters. Because correlational analysis focuses on the effects of individual independent variables, causality is additive. The net effects of all terms in the regression model are added to obtain the total explained variance in the dependent variable. Note further that causality is unifinal; there is only one regression equation to explain all variation in the dependent variable. Finally, correlational causality is symmetrical. The same regression equation explains both high and low levels of the outcome. For a linear effect, low levels of the independent variable explain low levels of the dependent variable and high levels of the independent variable explain high levels of the dependent variable. Note also that variables are nouns (e.g., level of *innovation*); they describe the distribution (variation) of a characteristic in a population. Instead, conditions are adjectives (e.g., *innovative* dyads); they qualify (characterize) cases (Goertz, 2020, p. 113).

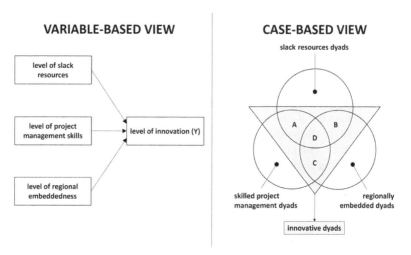

Figure 6.2   Variable-based and case-based analysis

COMPLEX CAUSALITY

Case-based methods follow a very different logic – one that is formalized with Boolean algebra rather than statistics. As argued above, regional embeddedness may well have an effect on knowledge creation in dyads; however, dyad partners may not be able to strengthen their embeddedness in regional networks to increase innovation. Nor do correlations tell us why or how an outcome occurs (Abbott, 1992). Knowledge creation that capitalizes on slack resources (i.e., resources internal to a firm) may result in a different kind of knowledge than knowledge creation that capitalizes on regional embeddedness (i.e., resources external to a firm). QCA is designed to capture these aspects of causality.

Look at the right pane in Figure 6.2. It suggests three explanatory conditions: being a slack resources dyad, being a skilled project management dyad, and being a regionally embedded dyad. A circle represents each condition, or rather, it represents the set of cases 'having' that characteristic. Area A is the intersection of the set of slack resources dyads AND the set of skilled project management dyads. Area B is the intersection of set of slack resources dyads AND the set of regionally embedded dyads. Area C is the intersection of the set of skilled project management dyads AND the set of regionally embedded dyads. Area D is the intersection of all three sets representing the explanatory conditions. Area D thus is part of Areas A, B and C. The outcome in this example is innovation, and the set of innovative dyads is represented by a shaded triangle. Note that the circles representing the three explanatory conditions only partially overlap with the outcome. This suggests that none of the explanatory conditions is a consistent subset of the outcome, meaning that none of the explanatory conditions is sufficient for knowledge creation. However, all intersections of the explanatory conditions are fully within the shaded area, suggesting that they are consistent subsets of the outcome. That is, the intersection of the set of slack resources dyads AND the set skilled project management dyads (Area A) forms a new set, and this new set is a consistent subset of the outcome. All inter-firm dyads that are members of the intersection represented by Area A are also members of the set of innovating dyads. The same goes for the intersections represented by Areas B and C; they are also consistent subsets of the outcome. By definition, therefore, all cases in the intersection represented by Area D are also members of the set of knowledge-creating dyads. But since any intersection of two of the three explanatory conditions is already sufficient for the outcome, the intersection of all three explanatory conditions does not suggest a separate explanation. Cases in Area D are overdetermined; these inter-firm dyads create knowledge for multiple (i.e., three) reasons (see below).

The solution for the set relationships in the right pane of Figure 6.2 is as follows: knowledge creation = [slack dyad AND skilled management dyad] OR [slack dyad AND regionally embedded dyad] OR [skilled management AND regionally embedded dyad]:

$$INN = [SLA \bullet MGT] + [SLA \bullet EMB] + [MGT \bullet EMB] \qquad (6.2)$$

The important thing from the perspective of causal explanation is that the three terms in the above solution explain knowledge creation in inter-firm dyads for different reasons. In this example:

- [Slack resources AND project management skills] (Area A) suggests that a dyad produced innovations because they managed the creative process where slack resources are developed into innovations – for example, by allowing staff to pursue pet projects next to their regular innovation projects. This suggests Area A as a managed creativity configuration.
- [Slack resources AND regional embeddedness] (Area B) suggests that a dyad produced innovations because their staff acquired new knowledge and ideas through regional networks. Innovation projects benefit from tapping into external sources of knowledge and ideas. This suggests Area B as an external inputs configuration.

- [Project management skills AND regional embeddedness] (Area C) suggests that a dyad produced innovations because it integrated regional partners into the innovation project of the dyad. This suggests Area C as a regional collaboration configuration.

These explanations are statements of sufficiency. For example, saying that [slack resources AND project management skills] (X) is sufficient for innovation (Y) is to say that: if X, then Y. Note that the above explanations are based on subset relationships between explanatory conditions and the outcome – that is, on general (cross-case) causal evidence. However, they also draw from what happens on the case level, on why or how the presence of a configuration of explanatory conditions makes it possible for cases (dyads) to innovate. In other words, the above explanations connect singular (case-level) and general (cross-case) causal evidence. If-then statements are observed on both the case level and across cases. This allows QCA researchers to dialogue both kinds of causal evidence in order to learn from cases (Ragin [1987] 2014; Rohlfing and Schneider, 2018).

Causal explanation in QCA thus is configurational rather than additive; it is equifinal rather than unifinal; and it is asymmetrical rather than symmetrical (Greckhamer et al., 2018; Rutten, 2020). In other words, causality is QCA complex. While causality in correlational methods is about identifying the effect of each independent variable, explanatory conditions in QCA only explain the outcome in conjunction with other explanatory conditions. It is important, therefore, not to refer to explanatory conditions in QCA as causal conditions. Individual conditions do not cause the outcome; they are not causes. Instead, their presence may be necessary for sufficiency as part of a configuration. If the label 'cause' can be attached to anything in QCA (see Chapter 3), it is configurations of explanatory conditions that are subsets of (i.e., sufficient for) the outcome (Duşa, 2022; Rutten, 2023).

Equifinal causality means that there are always multiple configurations explaining the outcome, and each configuration may explain the outcome for (very) different reasons. In the above example, three configurations explain innovation for three different reasons. This suggests that there are multiple kinds of innovation processes that produce different kinds of innovation. It may be that Area A [slack resources AND project management skills] allows the creation of more radical innovations than Area C [project management skills AND regional embeddedness]. Instead, Area C may explain incremental innovations that follow from regular innovation projects. Configurational and equifinal causality suggests that an explanatory condition – for example, regional embeddedness – may contribute to innovation in conjunction with some conditions but not in conjunction with others. So, in QCA, the question, 'Does, for example, regional embeddedness matter for innovation?', can only be answered as: 'It depends'. In case-based research, there is no such thing as an independent effect of, in this example, regional embeddedness on innovation.

Configurational and equifinal causality build on the notion of INUS conditions. In the configuration [project management skills AND regional embeddedness], both explanatory conditions are individually necessary but only jointly sufficient. In turn, the configuration is sufficient but not necessary; it explains the outcome (i.e., it is sufficient) but so do two other configurations (i.e., the configuration is not necessary). This makes, for example, regional embeddedness an INUS condition. It also suggests that a Boolean-algebraic conjunction (configuration, i.e., two terms combined with a logical AND) is something very different from a statistical interaction. An interaction is agnostic as to whether the individual terms in the interaction have an effect on the outcome. In fact, they usually do. However, if a Boolean-algebraic conjunction is sufficient for the outcome, it means that the individual terms in the conjunction cannot themselves be sufficient. They are INUS conditions that only explain the outcome in conjunction with each other.

Asymmetrical causality means that the configurations explaining the presence of the outcome are not the same as those explaining the absence of the outcome. This is because, in real life, the reasons we fail differ from the reasons we succeed. In correlational methods, the same regression equation explains both high and low levels of the outcome. Instead, in QCA, researchers perform a separate analysis for the absence of the outcome. Only in studies where researchers have a fully specified truth table is the solution for the absence ($\sim Y$) of the outcome the set-analytical complement of the solution for the presence (Y) of the outcome. But that almost never happens; except, of course, in this stylized example, where the solution for the absence of innovation is:

$$\sim INN = [\sim SLA \bullet \sim MGT] + [\sim SLA \bullet \sim EMB] + [\sim MGT \bullet \sim EMB] \qquad (6.3)$$

CONCLUSION

Variable-based causal logic aims to isolate the contribution of each independent variable to the variation in the dependent variable. However, on the case level, there is no such thing as an independent variable. Variables vary, cases do not; nor are their characteristics independent of each other. Co-variation happens on the level of a population and the effect size of an independent variable says nothing about what will happen if one manipulates that variable in individual cases. Correlation coefficients are not case-level probabilities. In other words, the causal evidence that variable-based (correlational) methods produce is decisively general. This kind of general causal evidence is notoriously difficult to connect to case-level (singular) causal evidence. Instead, case-based research recognizes that cases are holistic and that independent variables may not even be manipulable on case level. Case-based research acknowledges that, because cases are complex (i.e., 'composed' of interrelated characteristics) causality must also be complex. Causal explanation must recognize that causality is (1) configurational – that outcomes are explained by configurations rather than individual explanatory conditions; that causality is (2) equifinal – that multiple configurations explain the same outcome for different reasons; and that causality is (3) asymmetrical – that the configurations explaining the presence of the outcome do not also explain its absence. Complex causality requires a different language – viz., the language of sufficiency and necessity, formalized with Boolean algebra – because statistics is unable to capture configurational, equifinal and asymmetrical causality. Moreover, the language of sufficiency and necessity allows the connection of singular (case-level) and general (cross-case) causal evidence. General causal evidence produced by identifying supersets and subsets of cases suggests causality in the form of if-then statements. A subset relationship means if X in a population of cases, then also Y. But because this general causal evidence is observed from cases, we can also see the same if-then pattern on the case level, on the level of singular causal evidence. Complex causality thus achieves what no other causal language can do – viz., to establish a direct connection between singular and general causal evidence.

GLOSSARY OF KEY CONCEPTS

Asymmetrical causality	Configurations that explain the presence of the outcome are different from those explaining the absence of the outcome
Complex causality	The case-based approach to causality. Complex causality challenges the net-effects approach to causality of correlational (variable-based) methods. Instead of calculating correlations between variables, in order to isolate the individual effect of each independent variable, complex causality suggests that explanatory conditions only explain the outcome in combination with other explanatory conditions. Complex causality is (1) configurational; (2) equifinal; and (3) asymmetrical
Condition	A condition characterizes or qualifies cases. An innovative region is a region (case) that qualifies (is recognized) as innovative. Analytically, there is no difference between sets and conditions; however, the terms are not interchangeable. One speaks of the set of innovative regions and of innovative region as an explanatory condition (rather than an explanatory set)

Configurational causality	Explanatory conditions only explain the outcome in configurations of multiple explanatory conditions. The presence of an explanatory condition may contribute to the presence of the outcome in combination with one condition. However, the absence of the same explanatory condition may also contribute to the presence of the outcome in combination with another condition
Equifinal causality	Different configurations explain the same outcome
Explanatory condition	A condition whose presence explains the presence of the outcome
Necessity	This describes superset relationships. It suggests that an explanatory condition is a superset of the outcome. If a condition is necessary, it means that the outcome cannot occur if the condition is not present
Outcome condition	Or in other words, outcome is a condition whose presence a researcher sets out to explain
Set	A set is a population of cases that share a characteristic. The set of innovative regions describes the population of regions that are innovative
Sufficiency	Describes subset relationships. It suggests that an explanatory condition is a subset of the outcome. If a condition is sufficient, it means that the outcome will occur when the condition is present
Variable	A variable describes the distribution of a characteristic in a population. Variables abstract from cases. Variables and conditions both capture analytically relevant characteristics but in very different ways. One can have the variable (level of) innovation to describe the distribution of innovativeness in a population of regions. One can have the condition innovative regions to describe the set of regions that are innovative. Note that variables are nouns (level of *innovation*) and that conditions are adjectives (*innovative* region); they qualify cases

7. Set analysis

Set analysis is the empirical heart of QCA. Calculating subset and superset relationships identifies configurations that are mathematically sufficient and conditions that are mathematically necessary, respectively. This chapter takes readers through those elements of set analysis that are relevant for QCA. Set analysis in QCA develops the general (cross-case) causal evidence from which researchers interpret causal claims – that is, statements of sufficiency and necessity. Set analysis and its formal language, Boolean algebra, are the quantitative element of QCA, but they do not make QCA a quantitative method (Ragin [1987] 2014; Rohlfing and Schneider; 2018; Rubinson et al., 2019; Rutten, 2023). As argued, they provide part of the evidence that is required to learn from cases. Having said that, it is important that QCA researchers perform set analysis correctly. Hence this chapter.

THE CONSISTENCY OF SET RELATIONSHIPS

Set theory expresses causality as statements of necessity and sufficiency. A subset relationship between an explanatory condition and an outcome suggests the conditions as sufficient for the outcome, while superset relationships suggest necessity. However, QCA is a qualitative method and not a kind of 'data science'. Identifying superset and subset relationships is merely an important first step. They must be interpreted into causal statements on the basis of a dialogue between knowledge of cases, context and concepts (Ragin [1987] 2014, pp. 169–70; 2000, p. 84). In other words, there is a difference between mathematical sufficiency and necessity (consistent subset and superset relationships) on the one hand, and a statement of sufficiency or necessity on the other (Duşa, 2022; Rutten, 2023). A statement of sufficiency or necessity means that set relationships can be interpreted into a plausible explanation of the outcome. Mathematical sufficiency and necessity are the result of QCA's algorithm – that is, of applying formal (propositional) logic on a truth table describing a case population. It does not necessarily mean anything. Meaning follows from substantively interpreting the mathematical output.

Substantive interpretation of mathematically identified set relationships is crucial because set relationships are never perfectly consistent. Social reality is heterogeneous and contingent and no two cases are ever identical (Abbott, 1992; Ragin, 2000, p. 52). This is because every event that happens in social reality, and which we can study as a case, is a unique time- and place-contingent 'assemblage' of people, their relationships and their context (Bhaskar [1975] 2008, p. 112; Delanda, 2016). Even disregarding the limitations and imperfections of data, there is no reason why there would ever be a perfectly consistent set relationship across multiple cases. Because social reality is an emergent and open system (Elder-Vass, 2005; Porpora, 2018), the same cause may work differently in different cases, even when they are comparable cases (Ragin [1987] 2014, p. 52). The alternative is to confess to the kind of ontological determinism (Beach and Pedersen, 2016, pp. 19–24) underlying the unified empirical reality of correlational methods (see Chapter 1), a position that critical realism strongly rejects (Archer, 1995; Bhaskar [1975] 2008). This makes it crucial for researchers to ask when they identify a mostly consistent (superset or subset) relationship: what does this mean? Given the uniqueness of cases, there will always be some contradictory cases in a set relationship. For a statement of sufficiency, a contradictory case is a case where the explanatory condition (X) is present but not the outcome (Y). The presence of X combined with the absence of Y challenges the statement of sufficiency (if X, then Y) that is implied by the subset relationship. The question is, how many contradictory cases can one have and still speak of a consistent set relationship? How many $(X,\sim Y)$ cases still allow the subset relationship (observed in the domain of the Empirical) to be interpreted into a statement of sufficiency (a causal relationship in the domain of the Real)?

SUPERSET RELATIONSHIP (NECESSITY)

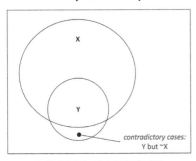

X: set of regions with strong institutions
Y: set of innovative regions

SUBSET RELATIONSHIP (SUFFICIENCY)

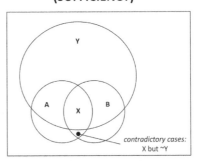

A: set of R&D-performing regions
B: set of regions with higher-educated workforce
X: A ∩ B
Y: set of innovative regions

Figure 7.1   Inconsistent set relationships

As argued, a few such cases are unproblematic. The left pane of Figure 7.1 suggests that having strong regional institutions (X) is a necessary condition for being an innovative region (Y). However, some regions may be innovative without having strong regional institutions. This may be because innovative firms in regions without strong institutions acquire their knowledge from elsewhere rather than develop it themselves, or because political chaos eroded the region's institutions but has not (yet) affected regional innovation efforts. These regions appear as contradictory cases; however, they do not defeat the claim that strong regional institutions are necessary for innovation. Other causal powers may 'interfere' with the causal power of interest without negating its efficacy (see Chapter 3). Similarly, the right pane of Figure 7.1 suggests that [being an R&D-performing region AND a region with a higher-educated workforce] is sufficient for being an innovative region. However, in some regions, these conditions are present but they are not innovative. This may be because a key innovative firm has left the region or because the economic situation does not favour regional firms starting new innovation projects. Again, these regions become contradictory cases but they do not defeat the statement that [performing R&D AND having a higher-educated workforce] is sufficient for regional innovation (i.e., for making regional innovation possible). Because it is not practical (or is simply unfeasible) to subject every contradictory case to a closer inspection, QCA works with a consistency threshold. If the number of contradictory cases is small enough, we still have a mostly consistent or almost consistent set relationship. We can still interpret this set relationship into a statement of sufficiency or necessity. Mathematical consistency does not have to be perfect, because QCA does not collapse causal claims into set relationships.

To explain how the consistency threshold works, let's convert the Venn diagrams of Figure 7.1 to the 2 × 2 tables of Figure 7.2. Cell (i) contains the cases where the explanatory condition (X) and the outcome (Y) are both present. These cases suggest that there may be a superset relationship (left pane) or a subset relationship (right pane) between X and Y. For both sufficiency and necessity, you will want most of your cases in Cell (i). Cases in Cell (i) are confirming cases. They provide confirming singular causal evidence for the general causal claim that X is sufficient (or necessary) for Y. They confirm the logical statement: if X, then Y (or iff X, then Y). For the left pane of Figure 7.2, Cell (i) is the part of the circle for Y that is inside the circle for X in the left pane of Figure 7.1. From a superset perspective, cases in Cell (iii) are problematic. These cases are equifinal cases; they 'have' the outcome (Y) but not the condition (X). These cases achieved the outcome for a reason other than the one implied by the explanatory condition. These cases defeat a statement of necessity. Their singular causal evidence contradicts the general causal claim: iff X, then Y. Cell (iii) are the cases in the circle for Y that is outside the circle for *X* in the left pane of Figure 7.1. For superset consistency (necessity), cases in Cell (ii) and Cell (iv) are inconsequential. These cases do not 'have' the outcome (~*Y*), so whether they 'have' the condition (*X* or ~*X*) does not matter. These cases are outside the circle for *Y* so they can never 'move' this circle outside the circle for *X*.

SUPERSET RELATIONSHIP

	Cell iii	Cell i
Y **outcome present**	*cases defeating* X ⊃ Y	*cases suggesting* X ⊃ Y
	Cell iv	Cell ii
~Y **outcome absent**	*cases irrelevant* *for superset* *consistency*	*cases irrelevant* *for superset* *consistency*
	~X **condition absent**	**X** **condition present**

SUBSET RELATIONSHIP

	Cell iii	Cell i
Y **outcome present**	*cases irrelevant* *for subset* *consistency*	*cases suggesting* X ⊂ Y
	Cell iv	Cell ii
~Y **outcome absent**	*cases irrelevant* *for subset* *consistency*	*cases defeating* X ⊂ Y
	~X **condition absent**	**X** **condition present**

Figure 7.2   Superset and subset consistency

For sufficiency (the right pane of Figure 7.2), cases in Cell (i) again suggest a causal (i.e., subset) relationship between *X* and *Y*. Also for sufficiency, the more cases in Cell (i) the better. These cases provide confirming singular causal evidence for the general causal statement that *X* is sufficient for *Y* (if *X*, then *Y*). But now cases in Cell (ii) are problematic. These cases 'have' the condition (*X*) but not the outcome (~*Y*). Therefore, these cases suggest that 'having' the condition (*X*) does not 'cause' a case to also 'have' the outcome (*Y*), which implies that *X* is not sufficient for *Y*. Cell (ii) cases are contradictory cases; their singular causal evidence contradicts the general causal claim: if *X*, then *Y*. Cell (ii) cases are cases in the part of the circle for *X* (in the right pane of Figure 7.1) that is outside the circle for *Y*. Cells (iii) and (iv) are inconsequential for subset consistency. These cases do not 'have' the condition (*X*); they are not in the circle for *X* and, therefore, cannot 'move' the *X* circle outside the *Y* circle. Cell (iii) cases are equifinal cases. They suggest that some other factor than *X* 'caused' *Y*. Cell (iv) cases are irrelevant. Because neither *X* nor *Y* is present, one cannot learn from these cases why or how *X* 'causes' *Y*. In other words, the singular causal evidence from cases in Cells (iii) and (iv) neither confirms nor contradicts the general causal claim: if *X*, then *Y*.

Set analytically, Cell (iv) is always irrelevant. Trying to establish whether the presence or absence of X makes a difference for the presence or absence of Y, one cannot learn anything from cases that 'have' neither X nor Y ($\sim X, \sim Y$ cases). Instead, Cell (i) is always relevant (for both necessity and sufficiency). These cases 'have' both X and Y (X, Y cases) and from these cases one can learn the causal relationship between X and Y. For example, from these cases, one can learn why having strong regional institutions matters for being an innovative region. This is different for correlational methods, where cases in Cells (i) and (iv) are equally relevant for establishing the strength of a correlation between X and Y (Mahoney and Goertz, 2006). It underlines that, in set analysis, causality is asymmetrical, while it is symmetrical in correlational methods. The implication is that set-analytical and correlational researchers will partially select different cases for further investigation (Beach and Pedersen, 2018). Correlational researchers will include cases from Cells (i) and (iv) because high levels of X explain high levels of Y and low levels of X explain low levels of Y (symmetry). Instead, set-analytical researchers focus on cases in Cell (i). For correlational researchers, Cells (ii) and (iii) are problematic because they upset the correlation between X and Y. Selecting cases in these cells for further investigation would teach them little if anything about the correlation between X and Y. However, for set-analytical researchers, Cells (ii) and (iii) are very relevant. From Cell (ii) cases, researchers may detect conditions that negate the occurrence of the outcome (Goertz, 2017, pp. 63–6; Ragin, 2000, pp. 62–3). For example, the contradictory cases in the right pane of Figure 7.1 may all be not-urbanized regions. This may set them apart from the confirming cases that may all be urbanized regions. This suggests that the configuration explaining being an innovative region must be expanded with the condition 'urbanized'. It means that, in fact, [R&D-performing AND higher educated AND urbanized] is sufficient for being innovative. Consequently, X is now a configuration of three conditions, which means that the not-urbanized cases in Cell (ii) will 'migrate' to Cell (iv) because they are no longer X cases. Having thus 'emptied' Cell (ii) makes X a perfectly consistent subset of Y.

In a similar way, cases in Cell (iii) learn about necessity. Suppose a researcher wants to know whether there are necessary conditions for London neighbourhoods to be attractive residential areas. Suppose the researcher finds that a good many attractive neighbourhoods (Y) have a tube station (X) (Cell (i) cases). However, there are also many attractive neighbourhoods (Y) that do not have a tube station ($\sim X$) (Cell (iii) cases). Looking closer at the cases in Cell (iii), the researcher notices that all these cases have a London Overground station – the surface rail network that services the parts of London outside the Central London area. The researcher can now expand X to include London Underground (tube) stations OR London Overground stations. X now becomes a disjunction of two SUIN conditions. This 'meta-condition' may be labelled Transport-for-London (TfL) station. This moves the cases that have an London Overground station from Cell (iii) to Cell (i). The new condition TfL station (X) is now a fully consistent superset of the set of attractive residential areas (Y). Note that the disjunction London [Underground station OR London Overground station] is semantically meaningful. The individual terms in the disjunction are logically equivalent to one another. One can make a plausible argument why having a TfL station would be a necessary condition for being an attractive residential area. That would not be possible for a disjunction that says [Underground station OR lively pub].

In sum, connecting conditions with a logical AND makes them INUS conditions. The more INUS conditions there are in an X, the fewer cases the set of X will contain. Thus, making the set of X smaller also makes it a more consistent subset of Y – albeit with a lower coverage (see below). Connecting conditions with a logical OR makes them SUIN conditions. The more SUIN conditions there are in an X, the more cases the set of X will contain. Thus, making the set of X larger also makes it a more consistent superset of Y. Note that this is only meaningful when SUIN conditions are logically equivalent. INUS conditions need not be logically equivalent; however, the more INUS conditions an X contains, the more difficult it will be to interpret X into a plausible explanation of Y. Also note that sufficiency and necessity work in opposite directions. More INUS conditions produces a smaller set, which increases subset consistency for sufficiency. More SUIN conditions produces a bigger set, which increases superset consistency for necessity.

QCA software automates the process of finding set relationships (see Chapter 10). However, the mathematical output cannot necessarily be plausibly interpreted into statements of sufficiency and necessity (Rubinson et al., 2019). To do that, researchers must dialogue between knowledge of cases, contexts and concepts (Ragin, 2008, p. 149). In other words, to interpret the mathematical output of the QCA software, researchers must always 'go back' to their cases. QCA cannot be reduced to a mathematical exercise.

CALCULATING THE CONSISTENCY OF SET RELATIONSHIPS

Social reality is heterogeneous and contingent. Multiple factors are always simultaneously 'at work' in any one case (Bhaskar, 1986, pp. 27–8; Ragin, 2000, pp. 61–2). Moreover, all cases are unique time- and place-contingent events (Delanda, 2016). The same condition may 'work' differently in different cases (Decoteau, 2018; Gorski, 2018). Consequently, it is not reasonable to expect perfectly consistent set relationships to occur in social reality, nor is it reasonable to take perfect consistency as a benchmark to evaluate the consistency of an actual set relationship (Rutten, 2023). In critical realist metaphysics, there is no such thing as ontological determinism, where, if left to themselves, the same cause will always 'produce' the same outcome. The question thus is how consistent a set relationship must be to allow the interpretation of it into a statement of sufficiency (subset relationship) or necessity (superset relationship).

Let's look at Figure 7.3. It describes a fictional population of 150 regions. Of these regions, 47 are collaborative regions (i.e., regions where collaboration between innovating firms happens) and also innovative regions (i.e., regions where firms develop new products and services). This is Cell (i) in the left pane of Figure 7.3. It is also the bit of the set (circle) of collaborative regions that overlaps with the set (circle) of innovative regions in the right pane of the same figure. Put differently, these 47 regions are (1,1) cases ($X = 1$ and $Y = 1$). Performing a correlational analysis, one would look at these 47 (1,1) cases and at the (0,0) cases ($X = 0$ and $Y = 0$) in Cell (iv). These are the 73 cases that are outside the sets (circles) of innovative regions and collaborative regions. The strength of the correlation between (X) collaborative region and (Y) innovative region is easily calculated as:

$$Correlation\ XY = \frac{(73 + 47)}{(73 + 47 + 13 + 17)} = \frac{120}{150} = 0.80 \tag{7.1}$$

That is a very decent correlation, so variable-based researchers may interpret this as evidence for a causal relationship between collaboration and innovation.

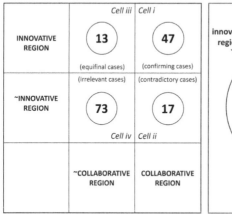 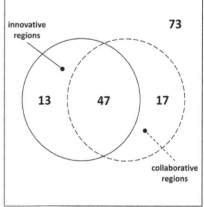

Figure 7.3   *Subset and superset consistency*

However, a set-analytical researcher would look at the data very differently. The 47 (1,1) cases (confirming cases) suggest a causal relationship between X

and Y. However, there are also 17 (1,0) cases (Cell ii) (contradictory cases) that defeat the causal relationship. This means that out of (47 + 17 =) 64 X cases, there only 47 cases that are also Y cases. Following Ragin's (2000) formula, subset consistency is calculated as:

$$Subset\ consistency\ X \subset Y = \frac{\sum (XY)\,cases}{\sum (X)\,cases} = \frac{47}{64} = 0.73 \tag{7.2}$$

Note that all of QCA's parameters and the formulae to calculate them were developed by Ragin (2000, 2008). A subset consistency of 0.73 is too low. The consistency threshold for subset relationships in QCA is 0.80. If substantive arguments permit, the threshold may be lowered to 0.75, but 0.73 is too low (Greckhamer et al., 2018; Ragin, 2000, pp. 35–6). This suggests that X is not a consistent subset of Y and that, therefore, being a collaborative region is not sufficient for being an innovative region.

I specifically say consistency threshold because consistencies higher than 0.8 are not necessarily better. Given the heterogeneous nature of social reality, a researcher should not expect to find (near) perfect consistencies (although, occasionally, it does happen). The consistency threshold of 0.8 distinguishes between subset relationships that are empirically valid descriptions of the cross-case patterns in the case population and those that are not. Any consistency ≥ 0.8 may be causally interpreted, and higher consistencies do not necessarily describe set relationships that are better interpretable. Any subset consistency ≥ 0.8 means that, given our knowledge of cases, context and concepts, we have good reason to believe that the presence of X makes the occurrence of Y possible (Rutten, 2023, p. 1713) (more on this possibilistic causality in Chapter 3).

Superset consistency is calculated in a similar way. Again, Cell (i) shows there are 47 (1,1) cases that suggest a causal relationship between X and Y (confirming cases). However, there are 13 (0,1) cases in Cell (iii) (equifinal cases) – innovative regions (Y) that are not-collaborative regions ($\sim X$). These regions are innovative for a different reason. This means that out of a total of (13 + 47 =) 60 Y cases, only 47 are also X cases. The superset consistency then is:

$$Superset\ consistency\ X \supset Y = \frac{\sum (XY)\,cases}{\sum (Y)\,cases} = \frac{47}{60} = 0.78 \tag{7.3}$$

This is too low for a statement of necessity. To say that X is necessary for Y makes a very strong statement; it suggests that Y cannot occur without X. For such a strong claim, we need strong evidence. Therefore, QCA's threshold for superset consistency is 0.9. Also here, 0.9 is a threshold. Higher superset consistencies do not make a condition more necessary. This result (0.78) means that X is not a consistent superset of Y and that, consequently, being a collaborative region is not necessary for being an innovative region.

In this example, a set-analytical researcher would find that being a collaborative region is neither necessary nor sufficient for being an innovative region (cf. Rutten, 2020). Whatever explains being an innovative region, it is not being a collaborative region. On the contrary, a correlational researcher would deduce that these factors are causally related (see above). It demonstrates that the same data may produce very different results depending on the method used to analyse them (Goertz and Mahoney, 2012a, p. 23) (which underlines the notion of epistemic relativism from Chapter 1). It also means that causality is and means something very different in correlational and set-analytical methods. When verbalizing their causal claims, QCA researchers must talk about sufficiency and necessity and never talk about causal effects (Rutten and Rubinson, 2022).

CALCULATING THE COVERAGE OF SET RELATIONSHIPS

In addition to consistency, the coverage of a set relationship must be considered. Coverage says something about the relevance of a set relationship. Of the 60 Y cases in Figure 7.3, only 47 are also X cases. Put differently, of the 60 Y cases, 47 are covered by X. This produces a subset coverage of:

$$Subset\ coverage\ X \supset Y = \frac{\sum (XY)\,\text{cases}}{\sum (Y)\,\text{cases}} = \frac{47}{60} = 0.78 \qquad (7.4)$$

Note that the formula for subset coverage is the same as the formula for superset consistency. The coverage of the subset relationship between X and Y is the same as the superset consistency of X and Y. After all, if all Y cases are covered by X, X is necessary for Y. A subset coverage of 0.78 is very high. It suggests that X is very relevant for the explanation of Y (even though we have seen that it is not sufficient). That many of the innovative regions (Y) are collaboration regions (X) suggests that being a collaborative region is a relevant condition. This is not the case for the subset relationship between being a city with a medieval centre (X) and being a tourist destination (Y). Pretty much all cities with a medieval city centre are also tourist destinations. Therefore, the set of medieval city centres is a (nearly) perfect subset of the set of tourist destinations. Being a city with a medieval centre is thus sufficient for being a tourist destination. However, the set of tourist destinations has many members. In addition to medieval city centres, they include natural parks, theme parks, holiday resorts, beaches, festivals, and so on. Medieval city centres make up but a small fraction of all tourist destinations. The coverage of this (nearly) perfect subset is thus very low. A low coverage is not necessarily problematic for a subset relationship, though. It may still be very relevant to know that being a medieval city centre is sufficient for being a tourist destination. That is, the empirical relevance of a subset relationship (i.e., its coverage) does not necessarily say anything about its theoretical (substantive) relevance.

In addition, superset relationships have a coverage. In the example in Figure 7.3, of the 64 X cases, only 47 are also Y cases. That is, of 64 X cases, only 47 are covered by Y. This works out as a superset coverage of:

$$\textit{Superset coverage } X \subset Y = \frac{\sum (XY)\text{cases}}{\sum (X)\text{cases}} = \frac{47}{64} = 0.73 \qquad (7.5)$$

Note that the formula for the coverage of a superset relationship is the same as the formula for the consistency of a subset relationship. After all, if all X cases are covered by Y, X is sufficient for Y. A superset coverage of 0.73 is very high. Because a statement of necessity is a very strong statement, researchers must only state that X is necessary for Y if the coverage of the superset relationship is high. The threshold for superset coverage is ≥ 0.5, but higher coverages are better. For necessary conditions, a higher superset coverage (empirical relevance) does suggest a higher substantive (theoretical) relevance. The importance of superset coverage can be demonstrated with the following example. Hosting a football club is a necessary condition for a city to become football champion, but this is a trivial statement. Of course, the set of cities hosting a football club is a perfect superset of cities that have won the football championship. However, the number of cities that host a football club is very much bigger than the number of cities that have won the football championship. Therefore, saying that hosting a football club is necessary for winning the football championship does not explain very much. Other factors do that, such as the quality of the players. A large set will always be a superset of a small set and therefore mathematically necessary. But it does not suggest a substantive explanation. Hence the superset coverage threshold of ≥ 0.5 for a statement of necessity.

THE RELATION BETWEEN CONSISTENCY AND COVERAGE

The fact that Ragin's formulae for subset consistency and superset coverage are the same, as are the formulae for superset consistency and subset coverage, suggests that consistency and coverage are related. Increasing subset consistency (making the set of X smaller, see above) decreases subset coverage. Increasing superset consistency (making the set of X bigger) decreases the superset coverage (i.e., the proportion of X cases covered by Y). This is visualized in Figure 7.4.

Look at Example (i). Being a higher-educated region (X) (i.e., a region with a higher-educated workforce) is not sufficient for being an innovative region (Y). The subset consistency $X \subset Y = 0.71$ (35/(35 + 14)) is too low (< 0.8). Nor is being a higher-educated region necessary for being an innovative region because the superset consistency $X \supset Y = 0.58$ is also too low (< 0.9). However, when we make the explanatory condition (X) a conjunction of [higher-educated region AND R&D-performing region] ($[X_A \cdot X_B]$), in Example (ii), the number of X cases decreases from (35 + 14 =) 49 regions to (21 + 4 =) 25 regions. A conjunction always describes fewer cases than a single condition. The number of Y cases, of course, remains the same (60), as does the overall number of cases in the case population (150). But now no fewer than 21 of the 25 X cases are also Y cases. This increases the subset consistency to 0.84 (21/(21 + 4)). At the same time, because the set of X is now smaller, it reduces the subset coverage from 0.58 to 0.35 (21/(21 + 39)).

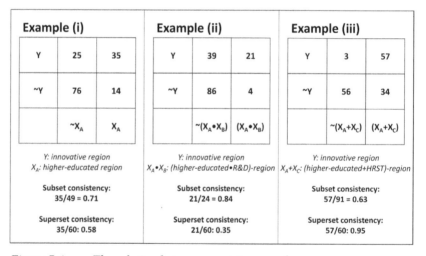

Example (i)			Example (ii)			Example (iii)		
Y	25	35	Y	39	21	Y	3	57
~Y	76	14	~Y	86	4	~Y	56	34
	~X_A	X_A		~(X_A•X_B)	(X_A•X_B)		~(X_A+X_C)	(X_A+X_C)

Y: innovative region
X_A: higher-educated region

Subset consistency:
35/49 = 0.71

Superset consistency:
35/60: 0.58

Y: innovative region
X_A•X_B: (higher-educated•R&D)-region

Subset consistency:
21/24 = 0.84

Superset consistency:
21/60: 0.35

Y: innovative region
X_A+X_C: (higher-educated+HRST)-region

Subset consistency:
57/91 = 0.63

Superset consistency:
57/60: 0.95

Figure 7.4   The relation between consistency and coverage

In Example (iii), the explanatory condition is a disjunction of [higher-educated OR HRST], where HRST stands for human resources working in science and technology occupations (the two are logically equivalent because an HRST occupation requires a higher education). There are still 60 innovative regions (Y cases) in this research population. But now 57 of these are also X cases, because a disjunction ($X_A + X_C$) always has more cases than a single condition. This equals a superset consistency of 0.95, generously above the ≥ 0.9 threshold for necessity. Of the 91 X cases in Example (iii), 57 are also Y cases, which yields a superset coverage of 0.63. This is well above the ≥ 0.5 threshold for superset coverage, which suggests that having skilled human capital (higher-educated OR HRST) is necessary for being an innovative region (note that 0.63 is [of course] lower than the subset consistency [= superset coverage] for $X_A \subset Y$). This example suggests that it is very difficult for a condition to be both necessary and sufficient. Nor is that what QCA is after. QCA develops configurational explanations because we expect that single conditions do not explain (are not sufficient for) an outcome. See Table 7.1 for consistency and coverage thresholds, and see the discussion on complex causality in Chapter 3.

Table 7.1   *Criteria for sufficiency and necessity*

Statement	Set Relationship	Consistency	Coverage
Sufficiency	$X \subset Y$ X is a subset of Y	Subset (or sufficiency) consistency ≥ 0.8 (≥ 0.75 if substantive arguments allow)	Subset coverage is not relevant for a statement of sufficiency
Necessity	$X \supset Y$ X is a superset of Y	Superset (or necessity) sufficiency ≥ 0.9	Superset coverage ≥ 0.5

FUZZY SET CONSISTENCY AND COVERAGE

Calculating consistency and coverage in fuzzy set QCA (fsQCA) follows the same logic as for crisp set QCA (csQCA). Fuzzy sets are discussed in greater detail in Chapters 8 and 9, but it is unproblematic to introduce the technicalities for fsQCA here. Set membership in fuzzy sets varies between 0 to 1, where 0 identifies cases that have no membership in a set (i.e., cases that have none of the characteristics that define the set) and 1 identifies cases that have full membership in the set (i.e., cases that have all of the characteristics that define the set). Fuzzy set membership values aim to capture that social reality has more nuances than just true and false. The statement 'This is a high-income region' may be partially true. In fuzzy sets in QCA, 0.5 is the semantical threshold (or crossover point) between logically false (0) and logically true (1).

Let's get back to the fictional London neighbourhoods from Chapter 6 and invent a couple more. Let's assign them membership in the set of neighbourhoods with lively pubs, the set of neighbourhoods with good public transportation, the set of neighbourhoods with safe streets, and the set of neighbourhoods that are attractive residential areas (see Table 7.2). Subset consistency in crisp sets is the degree to which the explanatory condition (X_A, lively pubs) is a subset of the outcome (Y, attractive residential area). This is the case when the set of X is smaller (i.e., has fewer cases) than the set of Y. Fuzzy subset consistency is no different. Subset consistency in fuzzy sets means that membership in $X \leq$ membership in Y. Take Hampton Village. It has 0.80 membership in the set of lively pubs (X_A) and 0.90 membership in the set of attractive residential areas (Y) – that is, membership in X_A (lively pubs) $\leq$ membership in Y (attractive residential area). This means that Hampton Village substantiates the statement that having lively pubs is sufficient for being an attractive residential area. Hampton Village would be in Cell (i) (1,1 cases) of a (crisp) 2 × 2 table. So would Elizabeth Road, as its membership in X_A (0.85) $\leq$ its membership in Y (0.85).

However, St. Barbara has 0.80 membership in the set of lively pubs (X_A) but only 0.25 membership in the set of attractive residential areas (Y). St. Barbara thus defeats the statement that having lively pubs is sufficient for being an attractive residential area. St. Barbara would be a (1,0) case in Cell (ii). So far so good. But now look at Newbury; it has 0.35 membership in X_A and 0.60 membership in Y. This would put it in Cell (iii), the (0,1) cases, of a 2 × 2 table because 0.35 (X_A) is below the semantical threshold (crossover point) of 0.5 while 0.60 (Y) is above it. In a crisp set study, Newbury is an equifinal case; for this case, another explanatory condition than X_A explains Y. Being in Cell (iii), this case would be excluded from the calculation of crisp subset consistency. However, because X_A (0.35) $\leq Y$ (0.60), Newbury does confirm the fuzzy set statement that having lively pubs is sufficient for being an attractive neighbourhood. The opposite is true for Wansbeck Commons. It has 0.75 membership in X_A and 0.55 membership in Y.

Both are $\geq$ 0.5, so Wansbeck Commons would be a case in Cell (i) (1,1 case) in a 2 × 2 table, and it would contribute to the consistency of the crisp subset relationship. However, because $X > Y$, it defeats the fuzzy set statement that having lively pubs is sufficient for being an attractive neighbourhood. Wansbeck Commons thus reduces the fuzzy subset consistency. Finally, consider Burnsley Heights. It has 0.25 membership in X_B (neighbourhoods with good public transportation) and 0.35 membership in Y (attractive residential areas). This places Burnsley Heights in Cell (iv) (0,0 case) in the 2 × 2 table. This case is irrelevant for calculating the crisp subset consistency of good public transportation $\subset$ attractive residential area (being a Cell (iv) case, it is irrelevant for any crisp calculation of consistency or coverage). However, because X_B (0.25) $\leq Y$ (0.35), it corroborates the fuzzy set statement that having good public transportation is sufficient for being an attractive residential area. Burnsley Heights thus contributes to the fuzzy subset consistency of $X_B \subset Y$. In short, cases are appreciated differently in crisp versus fuzzy sets. So, how do we calculate fuzzy subset consistency?

Table 7.2   Fuzzy set memberships of fictional London neighbourhoods

	X_A	X_B	$X_A \cdot X_B$	X_C	Y	Minimum $X_A Y$	Minimum $X_B Y$	Minimum $(X_A \cdot X_B)Y$	Minimum $X_C Y$
	Lively pubs	Good public transportation	Lively pubs and good public transportation	Safe streets	Attractive residential area				
Elizabeth Road	0.85	0.70	0.70	0.90	0.85	0.85	0.70	0.70	0.85
Greenfield Park	0.60	0.90	0.60	0.45	0.80	0.60	0.80	0.60	0.45
Hampton Village	0.80	0.50	0.50	0.80	0.90	0.80	0.50	0.50	0.80
Wansbeck Commons	0.75	1.00	0.75	0.80	0.55	0.55	0.55	0.55	0.55
Wakefield	1.00	0.60	0.60	0.60	0.60	0.60	0.60	0.60	0.60
Southbank	0.65	0.80	0.65	0.45	0.50	0.50	0.50	0.50	0.45
St. Barbara	0.80	0.50	0.50	0.60	0.25	0.25	0.25	0.25	0.25
Holloway Crescent	0.60	0.65	0.60	0.10	0.15	0.15	0.15	0.15	0.10
Horton	0.90	0.75	0.75	0.90	0.80	0.80	0.75	0.75	0.80
Newbury	0.35	0.80	0.35	0.75	0.60	0.35	0.60	0.35	0.60
Burnsley Heights	0.70	0.25	0.25	0.80	0.35	0.35	0.25	0.25	0.35
Reddington	0.05	0.70	0.05	0.45	0.10	0.05	0.10	0.05	0.10
Σ	8.05	8.15	6.30	7.60	6.45	5.85	5.75	5.25	5.90

First, we take the sum of set membership in X. For example, the sum of set membership in X_A is 8.05 (see Table 7.2). Second, we take the sum of the minimum set membership in X_A and Y. For Elizabeth Road, the minimum set membership of X_A (0.85) and Y (0.85) is 0.85; for Greenfield Park, the minimum set membership in X_A (0.60) and Y (0.80) is 0.60, and so on. The sum of these minimum set memberships is 5.85. Third, we divide $\sum$ minimum (X_A,Y) by $\sum (X_A)$. If the minimum (X_A,Y) would be determined by X_A for every case in the set, the numerator and denominator of the fraction would be the same and, hence, its outcome would be 1. This indicates that X_A is a perfect fuzzy subset of Y. The more the minimum (X_A,Y) is determined by Y, the lower the outcome of the fraction will be, which indicates an inconsistent fuzzy subset relationship. In this example, the fuzzy subset consistency for $X_A \subset Y$ is:

$$Fuzzy\ subset\ consistency\ X \subset Y = \frac{\sum minimum\ (Xi, Yi)}{\sum Xi} = \frac{5.85}{8.05} = 0.73 \qquad (7.6)$$

The threshold for fuzzy subset consistency is the same as for crisp sets, ≥ 0.8. The fuzzy subset consistency of $X_A \subset Y = 0.73$, thus is too low; consequently, having lively pubs is not sufficient for being an attractive residential neighbourhood. Note that fuzzy subset consistency is not a proportion, as is the case for crisp subset consistency. Instead, it expresses the degree to which set membership values in X are lower than set membership values in Y across all cases in the case population. Instead, crisp subset consistency excludes (0,1) and (0,0) cases from the calculation. Fuzzy subset consistency thus abstracts from cases to express the degree in which $X \leq Y$ in a population of cases, while crisp subset consistency addresses the cases head on (Ragin, 2008, pp. 49–51). Of course, this is also true for the calculation of fuzzy subset coverage and fuzzy superset consistency and coverage.

But first let's look at the intersection of the fuzzy sets of lively pubs (X_A) and good public transportation (X_B) in Table 7.2. Remember that (fuzzy as well as crisp) set membership in an intersection is determined by the minimum membership in the individual sets. Elizabeth Road has 0.85 membership in X_A and 0.70 membership in X_B; consequently, its membership in $(X_A \cdot X_B)$ is 0.70. The sum of set membership in [lively pubs • good public transport] is 6.30. The sum of minimum set membership in $((X_A \cdot X_B),Y)$ is 5.25. We can now calculate the fuzzy subset consistency of [lively pubs • good public transport] $\subset$ attractive residential area as $\sum$ minimum $((X_A \cdot X_B),Y) = 5.25$ divided by the $\sum (X_A \cdot X_B) = 6.30 = 0.83$. This is ≥ 0.8, which means that having [lively pubs AND good public transport] is sufficient for being an attractive residential area.

Fuzzy superset consistency is calculated in a similar way. If fuzzy subset consistency means that fuzzy set membership in $X \leq$ fuzzy set membership in *Y*, then fuzzy superset consistency means that fuzzy set membership in *X* ≥ fuzzy set membership in *Y*. After all, for superset consistency, membership in *X* must be larger than membership in *Y*. Look at condition X_C, having safe streets (Table 7.2). The sum of fuzzy set membership in X_C is 7.60. To know whether X_C is a consistent fuzzy superset of *Y*, we also need to know the sum of fuzzy set membership in the minimum of (X_C, *Y*). This is 5.90. We must now divide the minimum (X_C,*Y*) by *Y*. If the minimum of (X_C,*Y*) is determined by *Y*, the numerator of the fraction would be the same as the denominator. It means that for all cases X_C ≥ *Y*, which would make X_C a perfect superset of *Y*. The more the minimum (X_C,*Y*) is determined by X_C, the lower the outcome of the fraction will be. As with crisp sets, superset consistency must be ≥ 0.9 for X_C to be necessary for *Y*. This turns out to be the case, as the formula for fuzzy superset consistency for X_C ⊃ *Y* shows:

$$Fuzzy\ superset\ consistency\ X \supset Y = \frac{\sum minimum\ (Xi, Yi)}{\sum (Yi)} = \frac{5.90}{6.45} = 0.92 \qquad (7.7)$$

To establish whether this means that having safe streets is necessary for being an attractive residential area, we must also calculate the fuzzy superset coverage. As with crisp superset coverage, this formula is the same as the formula for fuzzy subset consistency. Consequently, the fuzzy superset coverage for X_C ⊃ *Y* is:

$$Fuzzy\ superset\ coverage\ X \supset Y = \frac{\sum minimum\ (Xi, Yi)}{\sum (Xi)} = \frac{5.90}{7.60} = 0.78 \qquad (7.8)$$

This is well above the superset coverage threshold of ≥ 0.5. Therefore, based on these metrics, we can state that having safe streets is necessary for being an attractive residential area.

To complete the picture, let's calculate the fuzzy subset coverage for (X_A • X_B) ⊂ *Y*. This formula is the same as the formula for fuzzy superset consistency. Hence:

$$Fuzzy\ subset\ coverage\ X \subset Y = \frac{\sum minimum\ (Xi, Yi)}{\sum (Yi)} = \frac{5.25}{6.45} = 0.81 \qquad (7.9)$$

This is a very high subset coverage, which means that (X_A • X_B) is a very relevant condition for *Y*.

While the consistency and coverage of subset and superset relationships is visualized using 2 × 2 tables for crisp sets, fuzzy sets use *XY* plots. The functionality to produce *XY* plots of fuzzy set relationships is available in all QCA software. The *XY* plot for [lively pub • good public transport] (*X*) and attractive residential area (*Y*) is visualized in the left pane of Figure 7.5. Each case (neighbourhood) is a dot in the *XY* plot and the *X* and *Y* axes mark cases' membership in the fuzzy sets of X and Y. Fuzzy subset consistency means that $X \leq Y$. This means that, for a perfectly consistent fuzzy subset relationship, all cases are to the left of the $X = Y$ diagonal. After all, the area to the left of the $X = Y$ diagonal is the area where X values are lower than Y values. Since perfectly consistent subset relationships almost never happen, researchers should expect to find some of the cases positioned to the right of the $X = Y$ diagonal. These cases 'cause' the fuzzy subset relationship to become less consistent. The formula for fuzzy subset consistency works such that the further a case is positioned to the right of the diagonal, the more it decreases the consistency of the fuzzy subset relationship. Because the formula looks across cases, it may still be that it produces a fuzzy subset consistency ≥ 0.8 even though many cases are below the $X = Y$ diagonal. In that eventuality, researchers must be very cautious about declaring that X is sufficient for Y. Again, mathematical sufficiency does not necessarily mean that the set relationship can be interpreted into a statement of sufficiency.

Alternatively, the formula may produce a fuzzy subset consistency < 0.8 because of a few cases with very low Y values – that is, a few cases far below the $X = Y$ diagonal. Such cases greatly weaken the fuzzy subset relationship, but a researcher may be able to 'explain them away' based on substantive case knowledge. The best thing to do, then, is to eliminate these cases from the case population and recalculate the fuzzy subset consistency. The important point is to never go blind on the numbers but to always inspect the XY plot to see what is going on. The XY plot in the left pane of Figure 7.5 is unsuspicious for a fuzzy subset relationship. There are four cases below the $X = Y$ diagonal but only the two at the bottom are really problematic. These are cases where $X > 0.5$ but $Y < 0.5$ – that is, they are (1,0) cases. In fuzzy set terminology, these cases are contradictory in kind; they would also show up as contradictory cases in a 2×2 table. The top two cases are contradictory in degree: $X > Y$ – however, both X and $Y > 0.5$. These would be confirming cases (i.e., 1,1 cases) in a 2×2 table. That is, cases contradictory in degree do not logically contradict the statement that X is sufficient for Y (if X, then Y). Having cases contradictory in kind in your XY plot is much more problematic than cases contradictory in degree. If an XY plot shows many cases contradictory in kind, researchers should really question whether X is sufficient for Y, no matter how high the fuzzy subset consistency is. Cases contradictory in kind logically contradict the statement that X is sufficient for Y (if X, then Y).

To assess a fuzzy superset relationship, one must look at the area in the XY plot below the $X = Y$ diagonal. This is the area where X values are higher than Y values, so all cases in this area confirm the fuzzy superset relationship that $X \geq Y$. The right pane of Figure 7.5 shows the fuzzy superset relationship for safe streets $\supset$ attractive residential area. Again, this is an unproblematic XY plot because there are few contradictory cases – that is, cases to the left of the

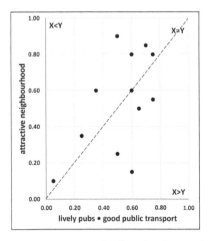 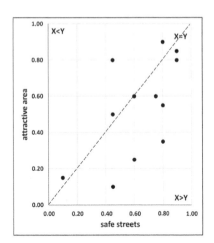

Figure 7.5   XY plots for fuzzy subset and superset relationships

$X = Y$ diagonal. Also here, a researcher must be conscious that having many cases with a low Y value (cases close to the X axis) makes X a superset of Y by default. This is suspicious no matter what the fuzzy superset consistency and fuzzy superset coverage. Furthermore, if only a few very contradictory cases (cases close to the X axis) 'cause' the fuzzy superset relationship to become inconsistent, a researcher may find reasons to eliminate these cases from the case population and recalculate the consistency and coverage of the superset relationship.

As argued in Chapter 3, casing is an ongoing activity throughout a QCA study. Researchers must never accept the metrics for consistency and coverage at face value but always inspect the XY plot. This may lead them to reconsider the inclusion of some cases in the case population. It may also lead them to reconsider the set membership values of cases – that is, to recalibrate them. QCA is a qualitative method where interpretation (the dialogue between knowledge of cases, context and concepts) takes precedence over the numerical (empirical) exercise of calculating consistencies and coverages (Ragin, 2000, p. 49).

SPURIOUS FUZZY SET RELATIONSHIPS

The calculation of fuzzy set consistency (and coverage) violates propositional logic. Cases where $X > Y$ but $Y > 0.5$ weaken fuzzy subset consistency even though their singular causal evidence confirms the statement: if X, then Y. Moreover, cases where $X < Y$ and where both X and $Y < 0.5$ contribute to fuzzy subset consistency, even though their singular causal evidence neither confirms nor contradicts the statement: if X, then Y. This can produce spurious results – set relationships that are mathematically consistent but substantively meaningless or even nonsensical. I have more to say on this in Chapter 9. Such violations of propositional logic produce two key problems for fuzzy set QCA: (1) simultaneous subset relationships; and (2) trivial necessary conditions. While spurious set relationships are easy to spot in small-N studies with intimate case knowledge, this is more challenging as researchers' distances to cases increases. Parameters to detect spurious set relationships then become necessary to help researchers dialogue ideas and (valid) evidence.

Simultaneous Subset Relationships: PRI

Simultaneous subset relationships in QCA refers to the explanatory condition (X) being a consistent subset of both the outcome (Y) and the negation of the outcome ($\sim Y$). This is, of course, logically nonsensical but a mathematical possibility in fuzzy set QCA. To address this phenomenon, Ragin developed the proportional reduction in inconsistency (PRI) parameter for fsQCA. The PRI is calculated with the following formula:

$$PRI(Y) = \frac{\sum \text{minimum } (Xi, Yi) - \sum \text{minimum } (Xi,\ Yi,\ \sim Yi)}{\sum (Xi) - \sum \text{minimum } (Xi,\ Yi,\ \sim Yi)} \qquad (7.10)$$

The first part of the formula is the same as the formula for fuzzy subset consistency. The second part includes $\sim Y$ in the calculation of the minimum set membership value. QCA researchers can compare the PRI(Y) value with the PRI($\sim Y$) value, which is calculated as follows:

$$PRI(\sim Y) = \frac{\sum \text{minimum } (Xi,\ \sim Yi) - \sum \text{minimum } (Xi,\ \sim Yi,\ Yi)}{\sum \text{minimum } (Xi) - \sum \text{minimum}(Xi,\ \sim Yi,\ Yi)} \qquad (7.11)$$

The fuzzy subset relationship ($X \subset Y$ or $X \subset \sim Y$) with the highest PRI value is the correct one. More often, QCA researchers only calculate the value for PRI(Y) and assess it against a threshold. Since PRI is symmetrical, any value for PRI(Y) ≥ 0.5 satisfies that X is indeed a fuzzy subset of Y and not of $\sim Y$ (Oana, Schneider and Thomann, 2021). However, to be safe, a PRI(Y) value of ≥ 0.6 is to be preferred. Some QCA methodologists set a higher PRI threshold (Pappas and Woodside, 2021). However, since PRI is more conservative than subset consistency, to me, a PRI threshold of > 0.8 seems unnecessary.

If X is a consistent fuzzy subset of Y, then the minimum for (X,Y) is determined by X. If $X \leq Y$, the values for Y will be high, particularly when $X > 0.5$. This means that the values for $\sim Y$ will be low (because $\sim Y = 1 - Y$). Consequently, the minimum for ($X,Y,\sim Y$) and for ($X,\sim Y$) will be determined by $\sim Y$. This means that the values for $\sum$ minimum ($Xi,\sim Yi$) and $\sum$ minimum ($Xi,\sim Yi,Yi$) will be (almost) the same. Subtracting $\sum$ minimum ($Xi,\sim Yi,Yi$) from

$\sum$ minimum $(X,\sim Y)$ thus produces a value of (almost) 0. The PRI$(\sim Y)$ will therefore be (almost) 0, suggesting that X is not a subset of $\sim Y$. Put differently, the more the minimum for $(Xi, Yi, \sim Yi)$ is determined by $\sim Yi$, the higher the PRI(Y). This is easily demonstrated with a fictional example. Suppose we want to investigate the relationship between having a hospital in your neighbourhood and being an attractive residential area. A hospital may contribute to the attractiveness of a neighbourhood because of the availability of medical services. However, residents also face the constant nuisance of noisy ambulances and increased traffic. Table 7.3 shows the fuzzy set memberships in these conditions, and their crisp set equivalents for comparison.

Table 7.3   *Simultaneous fuzzy subset relationships for Y and ~Y*

	Condition										
	Hospital nearby (X)		Attractive area (Y)		~Attractive area $(\sim Y)$		Minimum XY		Minimum $X\sim Y$		Minimum $XY\sim Y$
	Fuzzy set (fs) and crisp set (cs) membership											
	fs	cs	fs	cs	fs	cs	fs	cs	fs	cs	fs	cs
Northumberland Street	0.25	0	0.35	0	0.65	1	0.25	0	0.25	0	0.25	0
Wessex Square	0.45	0	0.55	1	0.45	0	0.45	0	0.45	0	0.45	0
Scotland Road	0.35	0	0.60	1	0.40	0	0.35	0	0.35	0	0.35	0
Jersey Lane	0.65	1	0.75	1	0.25	0	0.65	1	0.25	0	0.25	0
Yorkshire Avenue	0.40	0	0.45	0	0.55	1	0.40	0	0.40	0	0.40	0
$\sum$	2.10	1	2.70	3	2.30	2	2.10	1	1.70	0	1.70	0

The fuzzy subset consistency for hospital nearby $\subset$ attractive residential area is:

$$Hospital\ nearby \subset attractive\ residential\ area = \frac{\sum minimum\ (Xi, Yi)}{\sum (Xi)} = \frac{2.10}{2.10}$$
$$= 1 \quad (7.12)$$

This is a perfect fuzzy subset relationship; however, the fuzzy subset relationship for hospital nearby $\subset$ not-attractive residential area is also very consistent:

$$Hospital\ nearby \subset \sim attractive\ residential\ area = \frac{\sum minimum\ (Xi, \sim Yi)}{\sum (Xi)} \quad (7.13)$$
$$= \frac{1.70}{2.10} = 0.81$$

In other words, the subset consistency threshold does not conclusively say whether X is a subset of Y or $\sim Y$. However, the PRI values for Y and $\sim Y$ leave no doubt:

$$PRI(Y) = \frac{\sum \text{minimum } (Xi, Yi) - \sum \text{minimum } (Xi, Yi, \sim Yi)}{\sum (Xi) - \sum \text{minimum } (Xi, Yi, \sim Yi)} = \frac{2.10 - 1.70}{2.10 - 1.70} = 1 \qquad (7.14)$$

$$PRI(\sim Y) = \frac{\sum \text{minimum } (Xi, \sim Yi) - \sum \text{minimum } (Xi, \sim Yi, Yi)}{\sum (Xi) - \sum \text{minimum } (Xi, \sim Yi, Yi)} = \frac{1.70 - 1.70}{2.10 - 1.70} = 0 \qquad (7.15)$$

Clearly, in this example, the fuzzy subset relation hospital nearby $\subset \sim$attractive residential area is spurious, even though its consistency passes the thresholds. QCA researchers must always calculate the PRI(Y) value before claiming that X is sufficient for Y. No matter how consistent the fuzzy subset relationship, a PRI(Y) < 0.60 is deeply suspicious. Note that the problem of simultaneous subset relationships does not occur in crisp sets. The crisp set memberships in Table 7.3 conclusively show that 'hospital nearby' is only a consistent subset of 'attractive area':

$$\textit{Crisp subset consistency hospital nearby} \subset \textit{attractive area} = \frac{\sum (XY \text{ cases})}{\sum (X \text{ cases})}$$

$$= \frac{1}{1} = 1 \qquad (7.16)$$

$$\textit{Crisp subset consistency hospital nearby} \subset \sim\textit{attractive area} = \frac{\sum (X \sim Y \text{ cases})}{\sum (X - \text{ cases})}$$

$$= \frac{0}{1} = 0 \qquad (7.17)$$

Relevance of Necessity: RoN

A similar issue occurs with fuzzy superset relationships. They may be consistent (≥ 0.9) and their coverage may be high enough (≥ 0.5) but they may still be trivial. In fuzzy set QCA, trivialness of necessity may occur for two reasons. First, set membership in Y may be (very) low in (nearly) all cases. This makes the Y set a subset of any X set by default; however, this may not be taken to suggest necessity. In crisp set QCA, this situation will result in a superset coverage well below the 0.5 threshold. In most cases, the coverage of necessity is also a good safeguard against this kind of trivialness in fuzzy set QCA (see above), but it helps to always inspect the XY plot. Second, trivialness of necessity may also happen when membership in Y is (almost) equal to membership in X in (almost) all cases – that is, when X is only narrowly a fuzzy superset of Y. Such a high degree of overlap is problematic because it produces a (near) tautology where $X \approx Y$. This renders X irrelevant in a difference-making analysis like QCA. For example, the set of low-income EU regions is a superset of the set of EU regions that receive contributions from the EU's Regional Development Funds. But because almost all low-income regions receive regional development support, it is not meaningful to say that being a low-income region is necessary for receiving it. It actually says the same thing twice: these regions are less-developed regions. For this kind of trivialness, Schneider and Wagemann (2012, p. 236) developed a parameter called relevance of necessity (RoN) for fsQCA. RoN is calculated as follows:

$$RoN = \frac{\sum (1 - X_i)}{\sum (1 - minimum(X_i, Y_i))} \tag{7.18}$$

RoN is a more conservative metric than the coverage of necessity. It checks against X values that are (nearly) constantly high. Let's again demonstrate RoN with a fictional example. Table 7.4 shows three conditions that are all consistent fuzzy supersets of the set of streets with expensive houses (Y): being a street where residents have a high income (X_A), being a street where residents have big cars (X_B), and being a street with a paved road (X_C). The table shows the fuzzy set membership values of five fictional streets in these conditions.

The fuzzy superset consistencies are 1 for all three explanatory conditions:

$$\frac{minimum \sum (X_{Ai}, Y_i)}{\sum (X_{Ai})} = \frac{minimum \sum (X_{Bi}, Y_i)}{\sum (X_{Bi})} = \frac{minimum \sum (X_{Ci}, Y_i)}{\sum (X_{Ci})} = \frac{2.35}{2.35} = 1 \tag{7.19}$$

The fuzzy superset coverages differ but they are all > 0.5 and, therefore, unproblematic. The coverage of $X_A \supset Y$ is $\frac{\sum minimum(X_{Ai}, Y_i)}{\sum (X_{Ai})} = \frac{2.35}{2.70} = 0.87$; the coverage of $X_B \subset Y$ is $\frac{\sum minimum(X_{Bi}, Y_i)}{\sum (X_{Bi})} = \frac{2.35}{3.80} = 0.62$ and the coverage of $X_C \subset Y$ is $\frac{\sum minimum(X_{Ci}, Y_i)}{\sum (X_{Ci})} = \frac{2.35}{4.50} = 0.52$.

However, the RoN values for the three fuzzy superset relationships conclusively show that only 'high income' is necessary for 'expensive houses':

$$RoN\ high\ income \supset expensive\ houses = \frac{\sum (1 - X_{Ai})}{\sum (1 - minimum(X_{Ai}, Y_i))} = \frac{2.30}{2.65} \\ = 0.87 \tag{7.20}$$

$$RoN\ big\ cars \supset expensive\ houses = \frac{\sum (1 - X_{Bi})}{\sum (1 - minimum(X_{Bi}, Y_i))} = \frac{1.20}{2.65} \\ = 0.45 \tag{7.21}$$

$$RoN\ paved\ road \supset expensive\ houses = \frac{\sum (1 - X_{Ci})}{\sum (1 - minimum(X_{Ci}, Y_i))} = \frac{0.50}{2.65} \\ = 0.19 \tag{7.22}$$

Table 7.4   Relevance of necessity

	X_A High income	X_B Big car	X_C Paved road	Y Expensive houses	$1 - X_A$	$1 - X_B$	$1 - X_C$	Minimum X_A, Y	Minimum X_B, Y	Minimum X_C, Y	$1 -$ minimum X_A, Y	$1 -$ minimum X_B, Y	$1 -$ minimum X_C, Y
Estate Avenue	0.95	1	1	0.95	0.05	0	0	0.95	0.95	0.95	0.05	0.05	0.05
Villa Drive	0.85	0.95	0.95	0.75	0.15	0.05	0.05	0.75	0.75	0.75	0.25	0.25	0.25
Council Flat Lane	0.45	0.75	0.90	0.35	0.55	0.25	0.10	0.35	0.35	0.35	0.65	0.65	0.65
Renovation Road	0.30	0.85	0.85	0.25	0.70	0.15	0.15	0.25	0.25	0.25	0.75	0.75	0.75
Shack Street	0.15	0.25	0.80	0.05	0.85	0.75	0.20	0.05	0.05	0.05	0.95	0.95	0.95
Σ	2.70	3.80	4.50	2.35	2.30	1.20	0.50	2.35	2.35	2.35	2.65	2.65	2.65

These RoN values suggest that having a paved road is clearly a trivial necessary condition for being a street with expensive houses. Because pretty much all streets have paved roads, the fuzzy set membership values for condition X_C are (nearly) all high. The same is true for being a street where residents have big cars (X_B), because one can find big cars in nearly every street, regardless of whether the houses (or the cars) are expensive. Only being a street where residents have a high income is a relevant necessity condition for being a street with expensive houses.

Again, it is worth pointing out that calculating crisp superset consistencies and coverages, this kind of trivial necessity does not occur. Crispifying the fuzzy set membership values of Table 7.4 to $< 0.5 = 0$ and $> 0.5 = 1$ gives a crisp superset consistency for $X_A \supset Y$ of $\frac{\sum \text{minimum}(XAi, Yi)}{\sum(Yi)} = \frac{2}{2} = 1$. Also the crisp superset consistencies for $X_B \supset Y$ and $X_C \supset Y$ are 1. But now the crisp superset coverages are decisive. The coverage for $X_A \supset Y$ is $\frac{\sum \text{minimum}(XAi, Yi)}{\sum(XAi)} = \frac{2}{2} = 1$; however, the coverage for $X_B \supset Y = 0.5$ (borderline and, hence, not convincing) and the coverage for $X_C \supset Y = 0.4$ (too low).

In sum, PRI and RoN are parameters for fuzzy set QCA that help prevent researchers from making flawed inferences. Because of the way fuzzy subset and superset consistency are calculated, logically contradictory and dubious results are mathematically possible. Crisp sets rely on propositional logic for both singular and general causal evidence. However, fuzzy set relationships are calculated over all cases in the case population and mean something different than crisp set relationships, and this may conflict with the propositional logic of the truth table (see Chapter 10). Hence the need for PRI and RoN. The more important point is that QCA is not a quantitative method; researchers cannot rely on parameters alone and must always dialogue between knowledge of cases, context and concepts. PRI and RoN decide whether it is safe to interpret fuzzy set relationships into statements of sufficiency and necessity. They do not evidence that a set relationship is sufficient or necessary.

CONCLUSION

The set analysis required for QCA is fairly straightforward. The logic of superset, subsets and their consistency and coverage is enough for QCA. Only fuzzy set QCA requires PRI and RoN as additional parameters. Set analysis produces the cross-case – that is, general – causal evidence in QCA. Even though set analysis is a conspicuously quantitative element of QCA, it remains a qualitative method. The parameters only inform QCA researchers whether their cross-case evidence is empirically valid; that is, if it is a genuine rather than a spurious description of the subset and superset relationships between their cases. Only then may mathematically sufficient and necessary set relationships be interpreted into statements of sufficiency and necessity – that is, into causal claims (Rubinson et al., 2019). Obviously, it is crucial that QCA researchers correctly perform their set analyses. However, researchers must keep firmly in mind that interpretations of the set relationships make causal statements, not the set relationships themselves. Learning from cases is to attach meaning to the stylized facts of co-occurrence in subset and superset relationships.

GLOSSARY OF KEY CONCEPTS

Confirming cases	Cases in Cell (i). These are the (1,1) cases, where $X = 1$ and $Y = 1$. Confirming cases provide singular causal evidence that confirms the logical statement: if X, then Y (or iff X, then Y)
Contradictory cases	Cases in Cell (ii). These are the (1,0) cases, where $X = 1$ and $Y = 0$. Contradictory cases provide singular causal evidence that contradicts the logical statement: if X, then Y. This contradicts a statement of sufficiency that if X, then Y. However, contradictory cases do not contradict the logical statement: iff X, then Y. That is, they are inconsequential for statements of necessity
Contradictory in degree	For fuzzy sets only. $X > Y$ but $Y > 0.5$ (for sufficiency). $X < Y$ but $X > 0.5$ (for necessity). Cases contradictory in degree reduce the consistency of the fuzzy set relationship but do not logically contradict the statement that X is sufficient (necessary) for Y
Contradictory in kind	For fuzzy sets only. $X > Y$ and $Y < 0.5$ (for sufficiency). $X > Y$ and $X < 0.5$ (for necessity). Cases contradictory in kind reduce the consistency of the fuzzy set relationship and also logically contradict the statement that X is sufficient (necessary) for Y
Coverage	Indicates the empirical relevance of a set relationship
Coverage of necessity	Refers to the degree in which X is a subset of Y
Coverage of sufficiency	Refers to the degree in which X is a superset of Y
Equifinal cases	Cases in Cell (iii). These are the (0,1) cases, where $X = 0$ and $Y = 1$. Singular causal evidence from equifinal cases neither confirms nor contradicts the logical statement: if X, then Y. However, these cases do contradict the logical statement: iff X, then Y. In other words, equifinal cases are inconsequential for statements of sufficiency but contradict statements of necessity

Irrelevant cases	Cases in Cell (iv). These are the (0,0) cases, where $X = 0$ and $Y = 0$. The singular causal evidence from these cases neither confirms nor contradicts the logical statement: if X, then Y (or iff X, then Y). In fact, these cases have nothing to say on the causal relationship between X and Y, because X is not present and Y has not occurred
Mathematical necessity	The superset consistency ≥ 0.9 and the superset coverage ≥ 0.5. Mathematical necessity means that the superset relationship may be interpreted into a statement of necessity. It does not necessarily imply that X is necessary for Y
Mathematical sufficiency	The subset consistency ≥ 0.8, or ≥ 0.75 if substantive arguments permit. Mathematical sufficiency means that a subset relationship may be interpreted into a statement of sufficiency. It does not necessarily imply that X is substantively sufficient for Y
PRI	Proportional reduction in inconsistency. For fuzzy sets only. PRI(Y) indicates whether X is simultaneously a subset of Y and $\sim Y$. A low PRI(Y) value means that X is actually a subset of $\sim Y$
RoN	Relevance of necessity. For fuzzy sets only. RoN indicates whether X is a trivial necessary condition for Y. A low RoN means that fuzzy set memberships in X are nearly equal to fuzzy set memberships in Y
Statement of necessity	The mathematically sufficient superset relationship can be interpreted into a statement of necessity following a dialogue between knowledge of cases, context and concepts
Statement of sufficiency	The mathematically sufficient subset relationship can be interpreted into a statement of sufficiency following a dialogue between knowledge of cases, context and concepts – that is, X explains Y
Subset consistency (or sufficiency consistency)	The degree to which the set of X is a subset of the set of Y
Superset consistency (or necessity consistency)	The degree to which the set of X is a superset of the set of Y

8. Calibration and aggregation[1]

QCA is a threshold method; it investigates whether being above or below the threshold on a condition makes a difference for being above or below the threshold on the outcome (Goertz, 2020, p. 182; Ragin [1987] 2014, p. 83). Setting the threshold is the process of calibration, which is an interactive process rather than a one-shot 'conversion' of raw data (Ragin, 2000, pp. 166–71). All regions have a degree of economic development; however, only after a certain degree of economic development does a region qualify as an economically developed region. 'Sitting' above the threshold for regional economic development means that the statement, 'This is an economically developed region', is logically true. This chapter explains what calibration is and what it means. It also guides readers through the process of calibration. Most importantly, calibration is about meaning and interpretation; it cannot be done mechanically (Schneider and Wagemann, 2012, pp. 32–5). The above threshold is the crossover point, which distinguishes between economically developed and not-economically developed regions. Regions can also be economically developed in degree. Consequently, one can calibrate multiple (more than two) logical categories to capture the degree to which the statement, 'This is an economically developed region', is true. This gets one from crisp to fuzzy sets (Ragin, 2008, pp. 29–31; Smithson, 1987, p. 16). Yet the crucial difference is not between crisp and fuzzy sets but between multilevel (two or more categories) and continuous sets. The latter can only be meaningfully calibrated from continuous (i.e., ratio-scaled) raw data. However, fuzzy set QCA has the tendency to interpret all fuzzy sets as continuous (Smithson and Verkuilen, 2006, p. 44). In response, this chapter spends some time on how to calibrate from different kinds of (qualitative and quantitative) data and discusses the three methods of calibration (the manual, direct and indirect methods). In all cases, calibration starts with the definition of a set (Russo and Confente, 2019). Definition also connects calibration to aggregation. Sets, or concepts, are calibrated on the basis of their definition; on what it means to be a case of the set (concept) (Goertz, 2020, pp. 67–8; Ragin, 2000, pp. 160–67). Aggregation is about combining sub-concepts into concepts. This should not be done mechanically – for example, by averaging 'indicators' – but by using logical ANDs and logical ORs in order to stay true to the meaning of the concept (Goertz, 2020, pp. 14–20).

WHAT IS CALIBRATION ABOUT?

Calibration is about meaning and it is a profoundly qualitative aspect of QCA. Raw data, the data collected from cases, is meaningless. We may know that the GDP per capita of a region is £21 000. We may know that this is £1000 more than that of another region, but still not know whether the region is rich or poor. To know that, we need to set a threshold for being a rich or poor region. The threshold must be substantively informed; it must be based on a firm conceptual understanding of what it means to be a rich or poor region (Schneider and Wagemann, 2012, pp. 32–5). Setting the threshold may be relatively straightforward when concepts are mostly clear, such as rich or poor region. But what about concepts that are less straightforward to define and measure, such as democracy, conflict and sustainability, to name but a few? Calibrating such concepts requires interpretation – that is, conducting a dialogue between knowledge of cases, context and concepts to answer the question, for example, is this region a case of a democratic region (Ragin, 2000, p. 310)?

Calibration, thus, is interpretation; it is about connecting meaning to data (Goertz and Mahoney, 2012b). When we calibrate a region as a case of a democratic region, we are saying that the statement, 'This is a democratic region', is true. Set membership values 1 (true) and false (0) are logical statements, not empirical values. In fuzzy sets, a set membership value of 0.8 means that the statement is mostly true (and somewhat, i.e., 0.2, false) (Smithson and Verkuilen, 2006, p. 19). To explain calibration in more detail, it is easiest to start by saying what it is not. It is not a transformation of data; it is not about converting raw data into set membership values (Rubinson et al., 2019), even though in QCA practice this is often what happens, particularly when researchers use the so-called direct method of calibration (see below). Nor is calibration (necessarily) a one-shot process. Calibration, like QCA in general, is a dialogue. Calibration is part of QCA's aim to learn from cases. It is therefore perfectly acceptable to 'update' one's calibrations once or multiple times during a QCA study. Findings that are problematic, counterintuitive or otherwise difficult to interpret usually suggest issues with the calibration.

Calibration is a two-step process. The first step defines the concept. It requires researchers to define what it means to be a case of X. For example, what does it mean to be a low-income household? The answer to this question may be: a household that cannot make ends meet at the end of the month. The definition is about ontology, about meaning, which 'puts' it in the domain of the Real. Definition may be largely context independent. Failing to make ends meet defines a low-income household regardless of the nature of the means to make ends meet. It defines low-income families in the UK, which typically receive income from wages or welfare, as well as in developing countries, such as Indonesia, where low-income households tend to rely heavily on the informal economy and remittance.

The second step is about epistemology, about measurement. It answers the question of how we know a low-income family when we see one, which 'puts' it in the domain of the Empirical. The answer to this question is deeply contextual and can be answered in two ways. First, a researcher may inspect every single case (in the domain of the Actual) in the case population and establish whether the household can make ends meet. Because it is the most context sensitive, it is the most accurate way of calibrating a case as a member or not-member of, in this example, the set of low-income households. It is also a very labour-intensive way. Doing so requires setting a substantively informed threshold to distinguish between low-income and not-low-income households. Substantively informed means that the threshold is based on a dialogue between knowledge of cases, context and concept. For example, the threshold for low income may be between households that can afford housing, food and clothing but no other basic cost of living, and those that can. Second, a researcher can also use an 'external criterion'. Earlier (applied) research and policy documents may have developed such a criterion – for example, the minimum wage. The minimum wage is set (one would hope) to allow households make ends meet. Using such an external criterion as the (empirical) threshold is perfectly acceptable and the least labour-intensive; however, it is also the least accurate way of calibration because it severs the case from its context. After all, we do not know whether a particular minimum wage household can or cannot make ends meet.

The broader point is that researchers must convince themselves and their readers that the threshold they choose is meaningful. In any case, calibration always requires researchers to address two questions: (1) What does it mean to be a case of X (ontology)? And how do we know a case of X when we see one (epistemology)? A good way of calibrating is to work from ideal types. This makes concepts into idealized cognitive models (Lakoff, 1987, pp. 68–70) that we use to describe and interpret cases (events in the domain of the Actual). Defining the ideal type answers the first question. Assessing to what degree a particular case resembles the ideal type answers the second question. Calibrating from ideal types is an effective safeguard against regressing calibration to mere data conversion (Goertz and Mahoney, 2012b; Smithson, 1987, p. 80).

CALIBRATION AND LOGICAL CATEGORIES

Let's pursue the example of calibrating the set of low-income households. We have defined them as households that cannot make ends meet. Additionally, it is important to define what it means to be a not-low-income household.

This is important because most households will have both low-income and high-income characteristics. A not-low-income household may be defined as a household that can afford leisure and luxury on a regular basis. Households can only do that when they have no problems affording the cost of living. We must now answer the second of the above two questions and identify the threshold that distinguishes low-income from not-low-income households. This means we are looking for households that are just or narrowly in the set of low-income households. These households can afford the basic cost of living (i.e., housing, food and clothing) but nothing else – no Wi-Fi or a bus fare to travel to work or to school. Because these households need Wi-Fi and must travel on the bus, they will spend money on these items and depend on food banks and clothing banks for those costs of living. In other words, effectively, they cannot make ends meet. A household just below the threshold, or almost a low-income family, does not depend on food banks and clothing banks in order to afford other basic necessities, such as Wi-Fi and travel.

With this information, we can now conclusively answer for every case (household) whether the statement, 'This is a low-income household', is true (1) or false (0). We need to inspect every case carefully and, based on the empirical evidence from the case, identify it as a low-income or a not-low-income household. From a logical or threshold perspective, this is all we need to do. However, we may want to refine our calibration to identify more categories of low-incomeness. This works no differently than for two categories; we just need to define more categories and the thresholds between them. Table 8.1 calibrates households into eight categories of low-incomeness. Notice that elements of the definition of not-low-income households are used to calibrate the lowest category of the set of low-income households – that is, marginally low-income households.

All eight categories in Table 8.1 are logical categories that are identified with linguistic hedges. Linguistic hedges, or semantic modifiers (Lakoff, 1973; Zadeh, 1972), such as 'fully' and 'somewhat', modify the degree to which the statement, 'This is a low-income household', is true. Linguistic hedges thus define multiple logical categories and recognize that social reality is more colourful than merely true (1) or false (0). Multiple categories define multiple semantical thresholds. However, the principal semantical threshold is still the crossover point – the semantical threshold that distinguishes between categories where the statement, 'This is a low-income household', is more true than false (1) on the one hand, and where that statement is more false than true (0), on the other.[2] The principal semantical threshold thus sits between intensifying hedges (mostly, largely, predominantly) and diluting hedges (moderately, somewhat, marginally). This signals the transition between cases that are more 'in the set' and those more 'out of the set' (Ragin, 2000, p. 327; Smithson, 1987, p. 23; Zadeh, 1972).

Table 8.1   *Calibrating low-income households*

Category	Definition
Fully low-income household	Must choose between food and housing
Mostly low-income household	Can afford basic housing but must choose between other cost of living necessities (food, clothing)
Largely low-income household	Can afford basic housing and food but not clothing
Predominantly low-income household	Can afford basic housing, food and clothing but nothing else
Moderately low-income household	Can afford housing, food and clothing as well as other basic necessities
Somewhat low-income household	Can afford cost of living and other basic necessities with a small margin
Marginally low-income household	Can afford cost of living and other basic necessities and occasional leisure and luxury
Not-low-income household	Has enough budget for regular leisure and luxury

As argued, QCA is a threshold method and, as we will see in Chapter 10, the truth table minimization condenses all categories (all fuzzy set membership values) to 1s (true) and 0s (false). That is, we must always define the crossover point as the principal semantical threshold between true and false in order to perform a QCA study; and in order to investigate whether the presence (1) or absence (0) of X makes a difference for the presence (1) or absence (0) of Y. However, identifying multiple logical categories with semantical modifiers allows 'playing around' with the crossover point. For example, suppose the analysis of necessity learns that being a low-income family is not necessary for being an unhappy family, where the crossover point for low income is (at least) primarily low income. We can then lower the crossover point to (at least) moderately low income to investigate whether this condition may be necessary for being an unhappy family. Lowering the crossover point means that the set of X becomes larger (includes cases in more categories). So perhaps this X is necessary for being an unhappy family. If so, it would be a substantively important finding because it means that a degree of low-incomeness is necessary for being unhappy. Of course, lowering the crossover point must not become a fishing expedition; one must have substantive reasons for doing so.

Similarly, one may want to investigate whether different or similar configurations explain being an innovative region – that is, (at least) primarily innovative – versus being (at least) a largely innovative region. This raises the threshold for Y. The set of (at least) largely innovative regions includes fewer cases than the set of (at least) primarily innovative regions. Consequently, different rows may be true or false in the truth tables for those two outcomes and this will produce different solutions. The question is, how different? Suppose the solution for (at least) primarily innovative has two configurations: (1) [R&D • higher educated] and (2) [new business foundation • collaboration]. This suggests that (1) being an R&D-performing region AND being a region with a higher-educated workforce is sufficient for being an (at least) primarily innovative region. OR that (2) being a region with new business start-ups AND being a region where firms collaborate is sufficient for being an (at least) primarily innovative region. Now suppose that the solution for being an (at least) largely innovative region is (3) [R&D • higher educated • collaboration]. So we now have three configurations:

(1) [R&D • higher educated] → primarily innovative.
(2) [new business start-ups • collaboration] → primarily innovative.
(3) [R&D • higher educated • collaboration] → largely innovative.

Note that configuration (3) is a subset of configuration (1). This suggests that, in order to 'level up', from being a primarily innovative to being a largely innovative region, regions can 'augment' configuration (1) by also developing inter-firm collaboration. That is, they can level up by doing the same thing better. This is not the case for configuration (2). This configuration has no 'subset counterpart' in the solution for largely innovative. To level up, regions covered by configuration (2) must do something different from what they are currently doing. Obviously, this is theoretically very relevant to know. It suggests that some paths only lead to primarily innovative but not to a higher level of innovation (largely innovative). For those regions, levelling up requires path breaking – that is, doing something different.

   Thus, 'playing around' with the crossover point for the outcome allows QCA researchers to investigate equifinality on different levels. Again, this is not a fishing expedition; one must have substantive reasons for changing the crossover point. Randomly doing multiple QCA studies for different crossover points for the explanatory conditions and the outcome is not only extremely laborious, it is also futile. Changing the crossover point defines a different case population, because different cases will now be X and $\sim X$ cases. This will lead to different solutions by default. Therefore, 'playing around' with the crossover point must only be done when it is substantively meaningful. If so, calibrating multiple categories with linguistic hedges gives QCA researchers the opportunity to develop richer explanations.

FUZZY SET MEMBERSHIP VALUES

The default in fuzzy set QCA is to have set membership values but it runs the risk of suggesting the value as something 'hard' and 'objective' while ignoring that a degree of membership is a judgement, one that follows from dialoguing knowledge of cases, concepts and context. A qualitative judgement in the form of linguistic hedges is perfectly acceptable in fuzzy set theory (Goertz, 2020, pp. 98–105; Smithson, 1987, p. 16). In fact, set membership values suggest a precision and gradation that neither the definition of a concept nor its measurement may support. Converting ordinal scales to set membership values is particularly problematic (Smithson, 1987, p. 88). Only continuous scales used to measure clearly linearly graded concepts really lend themselves to a 'conversion' to fuzzy set membership values – and many concepts are not at all linear (Lakoff, 1987, pp. 68–70). In all other cases, calibration into categories (linguistic hedges) is a perfectly good option (Smithson and Verkuilen, 2006, pp. 20–21). One may still attach fuzzy set membership values to the categories, for computational purposes, only those values do not mean anything and the precision they suggest is spurious. Using qualitative data, calibration into categories is obvious (Russo and Confente, 2019). However, in the case of quantitative data, researchers too often and too easily mistake calibration for a data conversion and ignore making a connection to meaning (e.g., Pappas and Woodside, 2021).

A degree of membership, whether expressed as a linguistic hedge (category) or a set membership value is meaningful because of its definition. And unless calibrated from continuous data, any set membership value is largely arbitrary, *largely* because being above or below the crossover point (0.5) is very meaningful (see below). The number of categories (degrees of membership) of a fuzzy set is contingent on the number of categories one can meaningfully define. The eight categories of Table 8.1 can be numerated in three principal ways, as shown in Table 8.2.

It is customary in QCA to numerate logical categories in a symmetrical and evenly spaced way (A), and this is very good practice. However, the values as such have no meaning; they are merely attached to logical categories to allow calculating fuzzy subset and superset relationships. But there is no reason a researcher cannot assign set membership values according to distribution B or even C. It makes no difference for how the metrics in fuzzy set QCA work. This emphasizes that QCA performs a logical and not empirical analysis. Keep in mind that logical categories identified with the same semantical modifier – that is, the same meaning – must be assigned the same fuzzy set membership value across all sets in the same study (Smithson and Verkuilen, 2006, p. 27). Calibration is the process of putting all conditions on the same scale. Mostly developed regions and mostly innovative regions will have different raw data values but they will have the same fuzzy set membership value.

While assigning fuzzy set membership values to logical categories is the default approach in QCA, it is worth pointing out an important limitation. Even with fuzzy set membership values, logical categories are still ordinal scales

Table 8.2   *Set membership values for logical categories*

	(A) Symmetrical and Evenly Spaced	(B) Symmetrical but Unevenly Spaced	(C) Asymmetrical and Unevenly Spaced
Fully a case of X	1	1	1
Mostly a case of X	0.85	0.90	0.91
Largely a case of X	0.70	0.85	0.73
Predominantly a case of X	0.55	0.60	0.52
Moderately a case of X	0.45	0.40	0.47
Somewhat a case of X	0.30	0.15	0.36
Marginally a case of X	0.15	0.10	0.08
Not-a-case of X	0	0	0

(or, at best, interval scales). Fuzzy set metrics (see Chapter 7) 'behave' as ratio scales (Goertz, 2020, p. 145); however, the difference between a mostly low income (0.85) and a largely low income (0.70) is not the same as the difference between a somewhat low income (0.30) and a marginally low income (0.15). Even though the numerical difference is 0.15 in both cases, the difference between being unable (0.30) and being able (0.15) to afford leisure and luxury is of a qualitatively different nature than the difference between being unable (0.85) and being able (0.70) to afford food. That is, the empirical accuracy that fuzzy set membership values suggest is largely spurious. Smithson and Verkuilen (2006, p. 44) put it more politely but say the same thing: 'The extent to which we can effectively quantify fuzziness depends on the measurement level of the membership scales'.

But what if we have quantitative raw data? What if we calibrate our cases in the set of low-income households based on their income? That, of course, makes a difference because income is a ratio scale. To calibrate from ratio-scaled data, we first need to identify the three 'qualitative anchors' of a set. The first qualitative anchor is the threshold of full membership. Semantically, this still means that a household cannot afford the basic cost of living – that is, housing, food and clothing. We now connect this definition to a particular raw data value. Conducting a dialogue between knowledge of cases, context and concepts, we may deduce that £600 is a plausible empirical value for the threshold of full membership. The second qualitative anchor is the crossover point. This still distinguishes between households that can and cannot make ends meet. Dialoguing between knowledge of cases, context and concepts, we may identify £1600 as a plausible empirical value for the crossover point. The third qualitative anchor is the threshold of full non-membership.

This means that households have enough budget to afford regular leisure and luxury. Conducting the usual dialogue may point to £2600 as a plausible empirical value for the threshold of full non-membership. Alternatively, we may look for 'external criteria' in studies and policy documents. We may find that (in this example) the minimum wage is £1600 and use that as the crossover point. And we may find that a study on poverty identified £600 as the point where families run into very severe problems, and use that threshold for full non-membership. We may also find that the tourism sector does not target families with an income below £2600 in their advertising, and set that as the threshold for full non-membership. In other words, researchers can dialogue knowledge of cases, context and concepts to set substantive criteria for the qualitative anchors themselves, or they may look for external criteria in other studies, policy documents and so on – and be very creative and resourceful at it (in my example, both approaches identify the same £ value but that need not be the case with real-world data, which emphasizes that calibration is more about definition and interpretation than about data).

The qualitative anchors are definitions (ontology); they define what it means to be fully X (threshold of full membership – (1); to be not-X (threshold of full non-membership – (0); and what distinguishes cases that are narrowly X from those that are almost X (the crossover point, 0.5). The critical values (epistemology) are the raw data values attached to the qualitative anchors.

From the three critical values (£600, £1600 and £2600), we can now proceed in two different ways. Using the indirect method of calibration (Ragin, 2008, pp. 94–7), one 'sets' the critical values and then assigns set membership values to the raw data values between them in a linear way (see the relevant column in Table 8.3). Assigning set membership values to raw data values in the indirect method is linear. In this example, a difference of £100 equals a 0.5 set membership difference. The linearity of the indirect method of calibration is also its downside. Differences close to the crossover point have a higher impact on cases than differences close to thresholds of full (non-)membership. The difference between £1600 and £1700 has a bigger impact on the kind of lifestyle a household can afford than the difference between £2400 and £2500. The direct method of calibration (Ragin, 2008, pp. 84–94) accounts for this phenomenon by performing a logarithmic conversion of raw data into set membership values. The direct method can be performed in MS Excel in three steps; however, it is automated in most QCA software packages. The three steps of the direct method are as follows:

1. *Deviation score (DS)*. Subtract the value for the crossover point from the raw data value of the case. This identifies how much the case 'deviates' from the crossover point:

DS = Case's raw data value − Crossover point

2. *Log odds (LO)*. The logarithm of the odds ratio of the distribution. The *LO* is calculated differently for *DS* values above (positive *DS* values) and below (negative *DS* values) the crossover point:

$$LO \text{ (positive } DS) = DS * \left(\frac{3}{\text{threshold full membership − crossover point}} \right) \quad (8.1)$$

$$LO \text{ (negative } DS) = DS * \left(\frac{-3}{\text{threshold full non-membership − crossover point}} \right) \quad (8.2)$$

3. *Exponent (EXP)*. Takes the exponent of the *LO* to produce a fuzzy set membership value (*SV*) between 1 and 0:

$$SV = \frac{\exp LO}{1 + \exp LO} \quad (8.3)$$

Note that because of its logarithmic nature, the direct method of calibration actually produces set membership values between 0.95 and 0.05. This is inconsequential for the calculation and interpretation of fuzzy set relationships.

Table 8.3 compares the set membership values obtained with the direct[3] and indirect methods of calibration and those obtained with manual calibration into categories. The difference between the direct and indirect methods is relatively small. These calibrations say substantively the same thing. Manual calibration also produces very similar results. It is perfectly acceptable to use different methods of calibration for different sets in the same QCA study. Researchers can choose a method of calibration depending on the nature of their data. Nor must one use the direct method of calibration on ratio-scaled data. The direct and indirect methods of calibration still produce logical rather than empirical values, as all set membership values are logical statements. However, the number of logical categories that the direct and indirect methods of calibration produce is so fine-grained (continuous even, for the direct method) that it is no longer practical or possible to verbalize them. The English language (or any other language) does not have that many linguistic hedges. It suggests that, performing the (in)direct method of calibration, set membership values actually do have meaning. Again, that can only be true for calibrations performed on continuous raw data. For any other kind of (nominal, ordinal, interval) data, defining a meaningful number of categories (linguistic hedges) is a perfectly good option (Ragin, 2000, p. 167; Smithson, 1987, p. 27).

Converting ordinal or interval data into ratio-scaled fuzzy sets requires strong assumptions and the use of scaling techniques (Smithson and Verkuilen, 2006, p. 29). Simply performing the direct method of calibration on ordinal or interval data really makes little sense. Nor does it make sense to report set membership values with more than two digits. The direct method of

Table 8.3   *Fuzzy set membership values for different calibration methods*

Household Income in £	Indirect Method of Calibration	Direct Method of Calibration	Manual Calibration	Logical Categories
600	1	0.95	1	Fully low income
700	0.95	0.94	0.85	Mostly low income
800	0.90	0.92		
900	0.85	0.89		
1000	0.80	0.86	0.70	Largely low income
1100	0.75	0.82		
1200	0.70	0.77		
1300	0.65	0.71		
1400	0.60	0.65	0.55	Predominantly low income
1500	0.55	0.57		
1600	0.50	0.50		
1700	0.45	0.43	0.45	Moderately low income
1800	0.40	0.35		
1900	0.35	0.29		
2000	0.30	0.23	0.30	Somewhat low income
2100	0.25	0.18		
2200	0.20	0.14		
2300	0.15	0.11		
2400	0.10	0.08	0.15	Marginally low income
2500	0.05	0.06		
2600	0	0.05	0	Not-low income

calibration produces different set membership values for a household income of £1675 (0.443986) and £1676 (0.443246), but that is not a meaningful difference – both households live the same moderately low-income lifestyle. Set membership values are logical statements not empirical ones. Their accuracy is semantical rather than empirical. The fine-grainedness of a fuzzy set membership scale is a function of the fine-grainedness of the definition of the set, not of the fine-grainedness of the raw data (Goertz, 2020, p. 142). For some sets, like household income, a good degree of fine-grainedness is meaningful. For other sets – for example, democracy – a coarse scale is much better.

Researchers need to focus on their definitions, not, in the first place, on their data. In particular, the direct method of calibration risks focusing on the data and to suggest calibration as merely data conversion (Smithson and Verkuilen, 2006, p. 44).

Thinking of calibration merely as a data conversion technique, and using the direct method of calibration, has given rise to the particularly bad practice of using population distributions to set the qualitative anchors. Particularly in (very) large-N studies, where researchers have little or no recourse to cases, QCA researchers increasingly use distribution measures such as means, averages and percentiles for the qualitative anchors. The 90th percentile is used as threshold for full membership, the 50th for the crossover point, and the 10th for the threshold of full non-membership (e.g., Pappas and Woodside, 2021). Except for situations where percentages have a substantive meaning, this is a nonsensical approach to calibration for two reasons. First, calibration is about identifying semantical thresholds to distinguish between qualitatively different cases. Percentiles, means and averages are not about that. Cases on either side of a percentile, mean or average are often highly similar, which makes these metrics arbitrary criteria to distinguish between cases. Cases just above and below the average are all typical examples of average cases. Consequently, QCA studies based on distribution metrics, by definition, produce spurious results. QCA cannot be the method that uniquely accepts spurious results as genuine research findings. Second, suppose a household cannot make ends meet and it is also in the 51st percentile of low-income households. Setting the crossover point at the 50th percentile correctly calibrates this household as a low-income household, but now an economic recession hits the country, many people lose their job, and see their income reduced. The income of our household does not change but, because of the recession, most households now have a lower income than our household, which, accordingly, is now in the 49th percentile of household incomes. Setting the crossover point at the 50th percentile no longer recognizes our household as a low-income household but it still cannot make ends meet. A case is not a member of a set because it is in the 50th percentile, or sits above the average or the mean. It is a member of a set because it has certain characteristics (Ragin, 2023, p. 28).

Researchers using distribution metrics for calibration often argue that it does not matter much for the solution whether one uses the 50th percentile, the average or a substantive criterion to set the crossover point. This is often true. However, it underlines how thin the line is between genuine and spurious findings. This is because QCA is designed to be case sensitive. Calibrating a few or even one case on the other side of the crossover point can already lead to a different solution (Skaaning, 2011). As QCA is a case-based method, this sensitivity is a strength rather than a weakness (Rutten, 2023). However, it means that researchers must have very good arguments to calibrate cases on one side of the crossover point or the other. Particularly for large-N studies with little recourse to cases, researchers must make an effort to develop substantive or external criteria for their qualitative anchors. Being unable to do so, because one is primarily interested in data rather than meaning, questions the validity of using QCA.

THE CROSSOVER POINT, OR THE MEANING OF 0.5

As argued, the crossover point is QCA's most important semantical threshold. It distinguishes between cases that are more members than not-members of the set, and cases that are more not-members than members of the set. Ragin, therefore, suggests the crossover point as the point of maximum ambiguity (Ragin, 2000, p. 158). At this exact point, it is unclear whether a case is X or $\sim X$. The further a case is removed from the crossover point, the more obvious it is identified as a logical 1 (X) or a logical 0 ($\sim X$). However, closer to the crossover point, the matter becomes more ambiguous. It is pretty obvious that the UK has a free press and that North Korea does not. We may debate how free the UK press is, but there is no question on which side of the crossover point it is. But, writing in 2024, how about Turkey? *De jure*, Turkey has a free press. The country has no laws that explicitly curb the extent to which journalists are free to report what they want. However, journalists who report unfavourably about the government are regularly prosecuted on the charge of spreading false information. This obviously has an adverse effect on Turkey's membership in the set of free-press countries. But is this prosecution systematic enough to calibrate it below the crossover point? This is a judgement on the part of the researcher. And that is where the argument for the crossover point as the point of maximum ambiguity starts to unravel. If our definition of what it means to be a free-press country cannot conclusively calibrate Turkey on one side of the crossover point or the other, our definition is not precise enough (Goertz and Mahoney, 2012b).

Precise definitions do not mean objectively accurate definitions; they are idealized cognitive models (Lakoff, 1987, p. 68). Precise means plausible in the light of knowledge of cases, context and concepts, not an undisputed empirical value (see the notion of ontological uncertainty in Chapter 1). In fact, there really is no such thing as objective knowledge in the social sciences. Social scientists can only look at social reality through the lens of their concepts and theories (epistemic relativism) (Bhaskar, 1986, p. 24). Consequently, all measurement is theory and value laden and so is the definition of the crossover point (Rutten, 2023). This is certainly not a lapse into relativism; our knowledge of thresholds may be socially constructed but it captures real characteristics of real cases (Lakoff, 1987, pp. 260–61). QCA researchers must develop a plausible definition of the crossover point that allows them to conclusively calibrate all their cases. Developing such a definition is an iterative process wherein one learns from cases (judgemental rationality). The more one learns from one's cases, the clearer it becomes where the crossover point should be. Setting the crossover point is not about picking a raw data value that is 0.5; instead, it is about developing a plausible definition. And if all this still does not allow conclusively calibrating a case above or below the crossover point, then perhaps this is not a good case and it should be eliminated from the case population, because, apparently, one cannot learn enough from this case. Let's approach the meaning of the crossover point from a different angle. Being fully a case of X means that a case has all the characteristics that define X. Being not-a-case of X means that the case has none of the characteristics of X. Extending this argument, the crossover point is the point where a case has too few of the characteristics of X to qualify as a case of X but too many to qualify as not-a-case of X. But is that logically possible? Can one have too high an income to be a low-income household but have too low an income to be a not-low-income household? I think not. My view is not part of mainstream QCA, but I believe it logically impossible for a case to be at the crossover point, to be a 0.5 case. I think of 0.5 as a logical category that cannot contain any cases.

Nor does it make analytical sense to calibrate 0.5 cases. Suppose one has three explanatory conditions: A, B and C. This produces a truth table of $2^3 = 8$ rows. A case's membership in a configuration is determined by the minimum membership in the component conditions (see Chapter 5). Suppose a case has the following set memberships: $A = 0.8$, $B = 0.6$ and $C = 0.3$. Its membership in ABC then is 0.3, and its membership in $AB{\sim}C$ is 0.7 (as ${\sim}C = 1 - C$). It is easy enough to work out that $AB{\sim}C$ is the only row in which this case has > 0.5 membership (Ragin, 2008, pp. 128–31). Cases have > 0.5 membership in one truth table row only and this allows QCA researchers to investigate whether the presence or absence of (in this example) C makes a difference for the presence or absence of Y. However, if this case had 0.5 membership in C, it would also have 0.5 membership in ${\sim}C$ and thus be in both rows ABC and $AB{\sim}C$. It can now no longer be used for a difference-making analysis on C. For this reason, the truth table minimization ignores all 0.50 cases. Therefore, do not calibrate 0.5 cases. They are logically impossible and empirically irrelevant. To calibrate 0.5 cases effectively is to throw away data – because 0.5 cases are ignored in the truth table minimization.

But wait a minute. What if the crossover point is the minimum wage of £1600? A household that has a monthly income of £1600 surely 'sits' at the crossover point and must be a 0.5 case. No, it must not. The crossover point is not an empirical value but a definition. In this example, it means that a household cannot make ends meet. It may almost make ends meet and be £1 or even 1 penny short, which still means it cannot make ends meet and it is a low-income household. The problem with choosing the minimum wage as the crossover point is that we do not know whether a household that has an income of £1600 can or cannot make ends meet. It is a plausible threshold to distinguish between low-income and not-low-income households; however, some £1600-income households will make ends meet and some will not. £1600 is not the crossover point; it is a critical value, a plausible empirical value that is attached to the definition of the crossover point for a low-income household. Put differently, setting the crossover point at £1600 answers the question, how do we know a low-income household when we see one? It does not answer the question, what is a low-income household? Ontological statements ('The household cannot make ends meet') must not be collapsed into epistemological statements ('The household has an income of £1600'). The fact that some £1600-income households do make ends meet underlines epistemic relativism – that is, the limitations of our empirical knowledge. When using blanket values, such as the minimum wage, researchers must set an empirical value for the crossover point that does not exist in the data. This avoids calibrating 0.5 cases and throwing away data. For example, the database of household income is in pounds but not pennies. The crossover point may then be set at £1600.50. A £1600-income household is now calibrated as a low-income household, while a £1601-income household becomes a not-low-income household. We still do not know whether all £1600.50-income households cannot make ends meet; however, we have reason to believe that this is a plausible threshold and we do not have 0.5 cases.

Finally, note that because of the asymmetry of sets (see Chapter 6), changing the crossover point may calibrate different sets. Setting a higher crossover point may calibrate the set of high-income households. Most households will be not-low-income households but also not-high-income households. Their income is above the crossover point for low-income households (i.e., their income is too high) but below the crossover point for high-income households. QCA researchers may calibrate both sets. This allows them to investigate whether the absence of low income or the presence of high income explains, for example, being a happy household. This kind of dual calibration (calibrating two sets from the same data) may give a more refined understanding of the causal relationship between, in this example, income and happiness.

CRISP, MULTILEVEL AND CONTINUOUS (FUZZY) SETS

QCA distinguishes between crisp and fuzzy sets, and it further distinguishes between multilevel fuzzy sets and continuous fuzzy sets. Ragin advocates fuzzy sets and argues that crisp sets should only be used for categorical (i.e., two-value) concepts, because crisp sets do not capture the colourfulness of social reality (Ragin, 2008, p. 141). QCA researchers overwhelmingly follow

Ragin's advice, and fuzzy sets are by now the default in QCA. The problem with this approach is that it lumps together multilevel and continuous sets. However, crisp sets and multilevel sets have far more in common than multilevel and continuous sets. In fact, crisp sets are multilevel sets with just two categories. Contrary to continuous sets, multilevel sets are ordinal (or interval) scales, while continuous sets are ratio scales (Goertz, 2020, pp. 147–9; Smithson, 1987, p. 88). The problem of conflating multilevel and continuous sets into fuzzy sets is that it threatens to suggest all fuzzy sets as ratio scales. Yet, it is only meaningful to calibrate ratio-scaled sets from raw data that is ratio scaled (Smithson and Verkuilen, 2006). Ragin correctly argues that all fuzzy sets *behave* as ratio scales; however, that does not mean they *are* ratio scales. As argued, the difference between marginally (0.15) and somewhat (0.30) a low-income household is not the same as the difference between largely (0.70) and mostly (0.85) a low-income household – even though they are separated by the same 0.15 difference. Table 8.4 shows some examples of multilevel and continuous sets.

There is nothing wrong with the labels crisp and fuzzy sets, because they are accurate. However, it is important to realize that, methodologically, the real difference is between multilevel and continuous sets. This is because the nature of one's raw data determines whether it is meaningful to calibrate a continuous (fuzzy) set (Smithson and Verkuilen, 2006, p. 29).

Table 8.4   Multilevel and continuous sets

Two-value Set	Three-value Set	Six-value Set	Continuous Set
1 a case of X	1 fully a case of X	1 fully a case of X	1 fully a case of X
0 not-a-case of X	0.67 partially a case of X	0.8 mostly a case of X	$X > 0.5 - < 1$ more a case of X than not-a-case of X
	0 not-a-case of X	0.6 largely a case of X	$> 0 - < 0.5$ more not-a-case of X than a case of X
		0.4 somewhat a case of X	0 not-a-case of X
		0.2 marginally a case of X	
		0 not-a-case of X	
Crisp sets	Fuzzy sets		
Multilevel sets (ordinal scales or interval scales)	Continuous sets (ratio scales)		

At this point, it is worth mentioning that 'being a case of X' (being an instance of X) and 'being a member of the set of X' are not necessarily the same thing.

Cases above the crossover point are cases (instances) of X; they have enough of the characteristics of X to be recognized as a case (an instance) of X. Cases below the crossover point are not-cases (not-instances) of X, because they do not have enough of the characteristics of X to be recognized as a case (an instance) of X. This goes back to the above second question: how do we know a case of X when we see one? Well, we know it is a case of X if it 'sits' above the crossover point for X. However, all cases that have a membership > 0 in a set are members of that set, and also when their membership is < 0.5. This means that cases with a set membership in $X > 0$ but < 0.5 are members of the fuzzy set of X but not cases (instances) of X.

CALIBRATING FROM DIFFERENT KINDS OF DATA

QCA is pretty much agnostic about the data one calibrates from or how these data are collected. The only criterion is that data must be rich enough to be interpreted. And even then there is some leeway. Obviously, a database with the monthly income of all approximately 28.2 million UK households is not rich enough to be interpreted. It gives a single value only for each case and one cannot possibly go back to the cases. However, to calibrate from these data, a researcher can turn to earlier research and to policy documents on poverty, quality of life and so forth to interpret (i.e., calibrate) the data. Again, the point is that calibration cannot be reduced to a mechanical conversion of data. There must be some context to draw from. Absent that, researchers should not use QCA. Having said that, the kind of data one has matters for how one calibrates (Thomann and Maggetti, 2020). Let's look at three kinds of data in more detail.

Calibrating from Qualitative Data

Qualitative data may be obtained from interviews and ethnographic data, but also from written sources, such as policy documents, minutes of meetings, self-reporting from organizations and so forth. Calibrating from qualitative data requires researchers to develop very clear definitions of their concepts and then judge for each case whether the evidence (the data) suggests it is a member or not-a-member of the set, or the degree to which it is a member of the set. This is often a time-consuming process. Researchers may frequently revise or update their calibrations when dialoguing between knowledge of cases, context and concepts, or even go back to their respondents to collect more data. It is also the most rewarding, most satisfying and most valid way of calibrating. Calibrating from qualitative data is always manual. Of course, one can decide to quantify qualitative data. However, this inevitably comes at the expense of data richness, and data richness is the key to good and valid calibration. Quantifying qualitative data for the sole purpose of simplifying calibration is a very bad strategy. Grillitsch et al.'s (2023) paper is an excellent example of calibrating from qualitative data.

Calibrating from Likert Scales

Likert scale data are a good source from which to calibrate because Likert scales already have meaning (Ragin, 2000, p. 169). Likert scale categories mean something – for example, that the respondent fully agrees, mostly agrees, agrees nor disagrees, mostly disagrees or fully disagrees with a statement. That is, answering Likert scale questions, respondents declare themselves to have a specific degree of membership in a set. However, three things must be firmly kept in mind when calibrating from Likert scale data.

First, never use the neutral category for the crossover point. This merely creates lots of 0.5 cases, which will be ignored in the truth table minimization. Researchers must ask whether the neutral category means that the respondent is in or out of the set. Suppose we present respondents with the following statement on a five-point Likert scale: 'My household can make ends meet at the end of the month'. The neutral category – neither agree nor disagree – suggests that this household is able to make ends meet in some months but not in others. This means the household actually qualifies as a low-income household, one that is unable to always make ends meet. Therefore, the crossover point is not 3 on the Likert scale (agree nor disagree) but in between 3 and 2 (mostly disagree) – that is, the crossover point is 2.5. Since 2.5 is not a Likert scale category, thus setting the crossover point avoids calibrating 0.5 cases. If QCA researchers design their own Likert scale questions, they may consider using a four-value or a six-value Likert scale to avoid the neutral category altogether. Arguably, this defeats the original purpose of a Likert scale, but then QCA is a threshold method, not a correlational method.

Second, Likert scales are categorical (ordinal) scales rather than ratio scales. The distance between 1 (fully disagree) and 2 (mostly disagree) does not mean the same as the distance between 3 (neither agree nor disagree) and 4 (mostly disagree). Consequently, performing the direct method of calibration is not a good strategy for Likert scale data (Goertz, 2020, pp. 30–32).

Third, to aggregate answers from different Likert scale questions, averaging is not a very good strategy either. To answer 3 (neither agree nor disagree) on the statement, 'My household can make ends meet', and 3 on the statement 'My household can afford a holiday', gives an average of 3. Answering 5 (fully agree) and 1 (fully disagree), respectively, also gives an average of 3, but, arguably, these are two very different households. They should not have the same (degree of) membership in the set of low-income households. It is much better to use logical ANDs and logical ORs to aggregate answers from Likert scale questions, whereby it does not matter whether one aggregates first and then calibrates, or calibrates first and then aggregates. Also see the section on aggregation below.

Calibrating from Quantitative Data

Quantitative data are any kind of numerical data that are at least of ordinal scale. Calibrating such data, researchers again begin by clearly defining their sets and the three qualitative anchors (the thresholds of full [non-]member-ship and the crossover point). One approach is to calibrate multilevel sets. Researchers then define a number of meaningful categories and assess which raw data values are covered by each category. One can define the category of largely low-income households and – dialoguing knowledge of cases, context and concepts – deduce that a household income > £1000, < £1300 is in this category. In this example, substantive knowledge suggests that households with an income in this range have qualitatively similar lifestyles – a largely low-income lifestyle. If one has recourse to cases, one may find that the Ochmonek family has a monthly income of £1125, which puts it in the cate-gory of largely low-income households. However, they are helping the neigh-bours pay for a new washing machine because theirs broke down. This means the Ochmoneks must economize even more on the cost of living and this plausibly calibrates them into the category of mostly low-income households, even though their income is 'too high'. Similarly, the Collins family may have a monthly income of £1175 and also be in the category of largely low-income families. However, a brother may take them on summer holiday every year and invite them for Christmas dinner. This effectively makes the Collins a predom-inantly low-income household, even though their income is 'too low' for that category. In sum, it is the cases, not the raw data values as such, that decide the validity of calibration. If a researcher has ratio-scaled raw data, the direct method of calibration may be applied (see above).

The disadvantage of quantitative data is that they invite researchers to reduce calibration to a mechanical exercise in data conversion. However, calibration is always about interpretation, regardless of the nature of one's raw data. Particularly when all that researchers have are data in a database, with no recourse to cases, it is tempting to calibrate on the basis of population distributions. This is always a very bad idea (see above). Instead, researchers must search the (academic and professional) literature for plausible anchors, or talk to experts in the field. One may also look for gaps and breaks in the raw data; they may suggest boundaries between qualitatively different kinds of cases – that is, between categories. Preferably, one combines looking for gaps and breaks with talking to experts and searching the literature. The case for interpreting gaps and breaks in the data as category boundaries becomes that much stronger if one's case population coincides with an actual population

– for example, the population of countries in South America or regions of the European Union – because gaps in the data are not a function of missing cases (see Chapter 11).

AGGREGATION

Aggregating measurements into concepts is a topic worthy of a book of its own. Gary Goertz (2020) has written that book (*Social Science Concepts and Measurements*) and I recommend every social scientist take good notice of it. However, it is important to say a number of things on aggregation here, because aggregation is closely related to calibration. Informed by correlational thinking and thinking of concepts as latent variables, the default approach to aggregation in the social sciences is to average or index measurements. If measurements are indicators of the same underlying latent variable, they all mean the same thing. Consequently, they are interchangeable and can be averaged (Goertz and Mahoney, 2012b). The important thing is that different measurements of the same latent variable are correlated, to empirically 'evidence' they are merely different empirical apparitions of the same latent concept. However, this indicator (or latent variable) approach is deeply problematic for a set-analytical method like QCA. QCA works with conditions, not variables. Conditions are first about meaning (What does it mean to be a case of X?) and only second about measurement (How do we know an X when we see one?). Instead, variables are about the distribution of a characteristic in a population, and correlations between variables are meaningful as such (Goertz, 2020, pp. 111–14). That is, variables are much more about measurement.

The European Social Progress Index (EU-SPI) is a case in point of how indicator aggregation and set-analytical aggregation conflict. The EU-SPI is a composite of three indicators (sub-concepts): basic human needs, foundations of wellbeing, and opportunity (Annoni and Dijkstra, 2017). These three sub-concepts are each composed of a number of measurements. As the I in SPI suggests, all aggregation of measurements and sub-concepts is based on indices and averages of indices. This means that a low index score on basic human needs can be 'compensated' by a high score on, for example, opportunity, and still result in a good overall EU-SPI score for a region. Instead, a set-theoretical approach starts by asking: what does it mean to be a socially progressed region? Is it necessary to have satisfied [basic human needs AND foundations of wellbeing AND opportunity]? Or is it sufficient to have satisfied just two out of three of them? And, if so, does it matter which two? These are semantical questions that cannot be answered by looking at the data. They require a definition of what is a socially progressed region. To define the concept of a socially progressed region from its three sub-concepts, one has the following possibilities:

- [basic human needs AND foundations of wellbeing AND opportunity];
- [basic human needs AND (foundations of wellbeing OR opportunity)];
- [opportunity AND (basic human needs OR foundations of wellbeing)];
- [foundations of wellbeing AND (basic human needs OR opportunity)]; and
- [basic human needs OR foundations of wellbeing OR opportunity].

The EU uses the SPI to assess regions' strong and weak points. It does so by scoring all regions between 0 and 100, where 0 and 100 are the worst and best possible performance by an EU region. This sets the thresholds for full (non-) membership but fails to specify a crossover point, which means the raw SPI data can only establish relative differences between regions, despite the EU claiming otherwise (ibid.). Furthermore, the EU defines social progress as the capacity of a society to meet basic needs, provide the foundations for wellbeing and opportunities for citizens to reach their full potential. This suggests aggregating the three sub-concepts with logical ANDs; instead, they are indexed. From a QCA perspective, to define the concept of a socially progressed region in terms of its sub-concepts, a researcher must determine (define, conceptualize) whether the sub-concepts are INUS or SUIN conditions for the concept of socially progressed (Goertz, 2020, p. 28). Put differently, set-theoretical aggregation is semantical not empirical, and semantic calibration is causal. Using logical ANDs and ORs for aggregation is to use a causal language for aggregation. That is, semantical aggregation worries about the causal relations between sub-concepts and the meta-concept.

The latent variable approach is empirical; it does not worry about meaning so much. The more and more strongly plausible indicators correlate, the better they are considered a measurement of the latent variable. Instead, conditions are semantical; they are primarily about meaning. There is nothing wrong with using a single measurement for a condition because it ensures that meaning and measurement overlap. The label (meaning) of a condition must always closely follow the label of the measurement. Using logical ANDs and ORs is a perfectly good set-theoretical approach to aggregation. However, it challenges researchers to think very carefully about what the meta-concept means and how to label it.

CALIBRATION GOOD PRACTICE

To guide researchers through their calibration, Figure 8.1 offers a calibration good practice flow chart. The key to good calibration is transparency. Calibration is about making choices. These choices must be profoundly guided by knowledge of cases, context and concepts. They must be plausible in the light of this knowledge. Researchers must explain their key calibration choices on the pages of their papers. Ideally, a QCA paper contains a calibration table (see Table 8.5) or otherwise makes this information available in the paper. A more detailed explanation of how sets were defined and how cases were calibrated into sets can be presented in an (online) annex. Calibration starts with the definition of the set and then proceeds slightly differently for each of the three methods of calibration (manual, direct, indirect). But in all cases, calibration is about connecting meaning to raw (qualitative or quantitative) data and assigning set membership values to meaning. Figure 8.1 features dotted feedback lines to visualize that calibration is an iterative process, a dialogue wherein one learns from cases. A particular case may not fit a category and this may lead researchers to re-evaluate their calibrations, or the definition of their case population.

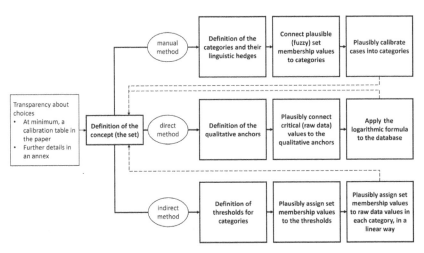

Figure 8.1   Calibration good practice flow chart

The calibration table (Table 8.5) specifies the minimal information that researchers must provide on their calibrations. The first three rows are templates for the three different methods of calibration. The bottom row is an example for the condition low-income household. Performing manual calibration on qualitative data, it may be challenging to fill out the cell 'Raw data value' in the first row. Instead, researchers can briefly characterize a typical case in each category. If one chooses not to assign fuzzy set membership values to categories, one numerates the categories 1 and 0 according to where one sets the crossover point.

Table 8.5　　Calibration table

Condition (Set)	Definition	Definition of Categories, Qualitative Anchors	Raw Data Value	Set Membership Value
Adjective CASE: • Explanatory condition • Manual calibration	What does it mean to be an *adjective* NAME?	A fully *adjective* NAME has characteristics *A* AND *B* AND *C*	Qualitative description or quantitative data value	1
		A mostly *adjective* NAME has characteristics A AND (*B* OR *C*)		0.67
		A somewhat *adjective* NAME has characteristics A OR *B* OR *C*		0.33
		A not-*adjective* NAME has none of the characteristics *A*, *B* and *C*		0
Adjective CASE: • Explanatory condition • Direct method	What does it mean to be an *adjective* NAME?	Full membership means that a case is [qualification]	80	1
		The crossover point means that a case is [qualification]	45	0.5
		Full non-membership means that a case is [qualification]	10	0

Condition (Set)	Definition	Definition of Categories, Qualitative Anchors	Raw Data Value	Set Membership Value
Adjective CASE: • Outcome condition • Indirect method	What does it mean to be an *adjective* NAME?	Fully *adjective* NAME means [qualification]	Likert 5	1
		Mostly *adjective* NAME means [qualification]	Likert 3, 4	0.67
		Somewhat *adjective* NAME means [qualification]	Likert 2	0.33
		Not-*adjective* NAME means [qualification]	Likert 1	0
Low-income HOUSEHOLD: • Explanatory condition • Manual calibration	The household cannot make ends meet	Fully *low-income* HOUSEHOLD must choose between housing, food, clothing	≤ £600	1
		Mostly *low-income* HOUSEHOLD relies on help for food and clothing	£601–1600	0.67
		Somewhat *low-income* HOUSEHOLD can afford necessities other than housing, food, clothing	£1601–2599	0.33
		Not-*low-income* HOUSEHOLD can afford leisure and luxury in addition to all basic necessities	≤ £2600	0

CONCEPTS, CONDITIONS AND SETS

At the end of this chapter, here are a few words on terminology. Throughout this chapter, I have used the terms concept, condition and set pretty much interchangeably because they are pretty much interchangeable. As social scientists, we define concepts to describe social reality. For example, the concept of low-income describes households unable to make ends meet. Concepts become (explanatory and outcome) conditions in a QCA study. The explanatory condition 'low-income household' may be one of several in a truth table explaining being a 'happy household'. All households (i.e., cases) that qualify as low-income households together form the set of low-income households. When we calibrate, we assess whether it is accurate to describe a household as 'low income' and assign it (a degree of) membership in the set of low-income households. Concept, condition and set thus almost say the same thing, *almost* because, although they mean the same thing (they have the same definition), we calibrate cases into the set of low-income households, not into the concept or the condition of low-income households.

GLOSSARY OF KEY CONCEPTS

0.5 cases	Should never be calibrated because 0.5 cases are ignored in the truth table minimization. Moreover, it is logically impossible for a case to be a 0.5 case. It is impossible for a case to have too few characteristics of X to qualify as a case of X and yet too many of the characteristics of X to qualify as not-a-case of X
Calibration	Interprets whether the statement, 'This is a case of X', is true or false, or the degree to which the statement is true
Continuous sets	Sets that are calibrated from continuous raw data. Continuous sets are always fuzzy sets
Critical values	The empirical values assigned to the qualitative anchors
Crossover point	The principal semantic threshold. It distinguishes between cases that qualify as instances of the set and cases that do not qualify as instances of the set
Direct method of calibration	A logarithmic conversion of raw data into set membership values based on the three critical values. The direct method of calibration is only meaningful when performed on ratio-scaled raw data
Dual calibration	Calibrating multiple sets from the same raw data, capitalizing on the asymmetry of sets. For example, calibrating the set of high-income households and the set of low-income households from the same income data

External criterion	A criterion or argument used for calibration that is external to the case population – that is, not based on distribution metrics such as means, averages and percentiles
Indicator aggregation	Aggregates measurements into concepts on the assumption that all measurements are indicators of the same underlying latent variable. It requires indicators to be strongly correlated. Indicator aggregation is problematic for qualitative methods such as QCA
Indirect method of calibration	Identifying semantical thresholds (based on gaps and breaks in the raw data and on substantive criteria). Assigning set membership values to these semantical thresholds. Assigning set membership values to all raw data values between the semantical thresholds in a linear way
Linguistic hedges (semantic modifiers)	Identify the different categories or levels of a set. Linguistic hedges modify the degree to which a case is a member of a set – for example, a largely low-income household and a moderately low-income household
Manual calibration	Assigning (a degree of) set membership to a case based on dialoguing knowledge of cases, context and concepts
Multilevel sets	Sets that consist of a number of ordinal (or interval) categories or levels. The number of categories or levels is a function of the definition (meaning) of the concept, not of the fine-grainedness of the underlying raw data. Crisp sets are multilevel sets with two categories. Multilevel sets with more than two categories are fuzzy sets
Qualitative anchors	The definitions of the threshold of full membership, the crossover point and the threshold of full non-membership
Semantical calibration	Aggregates sub-concepts into concepts with logical ANDs and logical ORs, based on the definition of the concept. Semantical aggregation follows the same set-theoretical logic as does QCA
Semantical threshold	Distinguishes between two categories or levels of cases. Cases in different categories (levels) are qualitatively different in terms of the degree in which they have the characteristics that define a set
Set membership	A logical statement, not an empirical value. It qualifies a case as a member of a set, or the degree in which a case is a member of a set
Substantive criterion	A criterion or argument used for calibration that is based on dialoguing between knowledge of cases, context and concepts
Threshold of full membership	Cases that have all the characteristics that define a set 'sit' above the threshold of full membership
Threshold of full non-membership	Cases that have none of the characteristics that define a set 'sit' below the threshold of full non-membership

NOTES

1. This chapter is partially based on valuable inputs from Claude Rubinson, with whom I discussed calibration and aggregation over many hours.
2. Note that a case can have a degree of membership in multiple categories. The statement, 'This is a mostly low-income household', may be largely true and marginally false. Consequently, for the same case, the statement, 'This is a mainly low-income household', may be somewhat true and mostly false. This is sometimes referred to as a second-order uncertainty, or second-order fuzziness (Smithson, 1987, p. 17). It also hugely complicates QCA in general and calibration in particular, without any obvious analytical benefits. Consequently, it is perfectly acceptable to just stick with the first-order categories of Table 8.1.
3. A low income should give households a high membership in the set of low-income households. However, applying the direct method of calibration on the income data in the first column of Table 8.3 actually does the reverse. It calibrates the set of not-low-income families. Set membership values for low income are calculated as: 1 – [not low income].

9. Reservations against fuzzy sets in QCA

Developed as a crisp method, fuzzy sets quickly became the default in QCA after Ragin made a strong case for fuzzy set social science (Ragin, 2000, 2008), the principal argument being that crisp sets crudely dichotomize social reality. Fuzzy sets are also argued to be more accurate, because fuzzy subsets and supersets are calculated over all cases in the case population, not just those in the relevant cells. Mostly, however, I believe, fuzzy sets became popular because they appeal to the variable-based 'instincts' of the vast majority of social scientists (see Lucas and Szatrowski, 2014, for a completely mistaken critique of QCA and Ragin, 2014, for his response). It is overstating it to say that fuzzy sets introduced variable-based thinking in QCA, although they go some way in that direction (Ragin, 2000, pp. 161–2). However, fuzzy sets necessarily come with more elaborate parameters and, consequently, contributed to the metrification and quantification of QCA. Apart from weakening some of QCA's qualitative logic, I see a number of problems with fuzzy sets in QCA.

Principally, fuzzy set relationships abstract from cases and instead consider the average distance to the $X = Y$ diagonal of all cases in the case population. However, singular causal evidence and the truth table minimization follows a threshold (i.e., crisp) logic, also in fuzzy set QCA. Consequently, singular and general causal evidence are not really compatible in fuzzy set QCA, which complicates learning from cases. Second, I dispute that fuzzy sets are more accurate on both ontological and epistemological grounds. Fuzzy sets assume that all concepts are scalable on a linear, ratio scale, and that numerical equidistance on that scale equals semantical equidistance. This effectively commits fuzzy sets in QCA to the general linear reality (Abbott, 1988, 1998) of variable-based methods. Ontologically, many concepts are not linear but instead have a radial, chain or metonymic structure (Lakoff, 1987, pp. 91–6), which means that degrees of membership do not accumulate linearly. Epistemologically, unless calibrated from ratio-scaled raw data, fuzzy set membership values are examples of spurious specificity (Smithson and Verkuilen, 2006, p. 44). I will elaborate these points throughout this chapter.

I am not convinced that the marriage between fuzzy sets and the threshold logic of the truth table is a fortunate one. Nor do I believe that fuzzy sets dichotomize social reality. As I have argued earlier in this book, 1s and 0s are logical statements (true and false), not empirical values. When a household cannot make ends meet, the statement, 'This is a low-income household' is true (1). And this truth makes an important difference for how the members of the household live their lives. Social reality is not dichotomous; however, it is characterized by thresholds (thresholds as in having enough of the characteristics of X to qualify as a case of X). Either a household can make ends meet, or it cannot. Either a student passes their exam, or they do not. Either a country has a democratic government or it does not. Being above or below the threshold for democracy makes a world of difference for, among others, journalists working in that country. It is relevant to investigate whether being above or below the threshold on the explanatory condition makes a difference for being above or below the threshold on the outcome. This is what QCA does – in both its crisp and fuzzy guises. The truth table minimization condenses all fuzzy set values to 1s and 0s, to true or false, because it is a logical exercise (Ragin [1987] 2014, pp. 105–11). The 1s and 0s in the truth table take nothing away from the colourfulness of social reality; they merely identify analytically relevant thresholds, thresholds that make a difference for human agents being (un) able to exercise causal powers in their pursuit of desirable outcomes. Almost passing an exam does not get a student a diploma. Almost being a democracy spells certain trouble for journalists. Fussing about crisp sets dichotomizing social reality fails to appreciate QCA's threshold logic. And even though fuzzy sets behave as ratio scales, they are not (Smithson, 1987, pp. 87–8) – except when calibrated from ratio-scaled data. This makes the accuracy of fuzzy sets largely spurious.

If, after reading this chapter, one accepts my reservations, then do not use fuzzy sets in QCA. I have suggested, and reiterate at the end of the chapter, that calibrating categories or multilevel sets (using linguistic hedges) acknowledges the colourfulness of social reality without the need to use fuzzy set metrics.

FUZZINESS AND FUZZY SET METRICS

Lotfi Zadeh (1965) introduced fuzzy sets to capture the vagueness of real-world statements. To say that today is a warm day makes a vague statement because 'warm' does not specify a particular temperature. In England, any day between 20°C and 30°C counts as a warm day. Below 20°C it would be a mild (but not a cold) day and above 30°C is would be a hot (but not a sweltering) day. However, 20°C is not particularly warm, while 30°C is very warm. So a temperature in the mid-20°Cs most plausibly connects to the statement, 'This is a warm day'. Consequently, days with a temperature of 24–26°C have a membership of 1 in the fuzzy set of warm days. Set membership drops to 0.5 when moving towards 20°C or 30°C, and below 0.5 for days that are cooler or warmer. Nobody (in England) would say, this is a warm day, when the temperature is 15°C or 35°C, so these days (and all cooler or warmer days) have 0 membership in the fuzzy set of warm days. It also means that a day of 22°C has a degree of membership in the fuzzy set of mild days as well as in the fuzzy set of hot days. However, these fuzzy set memberships will be lower than the membership of this day in the fuzzy set of warm days. In other words, fuzzy sets capture a kind of uncertainty that is not probabilistic but possibilistic (Smithson, 1987, pp. 43–5). Fuzzy set memberships of the Zadeh kind specify the possibility of, in this example, a day being recognized as a warm day. And this is because the concept of a 'warm day' is fuzzy, or vague. It is not clearly defined what it means to be a warm day and has no clear upper and lower temperature boundary; it is fuzzy. Lakoff (1973) augmented Zadeh's fuzzy sets with linguistic hedges (semantical modifiers) (see also Zadeh, 1972). For example, a very warm day pertains to a day that is warmer than 26°C but not as warm as 30°C. In sum, fuzzy sets are a means to quantify the vagueness of statements expressed in everyday language so that these statements can be used in scientific analysis (Smithson and Verkuilen, 2006, p. 1). But that is not how fuzzy sets are used in QCA.

Concepts in QCA are very clearly defined to allow calibration (Goertz, 2020, pp. 133–4). The boundaries of QCA's fuzzy sets are not fuzzy but clearly defined thresholds of full (non-)membership. In fuzzy sets of the Zadeh kind, the crossover point really is the point of maximum ambiguity (Smithson and Verkuilen, 2006, p. 17). At 0.5 – that is, 20°C – we cannot conclusively decide whether a day is a warm day or a mild day. However, concepts in QCA are not fuzzy. Their precise definition eliminates 0.5 as an actual (precise) value. In QCA, we will precisely know whether a day is a warm day or a not-warm day because we will have precisely defined (calibrated) what it means to be a warm day and which empirical threshold connects to that definition (Ragin, 2000, pp. 161–3). Put differently, a calibrated fuzzy set is something of an oxymoron because calibration (i.e., to determine) eradicates fuzziness (vagueness). Degrees of membership in QCA's fuzzy set capture a precisely defined distance to the crossover point. There really is nothing fuzzy about QCA's fuzzy set – in the sense that Zadeh defined fuzzy sets. Sets in QCA are fundamentally crisp; however, cases can have degrees of membership in a crisp set depending on their distance to the crossover point (Ragin, 2000, pp. 154–7; 2008, pp. 30–34).

Describing (defining) reality in terms of degrees of membership in concepts is a perfectly legitimate effort (Lakoff, 1973; Zadeh, 1972). Problematically, however, fuzzy set scales behave as ratio scales (Smithson and Verkuilen, 2006, pp. 87–8). This is how fuzzy set metrics 'work': the distance between 0.2 and 0.3 means the same as the distance between 0.6 and 0.7. But this is only plausible for fuzzy sets that are calculated from ratio-scaled data. In all other sets, numerical equidistance does not mean semantical equidistance. Per the example in Chapter 8, the difference between being able and being unable to afford leisure and luxury (i.e., the difference between 0.15 and 0.30 membership in the fuzzy set of low-income families) is qualitatively different from the difference between being able and being unable to afford clothing (0.55 and 0.70 membership in the fuzzy set of low-income families).

Obviously, it makes perfect sense to calibrate degrees of membership in a set to account for the colourfulness of social reality. Different degrees of membership suggest qualitatively different states, where cases 'progress' from having no degree of membership (because they have none of the characteristics of the set) to having full membership in the set (because they have all the characteristics of the set) (Ragin, 2000, pp. 149–50). However, for two reasons, it is something else to suggest the degrees of membership as a ratio scale if the underlying data are not ratio scaled. First, the concepts used to describe cases (social reality) are often not linear but, instead, have a chain, radial or metonymic structure (Lakoff, 1987, pp. 91–6). Second, cases are holistic. While individual characteristics of cases, such as household income, may well be expressed on a continuous (ratio) fuzzy set scale, the households themselves are characterized by much more than just their income. Decomposing cases into individual characteristics brings on board some of the variable-based logic that QCA (and other case-based methods) aims to overcome (Ragin [1987] 2014). In QCA, cases rather than conditions are the principal analytically relevant entities. Since cases are holistically characterized by multiple, interconnected characteristics, it is not plausible to position cases relative to each other on a linear (ratio) scale. Doing so brings us back to the general linear reality of variable-based methods (Abbott, 1988, 1998). While possibilistic uncertainty of the Zadeh kind may well be expressed on a continuous (ratio) fuzzy set scale, this is not so for cases. The non-linear nature of the concepts used to describe cases and their holistic nature both argue against it.

THRESHOLD (CRISP SET) LOGIC VERSUS FUZZY SET METRICS

Another problem of fuzzy sets in QCA is that they allow logically contradictory results. Chapter 7 already discussed simultaneous subset relationships and trivially necessary conditions. Simultaneous subset relationships ($X \subset Y$ and $X \subset \sim Y$) are a logical contradiction, while trivially necessary conditions ($X \supset Y$) effectively say the same thing twice ($X \approx Y$) – they are tautologies. Yet, they are mathematically possible using fuzzy set metrics. The proportional reduction in inconsistency (PRI) and relevance of necessity (RoN) metrics are developed to address these issues. However, in my view, they remain epistemological patches (metrics) for ontological problems (logical contradictions). Another logical impossibility is that fuzzy sets can produce different findings than crisp sets. Calibrating crisp and fuzzy sets from the same data and using the same crossover point, it is still possible for fuzzy set QCA to produce a different result (solution) than crisp set QCA (see below). That should not happen. If it is logically true that X is sufficient for Y, it should be so irrespective of how the consistency of the subset relationship $X \subset Y$ is expressed. In QCA's threshold logic (see Chapter 10), sufficiency means that being above the threshold of X (the presence of X) makes a difference for being above the threshold of Y (the presence of Y). If these thresholds are the same in crisp and fuzzy sets, then using crisp or fuzzy set metrics should not produce different results. The statement X is sufficient for Y should be true in both approaches. However, this is not always the case because fuzzy set relationships are calculated from different (viz., all) cases than are crisp set relationships. And therein lies a key logical problem, as the fictional examples below show.

Table 9.1 shows the membership of fictional neighbourhoods in the fuzzy and crisp sets of high-income neighbourhoods (X) and neighbourhoods with expensive houses (Y). Using the formulae from Chapter 7, the fuzzy subset consistency $X \subset Y = 0.70$ but the crisp subset consistency $X \subset Y = 0.80$. This suggests that, using crisp sets, being a high-income neighbourhood is suffi-cient for being a neighbourhood with expensive houses; however, using fuzzy sets, this is not the case. What is behind this?

As Figure 9.1 clearly shows, many cases in Cell (i) (confirming cases) are contradictory in degree. They are below the $X = Y$ diagonal – that is, they reduce fuzzy set consistency. However, $Y > 0.5$ so these cases do not violate the logical statement: if X, then Y. As all cases $X < Y$ weaken fuzzy set consist-ency, the cases in Cell (i) below the diagonal push the fuzzy subset consistency of high-income neighbourhood (X) $\subset$ neighbourhood with expensive houses (Y) well below the 0.8 cut-off, even though, from a threshold perspective, all Cell (i) cases are confirming cases. They all confirm a causal relationship between being a high-income neighbourhood and being a neighbourhood with expensive houses. There may be several why the neighbourhoods in Cell (i) are below the $X = Y$ diagonal. Maybe the houses in these neighbourhoods depreci-ated in value because of developments nearby – for example, the construction of a motorway. Whatever the reason, from a threshold perspective, these neighbourhoods are unproblematic because they are still neighbourhoods with expensive houses. Neighbourhoods in Cell (ii) are contradictory cases. Maybe these are high-income neighbourhoods in remote locations, which reduces the house prices. Crisp or fuzzy, these neighbourhoods reduce the consistency of the subset relationship high-income neighbourhood $\subset$ neighbourhood with expensive houses. The neighbourhoods in Cell (iii) are equifinal cases. These are not-high-income neighbourhoods with expensive houses. Perhaps the houses appreciated in value after their not-high-income residents renovated them. The point is, from a threshold perspective, they are equifinal cases;

Table 9.1   *Fictional neighbourhoods*

	High-income Neighbourhoods (X)		Neighbourhoods with Expensive Houses (Y)		minXY	
	fs	cs	fs	cs	fs	cs
Crown Estate	0.90	1	0.80	1	0.80	1
Posh Park	0.90	1	0.70	1	0.70	1
Villa Meadows	0.90	1	0.60	1	0.60	1
Sunshine Bungalows	0.80	1	0.70	1	0.70	1
Lucky Streak Street	0.80	1	0.60	1	0.60	1
Sleepy Hallow	0.70	1	0.60	1	0.60	1
Affluent Avenue	0.60	1	0.90	1	0.60	1
Golden Corner	0.60	1	0.70	1	0.60	1
Mountain Hide Out	0.60	1	0.10	0	0.10	0
Secret Cove	0.80	1	0.20	0	0.20	0
Fixer Upper Fairway	0.30	0	0.70	1	0.30	0
Boom Town Bridge	0.10	0	0.60	1	0.10	0
Council House Projects	0.40	0	0.20	0	0.20	0
Crime Ridden Crescent	0.40	0	0.10	0	0.10	0
Rundown Row	0.20	0	0.10	0	0.10	0
SUM	9.00	10	7.60	10	6.30	8

Crisp $X \subset Y = (\sum \min XY)/(\sum X) = 8/10 = 0.80$

Fuzzy $X \subset Y = (\sum \min XY)/(\sum X) = 6.30/9.00 = 0.70$

houses in these neighbourhoods are expensive for reasons unrelated to residents' high income. So why should they contribute to the subset consistency of high-income neighbourhood ⊂ neighbourhood with expensive houses? Yet, they do in fuzzy sets because $X < Y$. Finally, from a threshold perspective, cases in Cell (iv) are irrelevant. They are not-high-income neighbourhoods with not-expensive houses. One cannot learn about a causal relationship between being a high-income neighbourhood and being a neighbourhood with expensive houses from these cases. So why should they contribute to or weaken the consistency of the subset relationship high-income neighbourhood ⊂ neighbourhood with expensive houses? In this example, the cases in Cell (iv) are below the $X = Y$ diagonal, meaning they weaken the consistency of the subset relationship – unjustly, from a threshold perspective, because they are causally irrelevant. Had these cases been above the $X = Y$ diagonal, they would have equally unjustly inflated the subset consistency.

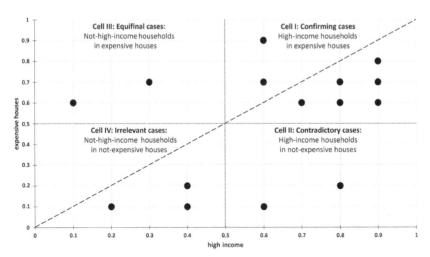

Figure 9.1   Crisp and fuzzy subsets for neighbourhoods with expensive houses

Calculating the consistency of set relationships over all cases, rather than only those in the relevant cells, fuzzy sets require another patch. Distinguishing between 'cases contradictory in degree' versus 'cases contradictory in kind' must help reconcile fuzzy set metrics with QCA's threshold logic. It must prevent fuzzy set QCA researchers making decisions on the consistency of set relationships that contradict QCA's threshold logic.

The disconnect between threshold logic and fuzzy set metrics is even more poignant in situations where fuzzy subset consistency is high enough for sufficiency but crisp subset consistency is not. Look at Table 9.2. It shows the membership of streets in the fuzzy and crisp sets of streets with lively pubs (X) and streets with attractive nightlife (Y). The fuzzy subset consistency of streets with lively pubs ⊂ streets with attractive night life is 0.87. However, the crisp subset consistency of the two sets is only 0.71, much too low for sufficiency. Inspecting the XY plot (Figure 9.2) shows nothing suspicious. Most cases are above the $X = Y$ diagonal ($X \leq Y$) and one case is contradictory in degree (in Cell i). Yet, from a threshold perspective, arguing that being a street with lively pubs is sufficient for being a street with attractive night life makes no sense at all. This becomes obvious when one looks at the cases.

If you want to have a good night out, you will want to go to the streets in Cell (i), the confirming cases. The pubs on Elvis Presley Street, The King's Corner, Blue Suede Shoes Avenue and Rock 'n' Roll Alley are lively and offer attractive night life. One would expect nothing less here. The pubs in Cell (ii) (contradictory cases) will certainly be very lively but for the wrong reasons.

Table 9.2   *Lively pubs and attractive night life*

	Streets with Lively Pubs (*X*)		Streets with Attractive Night Life (*Y*)		min*XY*	
	fs	cs	fs	cs	fs	cs
Rock 'n' Roll Alley	0.90	1	0.80	1	0.80	1
Elvis Presley Street	0.80	1	0.90	1	0.80	0
The King's Corner	0.70	1	0.80	1	0.70	1
Blue Suede Shoes Avenue	0.60	1	0.90	1	0.60	0
Broken Hearts Boulevard	0.90	1	0.20	0	0.70	1
Prisoner's Parade	0.60	1	0.40	0	0.40	0
Mafia Market	0.80	1	0.40	0	0.40	1
Theatre Row	0.40	0	0.60	1	0.40	0
Festival Square	0.30	0	0.90	1	0.30	0
Cinema Street	0.20	0	0.70	1	0.20	0
Carnival Close	0.10	0	0.80	1	0.10	0
Gallows Gate	0.30	0	0.40	0	0.30	0
Waste Treatment Way	0.20	0	0.40	0	0.20	0
Nerdy Drive	0.20	0	0.30	0	0.20	0
Cemetery Lane	0.10	0	0.30	0	0.10	1
SUM	7.10	7	8.80	8	6.20	5

Crisp $X \subset Y = (\sum \min XY)/(\sum X) = 5/7 = 0.71$

Fuzzy $X \subset Y = (\sum \min XY)/(\sum X) = 6.20/7.10 = 0.87$

Night life here might be exciting but not attractive for people wanting a good night out. Because there are three contradictory cases and only four confirming cases, from a threshold perspective, it is obvious that being a street with lively pubs is not sufficient for being a street with attractive night life. But the fuzzy subset consistency of these two sets shows something else. The streets in Cell (iii), Carnival Close, Cinema Street, Festival Square and Theatre Row, offer attractive night life, for reasons, however, that have nothing to do with lively pubs – that is, with the explanatory condition of interest. They are equifinal cases. So why would these cases contribute to the explanation of lively pubs → attractive night life? Yet they do in fuzzy set metrics. Finally, people looking for a good night out will certainly want to avoid the streets in Cell (iv). For obvious reasons, one learns nothing from the causal relationship between being a street with lively pubs and being a street with attractive night life from those cases. There may well be a pub on Cemetery Lane, where the bereaved

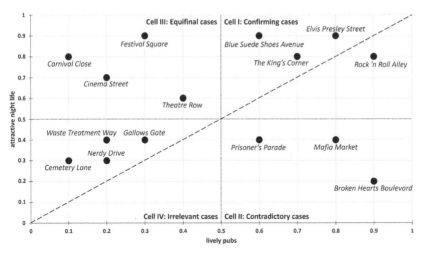

Figure 9.2   Crisp and fuzzy subsets for streets with attractive night life

gather after a funeral, but it is not lively and you do not go there for a good night out. However, since Cemetery Lane, Waste Treatment Way, Nerdy Drive and Gallows Gate all 'sit' above the *X = Y* diagonal, they contribute to the explanation of lively pubs → attractive night life in fuzzy sets.

In sum, from a threshold perspective, cases that have little or nothing to say on the causal relationship between lively pubs and attractive night life still 'cause' the fuzzy subset relationship between these two sets to be highly consistent. I do not think that is right. Another important point is that, without the benefit of case knowledge, relying merely on metrics, it would never have occurred to a researcher that, in this example, it is nonsensical to suggest that lively pubs are sufficient for attractive night life. In other words, insofar as fuzzy sets encourage researchers to rely on metrics, this is not a good development. QCA is a logical exercise, not an empirical one. And (fuzzy) subset relationships, however consistent, may still be logically nonsensical.

My examples may be very outspoken; however, they serve to demonstrate an important point – namely, that crisp and fuzzy subsets are different things. They may be calculated in the same way, but *X < Y* means something different in fuzzy sets than it does in crisp sets. This is because fuzzy (sub)set relationships are calculated over all cases in the case population, while crisp set metrics only consider cases in the relevant cells. Advocates of fuzzy sets argue that this makes fuzzy set metrics more accurate. My above examples demonstrate that this may not be so. I am not suggesting that fuzzy sets are necessarily wrong. What I am saying is that the marriage of the threshold logic of the truth table and the logic of truths-in-degree of fuzzy sets is not a very good one. Fuzzy set QCA conflates two different logics, which leads to fuzzy set QCA including cases in the calculation of fuzzy subset and superset relationships that, threshold-wise, should not be included. Since the basic logic of QCA is that of thresholds, one may wonder how including equifinal (Cell iii) and irrelevant (Cell iv) cases in the calculation of subset relationships helps researchers learn from cases. These cases do not elucidate whether being above the threshold for X (the presence of X) makes a difference for being above the threshold of Y (the presence of Y). Put differently, fuzzy set relationships produce a different kind of general causal evidence than do crisp set relationships. Fuzzy set general causal evidence is disconnected from cases. The consistency of fuzzy set relationships expresses the overall distance to the $X = Y$ diagonal of all cases in a case population. Instead, the general evidence expressed in the consistency of crisp set relationships is closely connected to the cases because it is calculated only from those cases that suggest singular causal evidence for (or against) the alleged causal relationship. Only $X = 1$ cases can produce singular causal evidence for sufficiency (if X, then Y), and only $Y = 1$ cases can produce singular causal evidence for necessity (iff X, then Y). In other words, crisp sets make a much stronger connection between singular and general causal evidence than fuzzy sets. This is what the above examples make clear. The cases in Cells (iii) and (iv) produce no singular causal evidence for the proposition, if X, then Y, and, therefore, are not included in the calculation of crisp subset relationships. Consequently, I prefer to calculate crisp rather than fuzzy set relationships. It consistently applies a threshold logic throughout the QCA study, which, I believe facilitates learning from cases because it produces logically compatible singular and general causal evidence.

MULTILEVEL SETS

Given the ontological (many concepts are not linear) and epistemological (for holistic cases, numerical equidistance does not equate to semantical equidistance) reservations against fuzzy sets, I think fuzzy sets are not a good combination with the propositional (threshold) logic of QCA. Fuzzy set relationships produce general causal evidence that is not readily compatible with the singular causal evidence that is collected from cases, which is propositional in nature. Fuzzy sets are far more obvious for set-analytical methods that abstract from cases, such as set coincidence analysis (Ragin and Fiss, 2017). Moreover, in QCA, the truth table minimization follows propositional (i.e., threshold or crisp) logic. QCA is a threshold method and the analytically relevant threshold is the one between diluting and intensifying linguistic hedges, which corresponds to the crossover point in fuzzy sets. QCA investigates whether being above this semantical threshold for X makes a difference for being above the semantical threshold for Y. It does not consider other degrees of membership in the investigation, which limits the analytical value of fuzzy sets. Furthermore, the value of calculating fuzzy set relationships in a threshold method is questionable, as I have demonstrated above. Consequently, I prefer calibrating with linguistic hedges to create multilevel sets – where all levels (degrees of membership) have a specific meaning but they form an ordinal scale only and are not numerated.

This multi-threshold or multilevel approach at once accounts for the colourfulness of social reality and conforms to QCA's threshold logic. To conduct the truth table analysis, researchers decide in which threshold they are interested. Perhaps they want to investigate whether being an (at least) moderately low-income household contributes to being a (an at least predominantly) happy household, in which case, the levels moderately low income and higher become 1s, and the levels somewhat low income and lower become 0s. This allows a crisp set QCA study to be performed and avoids the above problems. To refine the study – that is, to learn more from cases – QCA researchers may 'play around' with the crossover point, as I explained in detail in Chapter 8. In fact, I believe that this 'playing around' does more justice to the colourfulness of social reality then merely calibrating fuzzy sets. Performing different analyses for different thresholds (crossover points) gives a better understanding of how the causality 'works'. A fuzzy set analysis still only shows whether the presence or absence of an explanatory condition makes a difference for the presence or absence of the outcome. It does not allow specifying which degree of presence matters. Of course, one can alternate the crossover point in fuzzy sets too. But then one effectively calibrates multilevel sets.

CONCLUSION

I do not share the enthusiasm for fuzzy sets of the QCA methods literature and most QCA researchers. I think the fuzzy logic of truths-in-degree is a poor match with the threshold logic of the truth table analysis. Fuzzy set QCA has the ability to produce empirical results that contradict the formal, Boolean-algebraic (i.e., threshold) logic on which QCA rests. Most importantly, I fail to see how including equifinal (Cell iii) and irrelevant (Cell iv) cases in the calculation of set consistency helps us learn from cases. How can a cause that is not present (because set membership in $X < 0.5$) explain an outcome, particularly, for irrelevant cases, when the outcome has not even occurred (because membership in $Y < 0.5$). Because learning from cases in QCA requires dialoguing singular and general causal evidence, I think it is important that both kinds of causal evidence are compatible. Singular (case-level) causal evidence in QCA is threshold evidence, because cases are allocated to truth table rows that follow a threshold (i.e., true or false) logic. However, fuzzy set metrics develop general causal evidence that abstracts from cases – viz., it expresses the distance to the $X = Y$ diagonal across a population of cases. Instead, crisp set general causal evidence connects directly to QCA's singular causal evidence because crisp set relationships are calculated only over cases in the relevant cells; those cases producing singular causal evidence for or against the statement, if X, then Y. I believe that calibrating multi-level sets – that is, calibrating multiple thresholds (using linguistic hedges) – at once recognizes that social reality is not dichotomous and allows using crisp set metrics to align singular and general causal evidence. I also believe that alternating the crossover point (i.e., the principal threshold in a multilevel set) develops a deeper understanding of how causality 'works'.

GLOSSARY OF KEY CONCEPTS

Fuzziness	Or vagueness. The notion that concepts have no clear definition and no clear empirical boundaries. Instead, QCA works with clearly defined concepts to allow calibration. To calibrate (to determine) is to eliminate fuzziness (vagueness)
Fuzzy logic	Fuzzy logic says that statements are true-in-degree. Fuzzy logic allows using fuzzy concepts in scientific analysis
Multilevel sets	Sets that define multiple levels or categories with a threshold separating the levels. Levels suggest a degree of truth and are labelled accordingly; however, levels are not numerated – they do not receive a fuzzy set membership value
Propositional logic	Also known as formal logic, it is QCA's principal logic. It is expressed in statements of sufficiency (if X then Y) and necessity (iff X then Y). It suggests that propositions are either logically true or false and connects to Boolean algebra
Thresholds	These define semantically meaningful categories or levels. Being above the threshold for X means that a case has enough of the characteristics of X to be recognized (to qualify) as a case (an instance) of X. Thresholds connect to propositional logic. If a case is above the threshold for X, it means that the statement, 'This is a case of X', is logically true

10. The truth table analysis

The truth table analysis is the heart of a QCA study. All the work up to this point is to ensure the validity of the truth table analysis findings. The truth table analysis is much more than a Boolean minimization (Ragin [1987] 2014, pp. 105–18). Boolean minimization merely eliminates redundant conditions. However, researchers must first resolve contradictory rows, set consistency thresholds, and then interpret the minimization findings (the solution). All this requires dialoguing knowledge of cases, context and concepts. This chapter takes readers through the truth table analysis step by step. The chapter explains how the truth table is a tool to get from case-level (singular) to cross-case (general) causal evidence (Ragin, 2008, pp. 124–30). The truth table accounts for limited diversity in social reality – that some configurations are much more obvious than others, resulting in 'empty' rows (Ragin, 2000, pp. 81–7). The chapter explains how researchers can make counterfactual assumptions on empty rows, and the consequences this has for the solution that the Boolean minimization produces (Ragin, 2008, pp. 161–73). The chapter also discusses what comes after the Boolean minimization – viz., the interpretation of the solution into causal statements. The chapter presents truth table analysis as a sequence of steps. In reality, it is iterative and researchers find themselves going back and forth between the steps.

THE TRUTH TABLE AS AN INVESTIGATIVE TOOL

The truth table is QCA's investigative heart. It uniquely combines the analytical rigour of Boolean minimization with qualitative interpretation to infer causal claims (see Chapter 1). Most basically, the truth table presents all logically possible combinations of the explanatory conditions. Each row is a unique configuration of explanatory conditions. It is also a possibilistic causal claim – that this configuration is sufficient for the outcome. This claim may be logically true (1) or false (0). Formal, propositional logic minimizes the truth table from a large number of rows to a small number of configurations (Schneider and Wagemann, 2012, pp. 104–16). The output of the truth table analysis, the solution, expresses configurational and equifinal causality. Because a separate investigation must be performed for the presence and the absence of the outcome, the truth table analysis also expresses asymmetrical causality. In other words, the truth table is an investigative tool that acknowledges the complexity of causality. Mostly, the truth table is a tool to dialogue singular and general causal evidence. To explain the truth table, let's start with one based on fictional data (Table 10.1) that explains why people feel happy based on three explanatory conditions: being (1) a higher-educated person; (2) a stable-income-earning person; and (3) a person in a stable relationship. The outcome is being a person who feels happy.

The truth table describes the case population of a QCA study, or the universal set on which the investigation is performed. The case population contains all actual and counterfactual cases that conform to the definition of what is a case. This definition also includes a number of important scope conditions – that is, conditions that may be causally relevant but are held constant, because all cases must be qualitatively the same (on the same side of the crossover point) on all scope conditions (see Chapter 4). Even if they are not immediately causally relevant (in the investigation), scope conditions still narrow the causal explanation (Goertz and Mahoney, 2012a, pp. 210–14). The solution holds only for cases that conform to the scope conditions – which has consequences for generalizability. Let's say that, in this example, a case is a young adult (18–25 years) who recently (no more than nine months ago) moved to the Greater London area from North East England in search of work. That is, a case is an adult and the scope conditions are (1) young; (2) recently moved to London; (3) from North East England; (4) in search of work. This homogenizes cases on key background factors. The results of this study would be generalizable to young adults moving to cosmopolitan metropolitan areas (London-like) from relatively underdeveloped, peripheral regions in developed countries (North East England-like), in search of new opportunities (such as work). The result would be generalizable to young adults moving from, for example, Nebraska to San Francisco, or from Western Australia to Melbourne. They would also be relevant for but not fully generalizable to young adults moving from, for example, Sumatra to Jakarta, because Indonesia is a developing rather than a developed country.

CONDITIONS, ROWS AND LIMITED DIVERSITY

This truth table (Table 10.1) has eight rows because each of the three explanatory conditions may be present (1) or absent (0). As argued, 1 and 0 are logical statements (true and false), not empirical values (Ragin [1987] 2014, p. 15). It means that cases (young adults) in Row 1 have had enough education to be recognized (qualify) as higher educated, receive income regularly enough to qualify as stable-income earners, and have been in a relationship long enough to count as being in a stable relationship (Rubinson et al., 2019; Rutten and Rubinson, 2022). The number of rows in the truth table grows exponentially with the number of conditions as 2^k, where k is the number of conditions. Five

Table 10.1   Truth table for 'feeling happy' based on simulated data

Row	Higher Educated	Stable Income	Stable Relationship	Feeling Happy	Consistency	Confirming Cases	Contradictory Cases
1	1	1	1	?	—	—	—
2	1	1	0	1	0.67	Livia, Kareem, Ramon, Aleesha	Juanita (just broke up), Bruce (burnout)
3	1	0	1	?	0.83	Julia, Kofi, Priya, John, Saliha	Lucy (childless)
4	1	0	0	?	—	—	—
5	0	1	1	1	0.50	Judith, Nadya	Mike (failed degree), Elena (health issues)
6	0	1	0	0	—	—	—
7	0	0	1	?	—	—	—
8	0	0	0	0	0.67	Guy, Tariq	Nigel (Brexiteer), Joyce (won jackpot)

conditions produce a truth table of 32 rows, eight conditions already gives 256 rows. Even with many cases, this will still produce a lot of empty rows because of limited diversity. As explained in Chapter 1, some logically possible combinations of explanatory conditions (i.e., truth table rows) 'happen' only rarely or are not even possible, while other rows are far more obvious. In other words, limited diversity manifests itself as cases 'clustering' in some rows, while other rows are sparsely populated or empty. What variable-based (correlational) methods call multicollinearity is the norm in social reality (Ragin, 2000, p. 290). There really is no such thing as an independent variable on the case level because cases are holistic (ibid., pp. 194–202).

Empty rows may also happen because of a lack of cases rather than limited diversity and it is often difficult to say why a row is empty. Nor does it matter (Schneider and Wagemann, 2012, pp. 153–6). In the Boolean minimization, all empty rows are treated as logical remainder rows. Because they have no cases, there is no singular causal evidence to establish whether the row is logically true (1) or false (0). Researchers can make counterfactual assumptions on such rows. Having said that, one does not want too many empty truth table rows. Too many empty rows make it more difficult for the algorithm to correctly distinguish between causally relevant conditions and redundant conditions once researchers start making assumptions on logical remainder rows (Marx, Cambré and Rihoux, 2013, p. 38). There are no rules in QCA for how many logical remainder rows a truth table may have. Nor is there a benchmark for the minimum cases-to-conditions ratio (to avoid creating logical remainder rows). Marx et al. (ibid.) are more conservative than Mello (2021, p. 28) in this respect. However, when it comes to the number of conditions (and thus the number of truth table rows) one can have, QCA does have the following rules of thumb:

- If one has properly defined the case population, then it has the limited diversity that it has and this is what the truth table shows.
- If conditions are causally relevant, they must be included, if not as explanatory conditions then as scope conditions or confounding conditions (see Chapter 11). The operative word in the previous sentence is 'relevant'. Researchers must have good reasons to include a condition (Ragin, 2023, p. 53). Including conditions just to see what 'works' is a bad idea; QCA is a dialogue, not a fishing expedition.
- Keep the number of explanatory conditions limited. Lots of factors are always relevant but it is legitimate to focus on just a few. A statement of sufficiency says that this configuration makes the outcome possible (is sufficient) however many other conditions may also play a role. The contribution of other causally relevant factors does not negate the fact that this configuration is sufficient. However, they may reduce coverage.

- QCA's 'sweet spot' is four to six explanatory conditions. This is where the algorithm most effectively distinguishes between causally relevant and logically redundant conditions because it limits the number of logical remainder rows on which counterfactual assumptions must be made. More importantly, this is also where the solution is easiest to interpret into a causal explanation. Four to six explanatory conditions usually produces a solution that has configurations of two, three or four conditions. It is relatively easy to interpret what this means. With five or more conditions, that becomes progressively harder, which defeats one of QCA's key strengths – to attach meaning to configurations (Furnari et al., 2021). Researchers must move beyond merely identifying cross-case patterns and explain why the outcome is possible.
- Keep in mind that QCA was originally developed for mid-size Ns, roughly 15 to 50 cases. This number of cases, with four to six explanatory conditions still works best. With these numbers, one has intimate knowledge of cases, context and concepts with which to learn from cases. I would argue that the bare minimum for QCA is nine cases with three explanatory conditions.

FROM CASES TO ROWS

All rows in the above truth table (Table 10.1) show contradictory singular causal evidence; some cases 'have' the outcome and others do not. This is also what one may expect from real-world data. I have identified confirming and contradictory cases for didactical purposes, but truth tables normally only report the number of cases in each row. There are two strategies to determine whether a row is sufficient (logically true) or not. The first strategy sets a consistency threshold, usually ≥ 0.8, but researchers may set a higher or somewhat lower threshold. The consistency threshold is not a rigid cut-off point. With a consistency threshold ≥ 0.8, it is usually unproblematic to declare rows with a consistency of 0.79 or 0.78 sufficient, particularly when supported by substantive knowledge or when there is a gap to the next highest consistency – for example, after 0.78, the next highest consistency is 0.71. Suppose we had cases in Row 1 and that the consistency of the row was 0.75. All conditions being present in this row makes it highly plausible that the row is sufficient for feeling happy. Equally, rows with a consistency somewhat above the threshold may still be considered not-sufficient (false) if that is what substantive knowledge suggests. In sum, setting a consistency threshold is a good strategy but it must not be applied rigidly (Rubinson et al., 2019). In large-N studies (N ≥ 50), researchers may also set a frequency threshold. Particularly with little recourse to cases, this is a good strategy to eliminate the influence of sparsely populated rows (Ragin, 2000, p. 81). In the truth table minimization, each row has the same weight; a row is logically true or false, however few or many cases populate it. The validity of the statement, 'This row makes the outcome possible', rests on its substantive plausibility not on the number of confirming cases in the row (Rohlfing and Schneider, 2018). However, with larger Ns, sparsely populated rows may still evidence limited diversity and these rows are best considered logical remainder rows. The higher the N, the higher the frequency threshold can be, as long as the number of cases in the remaining populated rows is at least 80 per cent of the case population (give or take a per cent or two) (Greckhamer, Misangyi and Fiss, 2013; Rutten, 2022). Finally, fuzzy set truth tables must also set a proportional reduction in inconsistency (PRI) threshold for each row. This threshold may be a little lower than the consistency threshold, say 0.7, but should never be below 0.6.

The second strategy is to interpret all cases in each row. Going back to the cases will reveal whether the outcome is possible in the 'negative' cases. In those cases, some other factor may have interfered with the causal power that the configuration (row) describes (Ragin [1987] 2014, p. 88). This would not negate a statement of sufficiency. Or perhaps going back to the cases reveals that, for this row, the outcome is not possible, even though some cases may 'have' the outcome. Let's go to the cases in the above truth table (Table 10.1). Cases (young adults) in Row 2 are [higher educated AND stable income AND not-stable relationship] cases. Since knowledge of concepts and context suggests that it is the presence of the explanatory conditions rather than their absence that contributes to causal power emerging, it is not unreasonable to suggest that just the presence of [higher educated AND stable income] is sufficient for feeling happy. This is basically what one observes from the cases in Row 2. Four of the six young adults (cases) in this row feel happy, the remaining two do not. This means that the subset consistency of Row 2 is 0.67, well below the 0.8 threshold. However, when we inspect the contradictory cases, we find that Juanita is not-happy because she only just broke up with her girlfriend, while Bruce is not-happy because he worked himself into a burnout. But these factors have nothing to do with the explanatory conditions of the row (i.e., the causal power of interest). If we counterfactually removed these factors from Juanita and Bruce, there is no reason why they could not feel happy. Dialoguing knowledge of cases, context and concepts, one can comfortably declare that Row 2 is sufficient for the outcome – that the statement [higher educated AND stable income AND not-stable relationship] is sufficient for feeling happy, is logically true.

Now look at Row 8. In this row, all conditions are absent and we would expect the row to be not-sufficient for the outcome. Indeed, Guy and Tariq are not-happy but Nigel and Joyce are happy. The subset consistency of this row is 0.50 – too low for sufficiency. Inspecting Nigel reveals that he is a Brexiteer and is happy because the UK left the EU, while Joyce is happy because she won the lottery jackpot. Their feeling happy thus has nothing to do with the absence of the explanatory conditions in Row 8 and we can safely conclude that this row is not-sufficient for the outcome. We can perform this dialogue for all populated rows and get the outcome column (feeling happy) that we see in Table 10.1. The first strategy – setting consistency, frequency and PRI thresholds – is typically how fuzzy set QCA gets from singular to general causal evidence on the level of truth table rows. Crisp set QCA typically uses the second strategy – of dialoguing knowledge of cases, context and concepts. In reality, of course, it is best to always combine both strategies.

MINIMIZING THE TRUTH TABLE

The truth table minimization is a Boolean-algebraic exercise that is performed by the Quine – McCluskey algorithm (QMA) in all QCA software (or variations on QMA to suit specific software but which produce exactly the same outcomes) (Schneider and Wagemann, 2012, pp. 104–5). The QMA considers each truth table row as a primitive expression. It searches for prime implicants that cover multiple rows (primitive expressions) with the same outcome. Prime implicants simplify the primitive expressions by eliminating logically redundant conditions. The QMA then investigates which prime implicants may be logically redundant and eliminates them. What remains is a smaller number of more parsimonious configurations. This is the algorithmically derived solution. Because only logically redundant conditions and prime implicants are eliminated, the solution preserves the logical truth of the primitive expression – that is, of the truth table. This is easily explained with an example from Schneider and Wagemann (2012, pp. 108–11), shown in Figure 10.1 (I have only changed the capitals identifying the conditions).

Looking at Figure 10.1, suppose a truth table of three conditions (A, B, C) has four rows that are logically true. These are the four primitive expressions in the first row of Figure 10.1. Removing all logically redundant conditions produces the three prime implicants in the second row. Follow the arrows to see which primitive expression is covered by which prime implicant(s). They are prime implicants because they imply the truth of the primitive expressions. The second row in Figure 10.1 does not contain any expression that contradicts the logical truth of the first row. A logical contradiction would be, for example, $[A\sim B] \rightarrow Y$, because no primitive expression contains the conjunction $[A\sim B]$. The prime implicant chart in the third row further simplifies the prime implicants. Note that all primitive expressions covered by prime implicant $[BC]$ are also covered by prime implicants $[AB]$ and $[A\sim C]$. If we eliminate prime implicant $[BC]$ we would still preserve the logical truth of all primitive expressions (of the truth table). Put differently, nothing is gained by including $[BC]$.

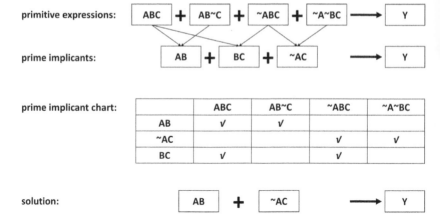

Figure 10.1   *Primitive expressions, prime implicants and solutions*

The remaining prime implicants speak the same logical truth as the primitive expressions but in a much simplified form.

Note that if we eliminated prime implicant [~*AC*], we would not preserve the truth of the primitive expression [~*A*~*BC*]. The prime implicant chart shows that only prime implicant [*BC*] is logically redundant. Eliminating [*BC*] produces the solution in the fourth row. We have thus simplified (or minimized) the truth table's four primitive expressions of three conditions each to just two configurations of only two conditions each, while preserving the logical truth. To make the point about preserving the logical truth, consider the following statement: 'Jack is tall (*A*), wears glasses (*B*) and has a beard (*C*)'. If this statement is true, than the statement, 'Jack is tall (*A*)' is also true.

Always perform the truth table minimization using software to avoid mistakes. The example shows that truth table minimization is a logical exercise, not an empirical one. It is also a logical exercise because it allows making counterfactual assumptions on logical remainder rows, for which no empirical evidence exists. To see how that works, let's return to the above truth table (Table 10.1). It has three rows, Rows 2, 3 and 5, that are logically true:

(Row 2) higher educated AND stable income
AND ~stable relationship → feeling happy   (10.1)

(Row 3) higher educated AND ~stable income
AND stable relationship → feeling happy   (10.2)

(Row 5) ~higher educated AND stable income
AND stable relationship → feeling happy   (10.3)

Keeping in mind what we have just learnt about logical minimization, these three statements (rows, primitive expressions) cannot be simplified. Between them, there is no logically redundant condition. Considering only populated truth table rows and making no assumptions on logical remainder rows, this is the solution. QCA labels this the complex or conservative solution. Not making any assumptions on logical remainder rows (i.e., being most conservative on counterfactual assumptions) produces the most complex solution (CS – i.e., a solution whose configurations include many conditions).

We could also assume that all logical remainder rows are true. That would minimize the maximum possible number of conditions from the most complex solution to produce the most parsimonious solution (PS). As long as the subset consistency of the configurations in this PS remains ≥ 0.8, it is, mathematically at least, sufficient. Assuming that Row 1 is sufficient for 'feeling happy' is uncontroversial. Conceptual knowledge suggests that it is the presence of the explanatory conditions rather than their absence that contributes to the emergence of causal power. This suggests that, if a case existed for Row 1, where all conditions are present, it is possible for this case to 'have' the outcome. This makes Row 1 an easy counterfactual. Assuming this row to be true does not increase the possibilistic uncertainty of the solution (Rutten, 2023). Instead, the other three logical remainder rows (Rows 4, 6 and 7) are difficult counterfactuals. In these rows, it would be mostly the absence of the explanatory conditions that contributed to the emergence of causal power. Assuming all counterfactuals (empty rows) to be true makes the most lenient counterfactual assumptions[1] and produces the PS. The PS for the above truth table is:

higher educated OR stable income OR stable relationship
$\quad\quad\rightarrow$ feeling happy $\quad\quad\quad\quad\quad\quad\quad\quad\quad\quad\quad$ (10.4)

However, those lenient assumptions very substantially increase the possibilistic uncertainty of the solution. The PS is unrealistically parsimonious, because assuming difficult counterfactuals to be true minimizes not only redundant but also causally relevant conditions (ibid.). Causal power is unlikely to emerge from this solution and, consequently, it would not be possible for cases to achieve the outcome. Still, one can learn from the PS which conditions must certainly be present to explain the outcome. Moreover, we can only say that counterfactuals are difficult or easy in the light of our knowledge of (other) cases, context and concepts. Rows are only 'impossible' and counterfactual assumptions 'untenable' relative to our definitions of what conditions (concepts) mean. What is not possible according to our definitions (idealized cognitive models [Lakoff, 1987, p. 68] and [epistemically relativist] knowledge), may well exist in social reality. Besides, if we could conclusively declare empty rows as easy or difficult counterfactuals, we would already have all the answers and there would be no need to analyse the truth table. Therefore, the

CS (no counterfactual assumptions) and the PS (assumptions on all empty truth table rows) are the logical extremes between which researchers must interpret a plausible solution – that is, the intermediate solution (IS).

To arrive at the IS, let's enter directional assumptions. As argued in the above example, substantive knowledge suggests that the presence rather than the absence of the explanatory conditions contributes to causal power emerging. We can now look at the conditions that appear in the CS but not in the PS. If directional assumptions suggest that their presence contributes to the emergence of causal power, they are unrealistically minimized from the PS and we must keep them. However, if substantive knowledge suggests that they need not be part of a configuration for causal power to emerge, they are correctly minimized from the PS. Thus, using directional assumptions to 'negotiate' between the complex and the PS produces the IS. The IS has a (very) low possibilistic uncertainty, because it is based on plausible counterfactuals (directional assumptions) only (Rutten, 2023).

To minimize [higher educated AND stable income AND ~stable relationship] to just [higher educated], the PS assumes both Rows 1 [higher educated AND stable income AND stable relationship] and 4 [higher educated AND ~stable income AND ~stable relationship] to be true. However, Row 4 is a difficult counterfactual, which makes the parsimonious statement that being higher educated is sufficient for feeling happy implausible. Directional assumptions suggest that the presence rather than the absence of the conditions contributes to causal power emerging. Consequently, [~stable relationship] is plausibly minimized but not [stable income]; this condition should be retained. This produces the following configuration in the IS: [higher educated AND stable income]. This is the most plausible explanation for [feeling happy] given our substantive knowledge. Using this logic to negotiate between the CS and PS produces the following IS for the above truth table:

(higher educated AND stable income)
OR (higher educated AND stable relationship)   (10.5)

OR (stable income AND stable relationship) → feeling happy   (10.6)

Figure 10.2 summarizes the above argument. Note that the three solutions are subsets and supersets of each other. The CS is a subset of the IS, which is itself a subset of the PS. This preserves the logical truth of the truth table across all three solutions. Following the rules of set analysis (see Chapter 7), as one goes from the complex to the intermediate to the PS, the coverage of the solution increases because supersets contain more cases. However, the subset consistencies of the solution types decrease, as more of the additionally covered cases will be contradictory cases, because the PS does not substantively explain the outcome.

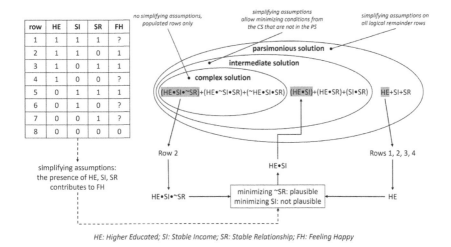

row	HE	SI	SR	FH
1	1	1	1	?
2	1	1	0	1
3	1	0	1	1
4	1	0	0	?
5	0	1	1	1
6	0	1	0	?
7	0	0	1	?
8	0	0	0	0

HE: Higher Educated; SI: Stable Income; SR: Stable Relationship; FH: Feeling Happy

Note: CS = complex solution; FH = feeling happy; HE = higher educated; PS = parsimonious solution; SI = stable income; SR = stable relationship.

Figure 10.2   Minimization and solution types

Set theory suggests there is more to logical remainder rows than easy and difficult counterfactuals. Remainder rows may be impossible, untenable and logically contradictory (Schneider and Wagemann, 2012, pp. 200–211). Trying to explain the effectiveness of team leaders from their personality characteristics, one may have 'narcissist' and 'empathic' as two of multiple explanatory conditions. However, there are no empathic narcissists. Consequently, truth table rows where 'narcissist' and 'empathic' are both present remain empty because they are impossible. Untenable logical remainders are configurations from which causal power cannot emerge. In the above example, if Row 8 were empty it would be an untenable remainder because the causal power to feel happy cannot emerge from this configuration. Remainder rows where a necessary condition is absent are logical contradictory rows. In the absence of a necessary condition, the outcome cannot occur and counterfactually assuming that it does contradicts the statement of necessity. However, social reality is a lot 'messier' than set theory would have it. Since we can only know social reality through the lens of our concepts (epistemic relativism, Chapter 1), we cannot definitively know that a logical remainder row is impossible, untenable or contradictory. It is only so in the light of our partial and perspectival knowledge. 'Things' are only impossible, untenable or contradictory if they do not exist in the domain of the Real, but we cannot directly observe this domain. Consequently, what we define as impossible, untenable or contradictory (from our idealized cognitive models) may well exist in social reality (even pregnant males are possible, if one accepts gender fluidity, which underlines that what we observe is contingent on how we define our concepts and measurements). In fact, given a large enough N, all impossible, untenable and contradictory rows will become populated, owing to the enormous diversity and heterogeneity of social reality (Bhaskar [1975] 2008, pp. 87–8; [1979] 2015, p. 128; Decoteau, 2018). The question is, is it plausible that such rows explain the outcome – plausible in the light of our knowledge of cases, context and concepts? In other words, the qualifications impossible, untenable and contradictory are relative to our definitions. In view of our epistemically relativist knowledge of cases, context and concepts, we really only have easy and difficult counterfactuals, and plausible and implausible explanations of the outcome. They are heuristic guidelines rather than mathematical axioms. Making assumptions on logical remainder rows and 'updating' them throughout a study (even when they are 'impossible', 'untenable' and 'contradictory') is part of learning from cases.

Making assumptions on logical remainder rows is largely automated in all QCA software. All that researchers need to do is make 'directional assumptions' on each explanatory condition. The software asks the researcher whether the presence or the absence of the explanatory condition is expected to contribute to the emergence of causal power to 'produce' the outcome. The researcher checks 'presence' or 'absence' for the directional assumptions for each condition. The software will then perform the minimization as explained above. Alternatively, researchers may indicate 'present or absent' when they do not wish to make directional assumptions because substantive knowledge suggests that both the presence and absence of the condition may contribute to the causal power emerging. If one checks 'present or absent' for all conditions, the IS will be identical to the CS. Because both their presence and their absence may contribute to the outcome, there is no ground on which conditions can be minimized. The IS is most commonly used in QCA. The CS is unnecessarily complex because making assumptions on easy counterfactuals is uncontroversial. The PS is unrealistically parsimonious because it is based on implausible counterfactuals (Ragin [1987] 2014, pp. 164–7).

It is important to realize that there is only one most CS and only one most PS. However, there are usually multiple ISs – that is, solutions 'in between' the CS and the PS. Any solution that is a superset of the CS and a subset of the PS is an IS. QCA software only shows one algorithmically derived IS. However, it is perfectly legitimate to refine this IS. As long as it remains a superset of the complex and a subset of the PS, the refined IS is logically true (Rutten, 2022) (it preserves the logical truth of the CS, and does not logically contradict the

PS). Refining the solution is part of QCA's learning from cases. If dialoguing knowledge of cases, context and concepts suggests that a configuration of the solution does not make sense, researchers may add a condition to a configuration or remove one from it. As long as the subset consistency of the refined configuration remains ≥ 0.8 (or ≥ 0.75), this is unproblematic. The software allows researchers to (manually) calculate the subset and superset consistencies of the refined configurations and solution.

THE SOLUTION TABLE AND ITS INTERPRETATION

The solution must be reported in a table (Ragin, 2008, p. 205). Figure 10.3 shows the solution table (or configuration chart [Fiss, 2011]) for the above IS. Configurations are in the columns, and each column shows which conditions are present (●), absent (⊗) or logically redundant (blank) in the configuration. The column also shows the configuration's coverage and consistency. With real-world data, many cases will be covered by more than one configuration. Such cases are 'overdetermined' (see Figure 2.1 in Chapter 2). They 'have' the outcome for more than one reason – that is, more than one causal power emerged in those cases. Some cases will be covered by a single configuration only, which means there is a difference between raw coverage (calculated over all cases that a configuration covers) and unique coverage (calculated only over the cases uniquely covered by this configuration) – except in the present example where each case is covered by a single configuration only. As argued in Chapter 7, even with a (very) low coverage, a configuration may still be theoretically relevant. Consistency, on the other hand, must be high enough, preferably ≥ 0.8, but ≥ 0.75 is also acceptable. Note that the consistencies of Configurations 1 and 3 are < 0.8. However, we have already explained away the contradictory cases in the above. Contradictory cases always upset a constant conjunction (domain of the Empirical) – that is, the consistency of a set relationship. However, investigating contradictory cases may reveal that this is unproblematic; that contradictory cases do not defeat the potentiality of the cause to make the outcome possible (domain of the Real). Instead, large(r)-N studies, with more distance to the cases, rely more strongly on consistency thresholds and less on 'explaining away' contradictory cases (Greckhamer et al., 2013; Rutten, 2022). Solution tables should mention the number of (contradictory) cases in each configuration. Small-N studies may identify the cases in the solution table.

Always mention the full Boolean expression for the solution, either as part of the truth table (as in Figure 10.3) or just below it. Also clearly identify the solution type, normally the (refined) IS. The solution coverage in this example

(intermediate solution)	Configuration 1 MATERIAL CONFIDENCE	Configuration 2 EMOTIONAL CONFIDENCE	Configuration 3 STABILITY
Higher educated	●	●	
Stable income	●		●
Stable relationship		●	●
Coverage	0.31	0.39	0.15
Consistency	0.67	0.83	0.50
Cases (*contradictory*)	Aleesha, Kareem, Livia, Ramon, *Bruce, Juanita*	Julia, John, Kofi, Priya, Saliha, *Lucy*	Judith, Nadya, *Elena, Mike*
Solution coverage	0.85		
Solution consistency	0.69		
[higher educated AND stable income] OR [stable income AND stable relationship] → feeling happy			

● condition present   ⊗ condition absent   [BLANK] condition logically redundant

Figure 10.3   Solution table

is 0.69. Using crisp set metrics, this means that the solution explains 69 per cent of the *Y* cases (cases that 'have' the outcome). Using fuzzy set metrics, a solution coverage of 0.69 may be interpreted as roughly 69 per cent of the cases 'sitting' above the *X* = *Y* diagonal. Note that the *Y* cases also include contradictory cases in *Y* = 0 rows of the truth table (i.e., Joyce and Nigel). The solution is never going to explain these *Y* cases because they populate rows that were not used to derive it. In other words, the solution will (almost) never explain all *Y* cases in the case population. The QCA literature does not set a threshold for solution coverage. However, I would argue that, if a solution explains less than 60–65 per cent of the *Y* cases, it does not explain very much. In my view, solution coverages ≤ 0.5 are very problematic because it means that half or more of the *Y* cases have the outcome for a different reason than the solution suggests. If the solution coverage is too low, reconsider the definition of a case (i.e., redo the casing), the calibration and the explanatory conditions of the study. Solution consistency is not particularly important, as long as the consistencies of the individual configurations are high enough – in which case the solution consistency will usually not be much lower anyway. A solution consistency of ≥ 0.7 is always unproblematic.

The next questions are: what does this mean, how do the three configurations explain the outcome, and why is it possible for young adults to feel happy when they 'have' these characteristics? In Chapter 3, I explained how a configuration is not a cause but describes a causal power that, when exercised, makes the outcome possible. The first configuration is [higher educated AND stable income]. Higher-educated people have the cognitive abilities to deal with life's challenges and opportunities. Having a stable income means that people are confident that they can pay their bills. What emerges from this configuration is confidence. [Higher educated AND stable income] persons are confident that they can face and enjoy life. The causal power to be confident emerges from this configuration. Configuration 2 is a variation of this causal power where confidence emerges from being in a stable relationship. This makes Configuration 1 the 'material confidence' configuration and Configuration 2 the 'emotional confidence' configuration. It is important to always label a configuration in such a way that the label captures the nature of the causal power. Configuration 3 is [stable income AND stable relationship]. People in a stable relationship have the emotional stability to deal with life's challenges and opportunities. Having a stable income means they do not have to worry about their material wellbeing. This makes Configuration 3 the 'stability configuration'. Exercising the causal power of stability makes it possible for young adults to feel happy. The point is, in QCA, researchers develop explanations on the level of a configuration (Furnari et al., 2021). They must ask: what does this configuration mean? And perhaps the same condition means something different in different configurations. In other words, when theorizing their findings, QCA researchers must radically break with causal-effects thinking. They must radically break with variable-based theorizing that develops causal explanations on the level of individual factors (e.g., independent variables or conditions).

EXPLAINING THE ABSENCE OF THE OUTCOME

Because causality in QCA is asymmetrical, QCA researchers must perform separate analyses for the presence and absence of the outcome. As we fail for reasons that are different from those when we succeed, different conditions will be necessary and different configurations sufficient for the presence and absence of the outcome. The analysis of necessity for not-the-outcome investigates which conditions are supersets of $\sim Y$. The analysis of sufficiency for $\sim Y$ is performed on the same truth table as the analysis of sufficiency for Y. However, now the 1s and 0s in the outcome column are mostly reversed. A row that is sufficient for Y cannot also be sufficient for $\sim Y$. Some rows may be sufficient for neither Y nor $\sim Y$ and they are available for minimizing the solutions for both Y and $\sim Y$. However, there may be some easy counterfactuals for Y that should not be available for counterfactual assumptions for the solution for $\sim Y$. Row 1 (all three explanatory conditions present) in the above truth table (Table 10.1) is such an easy counterfactual for Y. In the truth table for $\sim Y$, such rows should be identified as not-sufficient (0) for $\sim Y$. Because different logical remainder rows are used to simplify the solution for the presence and the absence of the outcome, the solution for $\sim Y$ will not simply be the complement of the solution for Y. Only when one has a fully specified truth table, with no logical remainder rows, will the solution for $\sim Y$ be the complement of the solution for Y. In that eventuality, we can simply apply De Morgan's Law (a Boolean-algebraic rule to negate a Boolean expression) to the solution for Y to find the solution for $\sim Y$. De Morgan's Law is based on the fact that the set of A and the set of $\sim A$ are each other's complements (Ragin [1987] 2014, pp. 98–9). So, following De Morgan's Law:

$$\text{If: } A \rightarrow Y, \text{ then: } \sim A \leftarrow \sim Y \tag{10.7}$$

$$\text{If: } (A \bullet B) \rightarrow Y, \text{ then: } (\sim A + \sim B) \rightarrow \sim Y \tag{10.8}$$

$$\text{If: } (A + B) \rightarrow Y, \text{ then: } (\sim A \bullet \sim B) \rightarrow \sim Y \tag{10.9}$$

If we apply De Morgan's Law to the above solution for 'feeling happy' (Y), we get the following solution for 'not-feeling-happy' ($\sim Y$):

$$\text{If: [higher educated} \bullet \text{ stable income] + [higher educated} \bullet \text{ stable relationship]} \\ + \text{[stable income} \bullet \text{ stable relationship]} \rightarrow \text{ feeling happy,} \tag{10.10}$$

$$\text{then: [} \sim \text{higher educated} \bullet \sim \text{stable income]} \\ + \text{[} \sim \text{higher educated} \bullet \sim \text{stable relationship]} \\ + \text{[} \sim \text{stable income} + \sim \text{stable relationship]} \rightarrow \sim \text{feeling happy} \tag{10.11}$$

However, if we minimize the truth table for 'not-feeling-happy' ($\sim Y$), we get a different solution – viz.:

$$\text{[} \sim \text{higher educated} \bullet \sim \text{stable income} \bullet \sim \text{stable relationship]} \\ \rightarrow \sim \text{feeling happy} \tag{10.12}$$

This solution is very different. Given that truth tables (almost) always feature empty rows, De Morgan's Law has little practical relevance for QCA. However, other set-analytical methods do apply it to obtain an explanation for the negated outcome (e.g., Mahoney and Barrenechea, 2019). Most notably, Ragin's method of analytic induction (Ragin, 2023) relies on De Morgan's Law for the negated solution because it considers positive cases only.

The consistency of the (intermediate) solution, which in this example counts only one configuration, is just 0.5; its coverage is a mere 0.29. However, this is completely unproblematic for the following reasons. First, the truth table contains only one populated row (Row 8) that is sufficient for $\sim$feeling happy.

The available logical remainder rows for ~feeling happy cannot simplify this configuration any further, so the solution for ~feeling happy is equal to Row 8. This row has a consistency of 0.5, because two of the four cases, Joyce and Nigel, are contradictory cases. But, as we have seen, Joyce and Nigel are happy for reasons unrelated to this row. So, in this example, the consistency of 0.5 is as high as we can get. Moreover, this solution explains all not-feeling-happy cases (Guy and Tariq) in Row 8. Other not-feeling-happy cases (Juanita, Bruce, Lucy, Mike and Elena) are contradictory cases in truth table rows that are sufficient for 'feeling happy'. These cases are never going to be explained by the solution for '~feeling happy' because this solution does not consider the rows populated by Juanita, Bruce, Lucy, Mike and Elena. Consequently, the solution for '~feeling happy' can only cover two of the seven 'negative' cases. Thus, also the coverage of 0.29 is as high as we can get for '~feeling happy' in this example. That is, always inspect the truth table when assessing consistencies and coverages, particularly for the explanation of ~Y.

How to interpret the solution for ~Y? In this example, it means that the causal power to feel happy cannot emerge when [~higher educated AND ~stable income AND ~stable relationship] describes a case. In other words, the solution for ~Y identifies constraints for X rather than an explanation for ~Y. The solution for ~Y explains why the causal power to make Y possible does not (cannot) emerge. It says something about the causal power (the 'cause') rather than suggest an explanation for why the outcome does not occur. Given that the solution for ~Y will contain mostly negated terms, it is very difficult to interpret it into an explanation of why the outcome does not occur – analogous to the above explanation of why the outcome (feeling happy) is possible. Negative cases are also much more heterogeneous than positive cases, which further complicates interpreting why the outcome did not occur (Ragin, 2023, p. 40). Thinking of the solution for ~Y in terms of constraints for X (for causal power) is much more straightforward. It also means that we need to worry much about the subset consistency and coverage of the solution for ~Y. After all, we are explaining the non-occurrence of the cause (causal power), not the non-occurrence of the outcome.

GLOSSARY OF KEY CONCEPTS

Cases-to-conditions ratio	QCA researchers must have a good cases-to-conditions ratio to avoid unnecessarily producing logical remainder rows. Three explanatory conditions and nine cases is the bare minimum for QCA. Four to six explanatory conditions and 20 to 50 cases is QCA's sweet spot. More than six explanatory conditions is likely to produce complex, difficult-to-interpret solutions however many cases one has
Complex solution	Or conservative solution. Follows when the truth table is minimized using populated rows only. The complex solution does not rely on any counterfactual assumptions. It is unnecessarily complex because making assumptions on easy counterfactuals does not increase possibilistic uncertainty
Configuration consistency	The subset consistency of the configuration. The solution table must report this consistency for each configuration
Configuration label	Each configuration in the solution must be given a unique number and a label (name) that captures the nature of the causal power it describes
Consistency threshold	The minimum subset consistency for a truth table row to be considered logically true. Setting a consistency threshold helps resolve contradictory rows. QCA's default consistency threshold is 0.8, and truth table rows that meet this threshold can usually be considered true. However, the consistency threshold must not be used mechanically as a cut-off point. Researchers must always inspect rows that are just below and above the consistency threshold for the (im)plausibility of their being true or false
Contradictory cases	'Have' a different outcome than the truth table row they populate. Researchers must 'explain away' contradictory cases to declare a row true or false. They must argue that contradictory cases 'not-having' (or having) the outcome is unrelated to their 'having' (or not-having) the configuration of explanatory conditions of their row
Contradictory row	A truth table row with contradictory singular causal evidence. Some cases in the row 'have' the outcome, while others do not. Contradictory rows must be resolved to declare a row logically true (1) or false (0)

De Morgan's law	A Boolean-algebraic rule to negate a Boolean expression. For fully specified truth tables (with no empty rows), applying De Morgan's Law to the solution for Y yields the solution for $\sim Y$. Only for fully specified truth tables are the solutions for Y and $\sim Y$ each other's complements and negating one produces the other. For QCA, De Morgan's Law has little practical relevance
Difficult counterfactual	A logical remainder row of which knowledge of cases, context and concepts suggests that it is logically false – that is, that the outcome is not possible for this row. Assuming difficult counterfactuals to be logically true strongly increases the possibilistic uncertainty of the solution
Directional assumptions	Based mostly on theoretical (conceptual) but also on empirical knowledge (of cases and their context), researchers establish whether the presence of an explanatory condition or its absence contributes to the emergence of causal power that makes the outcome possible
Easy counterfactual	A logical remainder row of which knowledge of cases, context and concepts suggests that it is logically true – that is, that the outcome is possible for this row
Frequency threshold	For large(r)-N studies ($N \geq 50$) researchers may set a frequency threshold for truth table rows. A frequency threshold sets the minimum number of cases in a row before it may be declared true or false. Rows with too few cases are considered logical remainder rows. Setting a frequency threshold eliminates sparsely populated rows that may be 'outliers'. After setting a frequency threshold, the remaining populated rows must contain at least 80 per cent of the cases in the case population. The frequency threshold must not be used mechanically as a cut-off point. Researchers must inspect rows just above and below the threshold for the (im)plausibility of their being true or false
Intermediate solution	Follows from using directional assumptions to minimize conditions that appear in the complex but not the parsimonious solution. The intermediate solution is QCA's preferred solution. It is the most plausible explanation of the outcome because directional assumptions are unlikely to minimize causally relevant conditions
Limited diversity	Some combinations of explanatory conditions are very common in social reality, while others are much less obvious or even impossible. It means that explanatory conditions are not independent; their (non-)occurrence is contingent on the presence or absence of other explanatory conditions. Because of limited diversity, cases tend to cluster in some truth table rows, while other rows remain sparsely populated or empty

Logical remainder rows	Truth table rows that are not populated with cases, either because of limited diversity or a lack of cases. Logical remainder rows cannot be declared logically true or false because no singular (case-level) causal evidence exists for these rows. Logical remainders are available for counterfactual assumptions. The truth table analysis is designed to deal with logical remainder rows
Parsimonious solution	Or lenient solution. Follows when the truth table is minimized using populated rows and making assumptions on both easy and difficult counterfactuals. The parsimonious solution is mathematically but not substantively sufficient for the outcome – that is, the outcome is not possible under the parsimonious solution
Preserving logical truth	The complex solution is a subset of the intermediate solution, which, in turn, is a subset of the parsimonious solution. Consequently, as the complex solution is known to be true (because it is based exclusively on populated truth table rows), the intermediate and parsimonious solutions cannot be logically false
Prime implicant	A configuration that is sufficient for the outcome after logically minimizing all available primitive expressions
Primitive expression	Or truth table row. A configuration that is sufficient for the outcome according to singular causal evidence from actual cases only
Proportional reduction in inconsistency (PRI) threshold	Fuzzy set QCA studies must also specify a PRI threshold. The PRI threshold may be lower than the consistency threshold but not lower than 0.6. Only truth table rows that meet the PRI threshold can be declared true. The PRI threshold must not be used mechanically as a cut-off point. Researchers must inspect rows just above and below the threshold for the (im)plausibility of their being true or false
Raw coverage	All cases that are covered (explained) by a particular configuration. Or the distance to the $X = Y$ diagonal for the cases above the diagonal in fuzzy set QCA. The raw coverage of each configuration must be reported in the solution table
Refining the solution	QCA software returns only one intermediate solution; however, any solution that is a superset of the complex solution and a subset of the parsimonious solution is an intermediate solution and, therefore, logically true. Using knowledge of cases, context and concepts, researchers may refine the algorithmically derived intermediate solution to get a better (more plausible) substantive explanation of the outcome

Solution	The union of all configurations that are sufficient for the outcome. The solution follows after minimizing all available prime implicants on the basis of counterfactual assumptions and directional assumptions
Solution consistency	The subset consistency of the solution. It must be reported in the solution table
Solution coverage	All cases covered (explained) by the solution – that is, by the union of all configurations in the solution. Solution coverage must be reported in the solution table. A solution coverage ≤ 0.5 means that the solution explains too little
Solution table	The findings of the truth table analysis must be reported in the solution table. The solution table shows the explanatory conditions in the rows. Each column represents a configuration in the solution. Symbols indicate whether a condition is present ($\bullet$), absent ($\otimes$) or logically redundant (blank) in a configuration
Truth table	QCA's key analytical tool. It describes all actual and counterfactual cases in the case population. A truth table has 2^k rows, where k is the number of explanatory conditions. This lists all logically possible combinations of the presence (1) and absence (0) of the explanatory conditions
Truth table analysis	The entirety of the steps that lead from developing and specifying the truth table to minimizing it and interpreting the findings. Truth table analysis is an iterative process
Truth table minimization	Or Boolean minimization. The mathematical step in the truth table analysis that minimizes logically redundant conditions to only retain causally relevant conditions. The minimization follows formal, propositional logic and must always be performed by software
Truth table row	The basic unit of analysis of a QCA study. A row is a logical statement (i.e., this configuration is sufficient for Y) that may be true (1) or false (0), regardless of how many (or few) cases populate the row. Truth table rows being true or false presents general (cross-case) causal evidence
Unique coverage	The cases uniquely covered by a particular configuration. More generally, and also applicable to fuzzy set QCA, the proportion of the solvution coverage uniquely explained by a particular configuration

NOTE

1.   It is common in QCA to refer to the complex solution as the conservative
     solution. This solution is Boolean-algebraically complex because it is
     based on the most conservative counterfactual assumptions – viz., none. By
     analogy, I like to refer to the parsimonious solution as the lenient solution.
     It is Boolean-algebraically parsimonious because of making the most lenient
     counterfactual assumptions. Alas, when I suggested this to Charles Ragin
     when I met him at the QCA experts meeting in Zurich, in December 2019,
     he strongly preferred calling it the parsimonious solution.

11. Calibration and confounding conditions in a large-N example

The aim of this chapter is two-fold. First, it explains how investigating confounding conditions enriches a QCA study. Confounding conditions are causally relevant, but they are not explanatory conditions in the truth table (Goertz, 2017, p. 107; Rutten, 2022). Investigating confounding conditions thus allows additional causally relevant conditions in a QCA study. The chapter also suggests how cases may be calibrated in large-N studies in the absence of external or substantive criteria. The chapter explains why calibrating from population distributions (means, averages and percentiles) is the worst calibration approach. By definition, it leads to spurious results. Instead, the ranking method that I introduced in my paper 'Applying and assessing large-N QCA' (Rutten, 2022) should be used as a calibration method of last resort. The chapter also explains why I believe that robustness tests are not particularly important for QCA. The validity of statements of sufficiency rests not on their empirical robustness but on their substantive plausibility. Second, this chapter demonstrates how to actually do a (large-N) QCA study. Using secondary data from Eurostat (the EU's statistical office), the chapter explains regional innovation. The example takes readers through the various steps of a QCA study and applies the knowledge learnt in the previous chapters. It also demonstrates what it means to dialogue knowledge of cases, context and concepts, and how to do it.

REGIONAL INNOVATION

Explaining why some regions are more innovative than others is one of the key concerns of economic geography. It has also been the focus of much of my scholarly and consultancy work (e.g., Rutten, 2019). The start of a QCA study is always a configurational question. Economic geographers know that 'conventional' economic factors, such as knowledge production (e.g., research and development) and labour productivity, contribute to the explanation of regional innovation. However, particularly since the work of Richard Florida (2002), the role of so-called 'soft factors' (such as openness values) is also considered. This is because regions are merely geographical spaces where innovation happens. Innovation is a human activity and it is organized in (networks of) firms (Hassink and Klaerding, 2012; Howells, 2012). Firms and their workers 'anchor' in specific places, the places where firms are based and where their workers live (Rutten, 2017). The configurational question to pursue is: are conventional economic and soft factors jointly necessary to explain regional innovation? Defining innovation as a human activity (i.e., as the outcome of knowledge creation) moves the study of regional innovation away from the abstract language of variables and their effects. Instead, we can ask which regional characteristics make it possible for human agents in a region to successfully engage in knowledge creation. This establishes a connection to activist causation and causal power. From regional characteristics, causal powers may emerge that, when exercised, allow human agents to engage in knowledge creation and 'produce' innovations. This frames how we theorize about regional innovation – not as effects of independent on dependent variables (passivist causation) but in terms of conditions that enable human agents to create knowledge. Activist causation does not have to pertain to human agents; organizations and other collectives may also be thought of as agents. Explanatory conditions capture 'things' that enable (or constrain) (human) agency. So rather than labour productivity having a positive effect on regional innovation, productive labour (remember that conditions are adjectives) allows (human) agents to spend more time and resources on knowledge creation.

Which conventional economic and which soft factors to focus on? As QCA can handle a limited number of conditions only (I recommend four to six), researchers must carefully consider which ones they choose and let theoretical and substantive arguments guide their decisions. QCA cannot be a 'fishing expedition' where researchers just 'throw in' some conditions and see what happens. Each explanatory condition must be (theoretically) meaningful (Ragin, 2008, pp. 124–5). In this example, I draw from 'conventional' economic geography theory for the 'hard' factors and from the European Social Progress Index (EU-SPI) for the 'soft' factors. For the 'hard' factors, I take human resources in science and technology (HRST) and labour productivity. Both are known to correlate strongly with regional innovation (Asheim and Coenen, 2005). HRST captures the regional production of knowledge. It suggests the presence of a broad regional pool of knowledge that knowledge workers can tap into for their knowledge-creation efforts. Productive labour captures a (technologically) advanced economy and suggests that firms have time and resources to spend on knowledge creation. The three dimensions of the EU-SPI capture the social development of regions (Annoni and Dijkstra, 2017). The assumption is that knowledge workers – the workers responsible for knowledge creation and innovation in organizations – prefer to live in socially developed regions because those regions best cater to their personal and professional needs. Socially developed regions thus provide an environment wherein knowledge workers can be creative and contribute to innovation (Florida, 2002). The EU-SPI effectively suggests all three dimensions as INUS conditions for social progress, but perhaps not all three are necessary for regional innovation.

The EU-SPI dimension 'basic human needs' captures the provision of nutrition and basic medical care, water and sanitation, shelter and personal safety. Thinking thresholds and calibration, we are not interested in the provision of basic human needs but the provision of human needs to the extent that places become pleasant enough for knowledge workers to live in. This yields the condition 'human needs provided'. The EU-SPI dimension 'foundations of wellbeing' captures access to education, to information and communication (i.e., Internet, media), health and wellness and environmental quality. The presence of this dimension suggests that places offer more advanced amenities. Again, we are not interested in merely the foundations of wellbeing but also in the presence of enough of it to make regions attractive for knowledge workers. This yields the condition 'wellbeing provided'. The EU-SPI dimension 'opportunity' captures the protection of personal rights, personal freedom and choice, tolerance and inclusion and access to advanced education. Opportunity thus suggests that knowledge workers can develop both their personal and professional lives. Opportunity, as defined above, also encourages creativity because new ideas 'bubble up' and cross over between communities in places that are tolerant and inclusive. This condition becomes the condition 'opportunities available'.

The outcome is 'regional innovation', which in this example is the regional innovation score (RIS) from the European Regional Innovation Scoreboard (European Commission, 2016, 2017). The RIS is a composite score of patent application, expenditure on research and development, product and process innovation, marketing and organizational innovation, and sales of innovative products. It captures regions' innovative performance in a broad sense. As a condition, the outcome becomes 'innovative region'.

Note that the RIS score and the EU-SPI dimensions are composite measures. The scores are aggregated from multiple indicators. In fact, they are index scores, which I have argued are not ideal for set-theoretic studies. It is possible to go back to the raw data and aggregate indicator scores with logical ANDs and ORs. It would require a rationale for each AND and OR, which, in this case, is not obvious. However, since RIS and EU-SPI scores are considered meaningful (they are used in EU regional policy), it is legitimate to use them as they are.

The causal argument that may be developed from the above is as follows. The presence rather than the absence of each of the five explanatory conditions contributes to the emergence of causal power for knowledge creation. It is unclear which configurations of explanatory conditions are sufficient for causal power to emerge; however, the expectation is that some combination of hard and soft factors is necessary. As QCA is more of an explorative method (a dialogue), developing explicit configurational hypotheses is not required. If the state of configurational theorizing in a field allows, it is possible to 'test' configurational hypotheses. However, it is not enough to merely conclude that a configurational hypothesis is confirmed (or rejected). Researchers must still interpret why this is so and what that means, which still requires dialoguing knowledge of cases, context and concepts. Testing hypotheses in variable-based (correlational) methods suggests a clear distinction between the theoretical moment (developing hypotheses) and the empirical moment (testing them). Given its qualitative nature, QCA deliberately blurs this distinction (Mahoney and Goertz, 2006).

CASING AND CONFOUNDERS

Cases in this study are EU regions. More precisely, a case is a sizable territorial subdivision of an EU (i.e., economically and institutionally developed) country. Depending on data availability per country, either NUTS 1 or NUTS 2 regions are used as cases, with NUTS 1 regions typically being larger regions. This is unproblematic because the variation between the two categories is not larger than the variation within them (Rutten, 2019). For example, Andalucía (Spain) (87 599 km^2, 8.5 million inhabitants) is a NUTS 2 region, while Saarland (Germany) (2570 km^2, 1 million inhabitants) is a NUTS 1 region. Countries not subdivided into NUTS regions are excluded (Cyprus, Estonia, Latvia, Lithuania, Luxembourg and Malta) so as not to conflate country-level and regional-level dynamics. This defines a case population of 212 regions. There is a good deal of variation between those regions and one could easily introduce scope conditions to define a more homogeneous case population. I have done so in my 2019 study 'Openness values and regional innovation', where I included only those EU regions that were strongly economically and institutionally developed (ibid.). However, since EU regions form a clearly defined set of regions on which, as a whole, social and economic policy is performed, they are meaningful as a case population. Carefully selecting cases based on scope conditions is a very good way of constructing a case population; however, some given populations are meaningful as they are (Ragin, 2000, pp. 43–9). Yet, we still want to account for confounding conditions. Confounders are conditions that affect both the explanatory and the outcome conditions. More broadly, in a QCA study, a confounder may be any condition that is causally relevant but not an explanatory condition (Rutten, 2022; Rutten and Rubinson, 2022).

Confounders play a role after the truth table analysis. For each configuration in the solution, researchers establish whether the cases covered by that configurations 'have' (1) or 'do not have' (0) the confounding condition. If the distribution of 1s and 0s is more or less even, the presence or absence of the confounder is logically redundant in the configuration. A skewed distribution suggests that the configuration only explains the outcome for cases that 'have' (or 'do not have') the outcome (depending on the direction in which the distribution is skewed) (Ragin [1987] 2014, pp. 37–8; Rutten, 2023). This study uses two confounding conditions: GDP per capita and population density. GDP per capita captures whether a region is affluent, and affluent regions are generally more socially progressive (Annoni and Dijkstra, 2017). To the extent that innovation depends on technology investments, affluent regions will also be more innovative. Population density captures the urbanization of a region (European Commission, 2016, 2017), although with exceptions and not for all residents, urban regions (in developed countries) generally have a better quality of life because of the wider availability of quality-of-life amenities – from hospitals and schools to culture (Florida, Adler and Mellander, 2017). Urban regions are also home to a larger diversity of social and economic communities. This facilitates ideas crossing over between communities and, in turn, knowledge creation and innovation. What role, if any, these confounders play in EU regional innovation will become apparent from the confounding conditions analysis. Technically, there is no limit to the number of confounders in a QCA study. However, it would be remarkable to have more confounding than explanatory conditions. As always, substantive arguments must support the inclusion of confounders.

DATA AND CALIBRATION

Table 11.1 shows how data for this study are sourced from various Eurostat databases. Note that all conditions are worded as adjectives of 'region', so that conditions qualify cases. The information provided in Table 11.1 is no different from what is expected in other kinds of (large-N) studies. As argued in Chapter 8, calibration is best done from substantive and/or external criteria. The principal point is that QCA is a threshold method and that calibration must identify meaningful thresholds. Cases above and below a threshold – in particular, the crossover point – must be qualitatively different cases. Means, averages and percentiles are not substantively meaningful thresholds. Cases just above and below the average are all typical examples of average cases, and the same goes for means and percentiles. This makes means, averages and percentiles arbitrary criteria for setting thresholds and, by definition, calibrations based on them produce spurious patterns (set relationships) (Rubinson et al., 2019). Many large-N studies use data that are distanced from the cases they were collected from, as in the example of the above Eurostat databases. Nor is it possible to go back to the cases. The share of HRST workers in the regional workforce is a fairly abstract measure. It meaningfully characterizes a territory (NUTS region) but the connection to the innovation efforts going on in the territory is only assumed. Nor are there any HRST workers to go back to. Facing these difficulties, and in the absence of external and/or substantive criteria, sadly, many QCA researchers turn to means, averages and percentiles for calibration. Some even recommend it (Pappas and Woodside, 2021), but it is simply wrong. Using arbitrary thresholds is nonsensical. QCA cannot be the method that uniquely accepts spurious empirical patterns as genuine research findings.

Without intimate case knowledge and substantive and external criteria, large-N QCA researchers still have a number of options for setting meaningful thresholds. First, researchers can consider the scales used to collect the data. Often, scales have meaning, and Likert scales most conspicuously. Unfortunately, Eurostat converted the 'raw data' into z-scores for their SPI and their Regional Innovation Scoreboard. Z-scores are stripped of all meaning and merely capture standardized distributions, making them useless for calibration. Second, researchers may speak to experts to investigate what their data mean. Other researchers, practitioners, consultants, policymakers – anyone with an informed opinion on the data – may have something meaningful to say. Calibration is about finding plausible thresholds, not about finding the exact and undisputed critical values. Given epistemic relativism (see Chapter 1), undisputed critical values do not exist anyway. Third, researchers may look for gaps in their data (Schneider and Wagemann, 2012, pp. 35–7). Such gaps may be meaningful; they may separate qualitatively different cases. Investigating the cases on both sides of a gap will inform whether this is so. Particularly when the case population coincides with an entire given population, gaps in the data are meaningful and do not suggest missing cases. Rutten (2022) elaborates the looking-for-gaps approach by ranking cases.

For example, averaging the RIS for 2019–21, the highest RIS is 153.4. As there are 212 cases in the case population (see above), the highest RIS is 153.4 and ranked 212, and the lowest RIS is 15.9 and is ranked 1. Plotting ranks on the Y axis and data values on the X axis produces an S-curve. The gaps and breaks in this line suggest thresholds between different kinds of cases (Figure 11.1). For example, the lowest-ranked moderately innovative region is the Czech region of Central Bohemia, the region surrounding the capital region of Prague. This suggests strong economic links between this region and the Czech economic heartland. The highest-ranked somewhat innovative region is Abruzzo, a region that culturally and economically belongs to less-developed Southern Italy. It is separated from Rome by the Apennine Mountains and its economy depends largely on tourism and agriculture. This suggests the gap between these two regions as a plausible threshold between somewhat and moderately innovative regions, rather than the gap in the middle of the

Table 11.1   *Where the data come from*

Condition	Description	Source	Measure
Human needs-provided region	Basic human needs from the EU-SPI	EU-SPI 2016	Index from z-scores for multiple subdimensions
Wellbeing-provided region	Foundations of wellbeing from the EU-SPI	EU-SPI 2016	Index from z-scores for multiple subdimensions
Opportunities-available region	Opportunity from the EU-SPI	EU-SPI 2016	Index from z-scores for multiple subdimensions
HRST region	Workers employed in science and technology occupations and/ or having a higher education	Eurostat online database	Percentage of working population (2018)
Productive labour region	GDP divided by the labour force	Eurostat online database	GDP in €/workforce in 1000s (2016)
Affluent region	GDP per capita	Eurostat online database, Office for National Statistics (for UK regions)	GDP in € in purchasing parities (2016), GDP in £ in purchasing parities (2016) converted to € from the 2016 exchange rate of £1 = €1.2002
Densely populated region	Population density	Eurostat online database	Inhabitants per square kilometre (2018)
Innovative region	RIS, average RIS scores for 2019–21	European Regional Innovation Scoreboard (2019–21 editions)	Index from z-scores for multiple subdimensions

category of somewhat innovative regions, between Alentejo (Portugal) and Basilicata (Italy), which are two quite similar less-developed rural regions.

In sum, also for large-N studies with more distance to the cases, there are still multiple ways of identifying meaningful thresholds. If you choose to do QCA, you do so to connect meaning to data (Ragin, 2000, pp. 161–2; Rutten and Rubinson, 2022). If you cannot plausibly connect meaning to data, use another method to analyse your data.

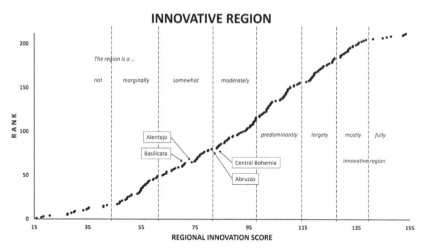

Figure 11.1   Calibrating by ranking

In this study, the ranking method was used to calibrate all explanatory, outcome and confounding conditions into eight categories. Following Figure 11.1, regions can be fully, mostly, largely, predominantly, moderately, somewhat, marginally or not-innovative regions. The threshold between moderately and predominantly innovative is the crossover point for all conditions. Note that this is the threshold between diluting and intensifying hedges (Lakoff, 1973). All categories 'predominantly' and higher become '1' (i.e., the statement, 'This is an innovative region' is logically true – viz., more true than false). Regions categorized as moderately and lower become '0' (i.e., the statement, 'This is an innovative region' is false – viz., more false than true) (see Chapter 8 for calibrating multilevel sets).

ANALYSIS OF NECESSITY

After all cases have been calibrated into a category, and the crossover point between true (1) and false (0) has been set, researchers first perform an analysis of necessity (see Figure 11.2). This analysis investigates whether conditions are supersets of the outcome. Using Ragin's fsQCA software (Ragin et al., 2023), this procedure is as follows:

1. Upload the calibrated data in the software, click the 'Analyze' tab and select 'Necessary conditions' (use .CSV files only in the fsQCA software).
2. The software now shows the 'Dialog' window (see the left pane of Figure 11.2). Select each condition to be investigated from the 'Add Condition' box and move it to the 'Conditions' box by clicking the -->.

3. When all conditions to be investigated are placed in the 'Conditions' box, select the outcome of interest in the 'Outcome' box.
4. Click 'OK' and inspect the results.

Researchers must perform separate analyses of necessity for the presence (innovative region) and absence (~innovative region) of the outcome. The software shows the superset consistencies and coverages for each condition, as shown in the right pane of Figure 11.2. To declare a condition mathematically necessary (a consistent and relevant superset of the outcome), superset consistency must be ≥ 0.9, and superset coverage must be ≥ 0.5. As Figure 11.2 shows, multiple conditions meet these thresholds. It is not at all uncommon to find no necessary conditions in a QCA study. Finding one or two necessary conditions is also plausible; however, finding that four of the five explanatory conditions are necessary is very suspicious. It more likely suggests a calibration issue rather than something substantive. Remember that the explanatory condition 'human needs provided' was calibrated from data capturing the provision of *basic* human needs. But we are not interested in merely basic human needs, rather in the provision of more substantial human needs to make an attractive home for knowledge workers. Perhaps the crossover point for human needs (rather than basic human needs) must be higher. If this were not an example to illustrate how QCA works, I would now have to recalibrate my cases – something that will happen at least once in most QCA studies. The same argument goes for 'wellbeing provided' and 'opportunities present'. Their crossover points seem to identify too basic levels of wellbeing and opportunities. That is, based on knowledge of concepts (the meaning of the explanatory conditions), it is not plausible to suggest these three explanatory conditions as necessary. Regardless of their superset consistencies and coverages passing the mathematical thresholds for necessity.

Productive labour only just passes the threshold for superset consistency. However, looking at gaps and breaks in the line is not an exact science. Moreover, would it really be impossible for a not-productive labour region to innovative? Nothing in the literature suggests so. Here too, substantive arguments suggest that it is not plausible to declare 'productive labour' necessary for 'innovative region'. Consequently, in spite of strong mathematical evidence, there are insufficient substantive arguments to declare any of these conditions necessary. In other words, QCA cannot be reduced to a mathematical exercise but must always be a dialogue between knowledge of cases, context and concepts – also in large-N studies with distance to cases.

	innovative		~innovative	
	consistency	coverage	consistency	coverage
human needs provided	0.96	0.74	0.28	0.26
wellbeing provided	0.93	0.77	0.22	0.23
opportunities available	0.93	0.80	0.19	0.20
HRST	0.87	0.79	0.19	0.21
productive labour	0.90	0.73	0.28	0.27
affluent	0.83	0.76	0.22	0.24
densely populated	0.68	0.70	0.24	0.30
~human needs provided	0.04	0.05	0.72	0.96
~wellbeing provided	0.07	0.07	0.78	0.93
~opportunities available	0.08	0.07	0.81	0.93
~HRST	0.14	0.12	0.81	0.88
~productive labour	0.10	0.11	0.72	0.89
~affluent	0.17	0.15	0.79	0.85
~densely populated	0.32	0.26	0.76	0.74

Figure 11.2   Necessary condition analysis

THE TRUTH TABLE

Table 11.2 is the truth table for 'innovative region'. It has five conditions and, consequently, $2^5 = 32$ rows. The first thing to notice is limited diversity. Of the 32 rows, only 19 are populated, but 65 per cent of cases cluster in just the first two rows and 84 per cent cluster in the first five rows. This kind of limited diversity is common in QCA. It evidences how strongly interconnected conditions are on the case level. There really is no such thing as an independent variable in social reality. Even a fairly large-N of 212 cases shows strong limited diversity. At this point in the analysis, the outcome column of a truth table is empty. We need to set consistency and frequency thresholds to decide whether a row may be declared sufficient (i.e., logically true). For larger-N studies (> 50), it is common to set a frequency threshold > 1. Sparsely populated rows may be exceptional cases that should not be included in the first step of the minimization, which considers populated rows only. However, in this example, the truth table describes the entire population of EU regions. Sparsely populated rows are not 'outliers' to be ignored but genuine features of the case population that should be included. Therefore, the frequency threshold is set at 1 and all populated rows are included in the first step of the minimization.

Note that this is a crisp set truth table where proportional reduction in inconsistency (PRI) values are not relevant. In fuzzy set truth tables, researchers must also set a PRI threshold. Unless one has reason to do otherwise, the consistency threshold in the truth table is 0.8. This produces five contradictory rows (Rows 1, 3, 4, 5 and 6). Rows 4 and 6 need no further consideration because of their low consistencies. These rows get a '0' in their outcome

Table 11.2 Truth table for 'innovative region'

Row	Human needs	Wellbeing	Opportunity	HRST	Productive Labour	No. of Cases	Innovative Region	Consistency
1	1	1	1	1	1	78 (36%)	1	0.884615
2	0	0	0	0	0	60 (65%)	0	0
3	1	1	1	1	0	16 (72%)	1	0.625
4	0	0	0	0	1	14 (79%)	0	0.071429
5	1	1	1	0	1	10 (84%)	1	0.7
6	1	0	0	0	1	7 (87%)	0	0.428571
7	1	0	0	0	0	5 (89%)	0	0
8	0	0	0	1	0	5 (92%)	0	0
9	0	1	0	0	0	3 (93%)	0	0
10	1	1	0	0	1	2 (94%)	1	1
11	0	0	1	1	1	2 (95%)	1	1
12	1	0	1	0	0	2 (96%)	0	0
13	1	1	1	0	0	2 (97%)	0	0
14	1	0	0	1	1	1 (97%)	1	1
15	0	1	1	1	1	1 (98%)	1	1
16	1	1	0	0	0	1 (98%)	0	0
17	0	1	0	0	1	1 (99%)	0	0
18	0	0	0	1	1	1 (99%)	0	0
19	0	1	0	1	1	1 (100%)	0	0

Row	Human needs	Wellbeing	Opportunity	HRST	Productive Labour	No. of Cases	Innovative Region	Consistency
20	0	0	1	0	0	0		
21	0	1	1	0	0	0		
22	1	0	0	1	0	0		
23	0	1	0	1	0	0		
24	1	1	0	1	0	0		
25	0	0	1	1	0	0		
26	1	1	1	1	0	0		
27	0	0	1	1	0	0		
28	0	0	1	0	1	0		
29	1	0	1	0	1	0		
30	0	1	1	0	1	0		
31	1	1	0	1	1	0		
32	1	0	1	1	1	0		

column. Technically, Row 1 is a contradictory row; however, at 0.89, its consistency is generously above the threshold so it may safely be declared sufficient and get a '1' in the outcome column. That leaves Rows 3 and 5 for further investigation. At 0.63, the consistency of Row 3 is mathematically far too low. It covers ten innovative and six not-innovative regions, all of them rural and suburban regions with a core city located within them. The 'positive' cases are Brandenburg, Chemnitz, Thuringia, North East England, Yorkshire and the Humber, East Midlands, West Midlands, South West England, Wales and Scotland. Their urban cores are relatively large – for example, Potsdam and the Berlin agglomeration for Brandenburg and Newcastle–Sunderland for North East England. The 'negative' cases are Mecklenburg–Western Pomerania, Lüneburg, Trier, Asturias, Cantabria and Western Slovenia. Their urban centres are relatively small – for example, Rostock for Mecklenburg– Western Pomerania and Ljubljana for Western Slovenia. Innovation in these regions may be happening mostly in their core urban areas. However, for the 'negative' cases, the urban core may be too small to 'lift' the entire region across the threshold for 'innovative region', but the causal power for innova- tion still also emerges in these smaller urban centres. Therefore, Row 3 may be declared sufficient. The same argument can be made for Row 5. In fact, two of the positive cases covered by this row (Zeeland and Drenthe) have small urban cores. However, they are also small regions, so the innovative activities in the small urban cores still 'lift' the whole region across the threshold for 'innovative region'. So Row 5, although mathematically insufficient, may also be declared sufficient.

At this point it helps to go back to the above causal argument. Innovation is defined as the outcome of a process of knowledge creation by knowl- edge workers. Being an innovative region suggests that knowledge creation 'happens' successfully in that region. That is, regional data are used to capture social interaction that does not necessarily 'happen' on that geographical scale. We thus need to develop a plausible argument that, given the conditions describing the region, it is possible for knowledge workers to successfully engage in knowledge creation. Dialoguing knowledge of cases, context and concepts suggests that the presence of [needs • wellbeing • opportunity • HRST] (i.e., Row 3) and the presence of [needs • wellbeing • opportunity • ~HRST] (Row 5) allows knowledge workers in the urban cores of a region to be innovative. The scale of their innovation activities may or may not be enough to 'lift' the region as a whole across the threshold for innovation. However, regional borders may not overlap with the economic spaces of knowledge workers. Yet, the dialogue makes it plausible to suggest that Rows 3 and 5 capture a causal power for innovation in regions' urban cores. Therefore, these rows may be declared sufficient (i.e., true). This is what dialoguing knowledge of cases, context and concept, by going back to the cases in Rows 3 and 5, may accomplish. Also in large-N studies, researchers must perform this dialogue.

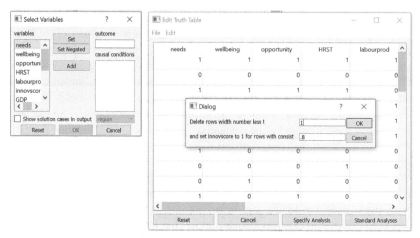

Figure 11.3   Truth table analysis (1)

In the fsQCA software, the analysis thus far performed is as follows:

1. Open the file, click the 'Analyze' tab and select 'Truth table analysis'. This opens the 'Select Variables' box (Figure 11.3) (of course, they are conditions not variables).
2. Select the explanatory conditions from the 'variables' column and click 'Add' to move them to the 'causal conditions' column (of course, they are explanatory conditions, not causal conditions).
3. Select the outcome from the 'variables' column and click on 'Set' (or 'Set Negated' to perform a truth table analysis for the absence of the outcome).
4. Check the box 'Show solution cases in output'. This identifies the cases in each truth table row and in each configuration of the solution.
5. Click 'OK' to start the truth table analysis.
6. In the next window, the 'Edit Truth Table' window, click the 'Edit' tab and select 'Delete and Code'. This opens the 'Dialog' window where researchers can set frequency and consistency thresholds. In this example, I keep the default values of 1 (frequency) and 0.8 (consistency). Clicking 'OK' puts a '1' in the outcome column for all rows that meet the frequency and consistency thresholds and a '0' in the remaining rows. The outcome column for unpopulated rows remains empty. These rows are available for counterfactual assumptions. Researchers can manually adjust the outcome value from '0' to '1' for rows that are mathematically

insufficient but where substantive knowledge suggests they do explain the outcome – Rows 3 and 5 in this example. Always carefully explain how the logical values '1' and '0' have been assigned to truth table rows in a research paper and explain how contradictory rows have been resolved.

7. For the next step of the analysis click 'Standard Analysis' at the bottom of the 'Edit Truth Table' window. This may result in a 'Prime Implicant Chart' appearing (Figure 11.4). This happens when the algorithm identifies multiple possible prime implicants to simplify the same primitive expression (truth table row). In the example in Figure 11.4, the primitive expression [~needs • ~wellbeing • opportunity • HRST • labourprod][1] may be simplified to three prime implicants. If researchers have substantive, theoretical or empirical arguments to prefer one particular prime implicant, they can select it by checking the box in front of it. Barring such arguments, simply click 'Select All' and 'OK'. The software now shows the 'Intermediate Solution' window. If knowledge of cases, context and concepts suggests that the presence of a condition contributes to the emerging of causal power, check 'Present' for that condition. Check 'Absent' if the absence of a condition contributes to the emerging of causal power. Going back to an earlier example, the absence of 'low income' contributes to the emerging of causal power for 'feeling happy'. If researchers cannot or do not want to commit to either the presence or absence of a condition contributing to causal power emerging, check 'Present' or 'Absent'. The algorithm will never minimize this condition away. When directional assumptions are made for all conditions, click 'OK' and inspect the solution.

The software shows the information in Figure 11.5 for all three solutions. It conveniently identifies the datafile ('File') used for the analysis and where it is located on your computer. 'Model' identifies the outcome and the explanatory conditions as: outcome = f(condition *i*, condition *ii*, condition *n*). It also shows that the Quine–McCluskey algorithm was used for the Boolean minimization. For the intermediate solution, the directional assumptions are also identified (note that by accepting Row 3 in Table 11.2 as 'true' we have effectively lowered the consistency threshold to 0.625). The next line identifies which of the three solutions is shown (the complex solution in Figure 11.5), followed by the frequency and consistency threshold for the truth table analysis. The subsequent lines identify the various configurations in the solution. For each configuration, raw and unique coverages and (subset) consistency are given. Note that the software reports six or even seven digits for these metrics but that is spurious specificity. Reporting two digits suffices. In addition, the solution coverage and (subset) consistency are given. The software further identifies the cases that each configuration covers – if you have checked 'Show solution

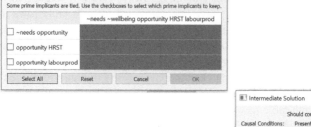

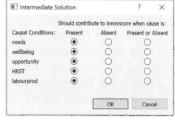

Figure 11.4   Truth table analysis (2)

cases in output' earlier. The set membership in both the configuration and the outcome is shown for each case. For example, but not shown in Figure 11.5, Lower Bavaria is identified in the software as '(1,1)'– indicating that it has a membership of '1' in the configuration as well as in the outcome. Cases whose membership in the configuration is ≤ its membership in the outcome are confirming cases. Disconfirming cases have a higher membership in the configuration than in the outcome (see Chapter 7). Since we have already dealt with contradictory cases in the truth table analysis, this information is useful but of no further consequence.

Table 11.3 shows the three solution types for the above truth table, and it demonstrates that the complex solution is a subset of the intermediate solution, which is itself a subset of the parsimonious solution. For reasons elucidated in Chapter 10, the intermediate solution is the one to interpret into a causal in explanation in QCA studies.

INTERPRETING THE SOLUTION

The intermediate solution has four configurations, all of which are mathematically unproblematic because of their high consistencies (ranging from 0.84 to 0.89). Their raw coverages are very high (0.73 to 0.82) while their unique coverages are very low, the latter usually being the case in a QCA study (Figure 11.6). It tells us that regions are innovative for multiple reasons; multiple causal powers emerge in any one region. This, in turn, suggests that different kinds of knowledge-creating (innovative) activities 'happen' in the same territory. Economic geography theory suggests it is quite plausible that differ-

```
**********************
*TRUTH TABLE ANALYSIS*
**********************
```

File: C:/Users/rprutten/surfdrive/Data/0word/QCA book/data chapter 11/calibrated crisp - predominantly = 1.csv
Model: innovscore = f(needs, wellbeing, opportunity, HRST, labourprod)
Algorithm: Quine-McCluskey

--- COMPLEX SOLUTION ---
frequency cutoff: 1
consistency cutoff: 0.625

	raw coverage	unique coverage	consistency
needs*wellbeing*~HRST*labourprod	0.09375	0.09375	0.75
~needs*opportunity*HRST*labourprod	0.03125	0.03125	1
needs*wellbeing*opportunity*HRST	0.822917	0.822917	0.840426
needs*~wellbeing*~opportunity*HRST*labourprod	0.0104167	0.0104166	1

solution coverage: 0.958333
solution consistency: 0.836364

Figure 11.5   Truth table analysis output

Table 11.3   Three solution types

Complex Solution
(1) needs • wellbeing • ~HRST • labourprod
(2) needs • ~wellbeing • ~opportunity • HRST • labourprod
(3) ~needs • opportunity • HRST • labourprod
(4) needs • wellbeing • opportunity • HRST
Intermediate Solution
(1) needs • wellbeing • labourprod
(2) needs • HRST • labourprod
(3) opportunity • HRST • labourprod
(4) needs • wellbeing • opportunity • HRST
Parsimonious Solution
(1) needs • wellbeing • labourprod
(2) needs • HRST
(3.1) opportunity • labourprod
(3.2) ~needs • opportunity
(4) opportunity • HRST

ent communities of knowledge workers in the same region employ different 'modes' of knowledge creation, as well as interactions happening between the various modes of knowledge creation (Asheim and Coenen, 2005; Morgan, 1997, 2004; Rutten, 2019). In fact, case-based researchers often expect their cases to be 'overdetermined' (see Chapter 2). Because of their holistic nature, multiple causal explanations apply to the same case (Goertz and Mahoney, 2012a). In QCA, configurations suggest generalizable causal explanations and the cases they cover provide singular causal evidence for them, and the same case may provide singular causal evidence in support of multiple configurations. The solution coverage (Figure 11.6) is very high (0.96), which means that the solution explains nearly all innovative regions (i.e., cases 'having' the outcome). At 0.84, the solution consistency is also high.

intermediate solution	I	IIa	IIb	III
OUTCOME: INNOVATIVE REGION	regionally embedded (1)	knowledge economy (2)	knowledge economy (3)	quality of life (4)
NEEDS PROVIDED	●	●		●
WELLBEING PROVIDED	●			●
OPPORTUNITIES AVAILABLE			●	●
HRST		●	●	●
PRODUCTIVE LABOUR	●	●	●	
Cases (confirming/contradictory)	90 (78/12)	79 (70/9)	81 (79/9)	94 (79/5)
Coverage (unique)	0.81 (0.09)	0.73 (0.01)	0.75 (0.03)	0.82 (0.10)
consistency	0.87	0.89	0.89	0.84
Solution coverage	0.96			
Solution consistency	0.84			
AFFLUENT	●	●	●	●
DENSELY POPULATED				

● condition present   ⊗ condition absent   [BLANK] condition logically redundant

Figure 11.6   Solution table for 'innovative region'

So what does all this mean? First of all, note that every configuration includes at least one social progress and one economic development dimension. This suggests that innovation 'happens' in regions that are both socially progressed and economically developed (which does not necessarily imply a one-directional causality – see Chapter 10). Consequently, successful regional innovation policy cannot exclusively focus on strengthening regional economies. It must also turn regions into attractive places for knowledge workers to live. It further suggests that all three social progress dimensions may be necessary for a basic level of social progress (see Chapter 8). However, once each dimension is present in its basic form, the presence of only one dimension in a more advanced form is required to make a region attractive for knowledge workers. Let's look at intermediate solution Configuration 1 in Table 11.3: [needs • wellbeing • labourprod]. It covers 90 regions of all kinds and sizes. However, regions uniquely covered by Configuration 1 (regions that are innovative for this reason only) are Lower Bavaria (DE22), Upper Palatinate (DE23), Detmold (DEA4), Arnsberg (DEA5), Trento (ITH2) and Zeeland (NL34).[2] Since these regions are uniquely covered by Configuration 1, they may be considered typical cases of that configuration. These regions are all non-core regions in their respective countries, though neither peripheral nor particularly rural. They may be home to innovative activities that are too expensive to perform in urbanized, core regions – for example, large R&D facilities (Florida et al., 2017; Shearmur, 2011, 2012). Their innovative activities may also be based on regionally embedded skills, competences and communities (Bennat, 2021; Punstein and Glückler, 2020). That HRST is logically redundant in this configuration suggests that these innovative activities are more applied and less high-tech. Regions covered by Configuration 1 are pleasant enough places to live in (human needs and wellbeing are provided); however, 'opportunities' being logically redundant suggests that the innovative activities are not entrepreneurially driven. They may result more from methodical improvements of products, practices and technologies. Configuration 1 also seems to capture innovative activities that are subsidiary to those in core firms and core regions. Core firms and regions may want to draw from the specific regionally embedded skills, competences and communities. All this suggests Configuration 1 as the 'regionally embedded innovation' configuration. It captures a causal power that emerges from knowledge creation that is embedded in regional communities of knowledge workers and their specific skills and competences and from these regions offering attractive living conditions for knowledge workers.

Note how this interpretation follows from a dialogue between knowledge of cases, context and concepts, even if knowledge of cases is limited. It demonstrates how inference in QCA is qualitative and interpretive rather than empirical. This is the kind of discussion that QCA researchers must conduct in their papers – and draw even more strongly from the literature than I did in this example. Interpreting configurations is an essential part of theorizing in a QCA study (Furnari et al., 2021; Ragin [1987] 2014). Drawing from the first stage of theorizing – where concepts are defined and their meaning explained – it develops configurational explanations that go beyond what may be achieved with correlational (variable-based) methods.

Intermediate solution Configuration 2 in Table 11.3 [needs • HRST • labourprod] and Configuration 3 [opportunity • HRST • labourprod] are very similar. They explain innovation in economically developed ('labourprod') and knowledge-intensive ('HRST') regions that are at least in some way attractive for knowledge workers [needs OR opportunity]. The presence of 'opportunity' in Configuration 3 suggests a more entrepreneurially driven kind of innovation; however, both configurations may be labelled 'knowledge economy' configurations. They seem to augment conventional knowledge-based explanations of regional innovation (e.g., Florida, 2002; Hassink and Klaerding, 2012; Howells, 2012) by including social progress. Knowledge creation is not a stylized concept but a social activity performed by knowledge workers – that is, by people who have a life, and regional economic theorizing needs to account for it. Configurations 2 and 3 may thus be written as: [HRST • labourprod • (needs + opportunity)], which makes 'needs' and 'opportunity' both SUIN conditions in the knowledge economy configuration.

In intermediate solution Configuration 4 in Table 11.3 [needs • wellbeing • opportunity • HRST], causal power for innovation emerges from the presence of all three social progress dimensions and the presence of HRST – that is, of knowledge workers. This suggests that knowledge workers enjoy the quality of life in these regions, and that may be the reason they are there. This is in line with Florida's (2002) argument that for the 'creative class' (Florida's terms for creative [innovative) knowledge workers), jobs follow people. The presence of knowledge workers from multiple knowledge domains may also mean that knowledge may cross over easily between different communities of practice to further fuel knowledge creation. Configuration 4 may be labelled the 'quality-of-life' configuration.

Dialoguing knowledge of cases, context and concepts thus interprets the (four) configurations into (three) different explanations of regional innovation. Figure 11.6 gives a unique number for each configuration (1–4), but also identifies that interpreting the configurations yields only three different explanations (I, IIa, IIb, III). Different explanations corroborate different economic geography theories. While variable-based theorizing may become a horse race – which variable from which theory has the largest effect – configurational theorizing recognizes the complexity of social reality and the need to draw from multiple theories to explain it (Ragin [1987] 2014). Note further that interpreting configurations is neither explicitly explanatory nor explicitly exploratory but has elements of both, because QCA blurs the distinction between the theoretical and empirical 'moments' of a study (see above). As good practice, always report the solution as a Boolean expression, as in this example:

$$[\text{needs} \bullet \text{wellbeing} \bullet \text{labourprod}] + [\text{HRST} \bullet \text{labourprod} \bullet \\ (\text{needs} + \text{opportunity})] + \\ [\text{needs} \bullet \text{wellbeing} \bullet \text{opportunities} \bullet \text{HRST}] \\ \rightarrow \text{innovative region} \qquad (11.1)$$

CORE AND CONTRIBUTORY CONDITIONS

Peer Fiss (2011) suggested that conditions featuring in the parsimonious solution are 'core conditions'. If even logically contradictory assumptions cannot minimize a condition, argues Fiss, it must be important. Core conditions are fundamental to the emergence of causal power. However, their empirical relevance does not necessarily elevate their explanatory significance. Core conditions are not more 'causal'. Conditions featuring only in the intermediate solution but which are minimized from the parsimonious solution, are contributory conditions. In solution tables, core conditions are visualized as large (e.g., as in Figure 11.7) while contributory conditions are small dots. Fiss' is an elegant argument and it recognizes that we can also learn something from the parsimonious solution, even if it does not causally explain the outcome. However, it is a strictly mathematical argument. Core conditions are core because they are in the parsimonious solution, not because a substantive argument suggests they have an elevated importance. This may lead to conflicts. For example, the parsimonious solution in Table 11.3 minimizes 'productive labour' from Configuration 2, which suggests it as a contributory condition, while 'needs' and 'HRST' are core conditions. In Configuration 3, the parsimonious solution minimizes 'HRST', suggesting it as a contributory condition, and now 'opportunity' and 'productive labour' are core conditions. However, on substantive grounds, I have suggested in the above that Configurations 2 and 3 capture the same causal power (the 'knowledge economy' configuration) and that 'needs' and 'opportunity' are SUIN conditions. This suggests 'needs' and 'opportunity' as contributory conditions and 'HRST' and 'productive labour' as core conditions (Figure 11.7).

	Fiss' (2011) mathematical approach				Substantive approach			
	1	2	3	4	1	2	3	4
needs	●	●		•	●	•		●
wellbeing	●			•	●			●
opportunity			●	●			•	●
HRST		●	•	●		●	●	●
productive labour	●	•	●		●	●	●	

● core condition   ● contributory condition

Figure 11.7   Core and contributory conditions

It should come as no surprise that I prefer the substantive approach to identifying core and contributory conditions. Having said that, Fiss's argument is set-theoretically perfectly sound. It is for researchers to decide which approach to core and contributory conditions best helps them interpret their findings. However, I would argue against identifying core and contributory conditions at all if that distinction plays no further role in explaining the outcome.

CONFOUNDING CONDITIONS

To investigate whether 'affluent' and 'densely populated' are indeed confounding conditions, consider the proportion of regions in each configuration that 'have' these conditions. Of the 90 cases covered by Configuration 1 (Figure 11.6), 78 are affluent regions (their GDP per capita is above the threshold for predominantly affluent), while 12 are not-affluent regions. That is, 86 per cent of the cases are affluent regions and 14 per cent are not-affluent regions. Multiplying the proportions of [confounder] and [~confounder] cases produces a score that is maximally 0.25 (0.50 * 0.50 – when 50 per cent of the cases 'have' the confounding condition) and minimally 0 (0 * 1 – when all cases either 'have' or 'do not have' the confounding condition). Dividing this product by 0.25 produces a score between 0 and 1 – the heterogeneity score (Rutten, 2022):

$$\text{heterogeneity score} = \frac{(\text{proportion confounder cases})*(\text{proportion ~confounder cases})}{0.25} \quad (11.2)$$

For Configuration 1, this works out as $\frac{(0.87 * 0.13)}{0.25}$ = 0.45. A heterogeneity score of 1 means that the cases covered by the configuration are maximally heterogeneous (a 50–50 split) in terms of their membership in the confounding condition. This suggests the confounding condition as logically redundant. 'Having' or 'not-having' the confounder is irrelevant for 'having' membership in the configuration. On the other hand, a heterogeneity score of 0 means that the cases covered by the configuration are fully homogeneous in their 'having' or 'not having' the confounder. This suggests that the confounding condition is set-theoretically relevant; only cases that 'have' (or 'do not have') the confounding condition 'have' membership in the configuration. Heterogeneity scores of '0' and '1' are ideal-typical cases; however, connecting to QCA's default consistency threshold, a heterogeneity score of ≥ 0.8 suggests that the confounding condition is logically redundant – that it is, in fact, not a confounder. Of course, 0.8 is not a hard cut-off. As with all QCA metrics, there is room for interpretation. Table 11.4 shows the proportions of confounder

Table 11.4   *Heterogeneity scores*

	Affluent Regions	~Affluent Regions	Heterogeneity Score	Densely Populated Regions	~Densely Populated Regions	Heterogeneity Score
Config. 1	77/90 (0.86)	13/90 (0.14)	0.48	55/90 (0.61)	35/90 (0.39)	0.95
Config. 2	70/79 (0.89)	9/79 (0.11)	0.39	51/79 (0.65)	28/79 (0.35)	0.91
Config. 3	72/81 (0.89)	9/81 (0.11)	0.39	53/81 (0.65)	28/81 (0.35)	0.91
Config. 4	79/94 (0.84)	15/94 (0.16)	0.53	57/94 (0.61)	37/94 (0.39)	0.95

and ~confounder cases and the corresponding heterogeneity scores for all four configurations.

The results are conclusive – the configurations describe causal powers that emerge in affluent regions. This means that 'affluent' is a confounder. However, 'densely populated' is not a confounding condition. Causal powers implied by the configurations emerge in densely and not-densely populated regions alike. It may be that a condition is a confounder in one configuration but not in another. This would have different implications for theorizing than the above result. Confounding conditions may be visualized in a solution table as in the example in Figure 11.6. Note how the solution table is densely packed with information. It is at once a description of the cross-case patterns in the case population and an interpretation of what they mean, the latter in the form of the configuration labels.

ROBUSTNESS TESTS

QCA uses several robustness tests. They are relevant for large-N studies based on samples rather than constructed case populations. The best thing to do is to construct a case population rather than using a sample, also in large-N QCA (see Chapter 4). Or to use the whole of a given population, as in this example, which is not a sample either. The rationale behind robustness tests lies in QCA's case sensitivity. Small changes in the number of cases, the crossover point and consistency and frequency thresholds in the truth table may substantially impact the solution. This happens when cases 'migrate' to the other side of the crossover point and when populated rows become empty, and vice versa. However, when one has carefully selected one's cases and when one has carefully calibrated them, all this is perfectly unproblematic. Having done so, one will always find the 'correct' solution; the solution that 'belongs' to the case population as the researcher defined it. Changes in the definition of cases, the inclusion or exclusion of cases, changes to the crossover point and changes to the consistency and frequency thresholds in the truth table define different case populations – and one would expect to find different solutions for them (Rutten, 2022, 2023; Skaaning, 2011). QCA's case sensitivity then becomes a strength. However, for a variety of reasons, QCA researchers may have to, or choose to, work with samples rather than constructed case populations. Robustness tests are helpful to identify how sensitive the solution is in those situations.

I have discussed QCA's most important robustness tests in my paper 'Applying and assessing large-N QCA' (Rutten, 2022) and I refer readers to that paper to learn more about them. Here I will only mention the most common robustness checks:

• Randomly delete 5 or 10 per cent of the cases and redo the superset and subset analyses. This procedure may be repeated several times.
• Set somewhat higher and lower but still plausible crossover points and redo the analyses.
• Set somewhat higher and lower consistency thresholds in the truth table and redo the analyses.
• Set somewhat higher and lower frequency thresholds in the truth table and redo the analyses.

The original solution is considered very robust when the exact same solution is produced for different case populations, crossover points and consistency and frequency thresholds. The solution is robust when different settings identify all configurations of the original solution as subsets or supersets of the original configurations – that is, when configurations for the alternate settings have fewer (supersets) or more (subsets) conditions. The solution is considered not-robust when one or more of the initial configurations are not identified in the alternate analyses, or when the alternate analyses produce one or more configurations that are not in the original solution. The question, of course, is: what does it mean when a solution is not robust, and does it matter? What it means is that changes in the case population, crossover point and frequency and consistency thresholds produce different solutions. That is simply how QCA works. However, even big differences following from small changes do not invalidate the solution. The solution is still the correct solution for the case population as defined by the researcher and, therefore, meaningful. It is far more damaging from a validity perspective if a researcher has no clear legitimization for how the case population is defined. Sloppy calibration and sloppy definitions of cases and populations produce spurious results in case-based methods – a flaw that no amount of robustness testing will remedy. Meaningful case and case population definitions always produce meaningful results, regardless of their robustness. Nor is QCA a method for empirical generalization (see Chapter 4), which greatly reduces the relevance of robustness tests in QCA.

In sum, as I see it, robustness tests are a feature to make QCA more empirical or at least to give the impression of empirical precision. However, given QCA's qualitative nature, the practical (methodological) relevance of robustness tests is (very) limited for interpreting the validity of a solution. Solutions are logical statements whose meaning is interpreted from dialoguing knowledge of cases, context and concepts. They are not empirical findings in the way that the findings of correlational methods are empirical. Therefore, QCA's findings do not require the empirical robustness that is expected of correlational methods. Robustness in QCA is much more a function of the plausibility of a researcher's choices and interpretations; of interpreting configurations (domain of the Empirical) into possibilistic claims about causal powers (domain of the Real).

EXPLAINING THE ABSENCE OF REGIONAL INNOVATION

Because causality in QCA is asymmetrical, a separate analysis is required for the absence of the outcome. This means that all the above steps must be repeated to explain the absence of regional innovation. The analysis of necessity (above) identified no consistent supersets of the set of not-innovative regions. Always check manually whether the truth table for the negation of the outcome does not contain any logical contradictions. A row that is true in the truth table for Y, must be false in the truth table for $\sim Y$. Nor can easy counterfactuals for Y be available for counterfactual assumptions for $\sim Y$. This is not the case in the present example, nor does the truth table for not-innovative regions contain contradictory rows that need further investigations (Table 11.5).

The truth table analysis for not-innovative regions produces two configurations: [$\sim$HRST • labourprod] and [$\sim$needs • $\sim$opportunity] (Table 11.6). It is enough just to report the intermediate solution for the absence of the outcome and refer all relevant tables and figures to an annex. Researchers only need to explain what the analysis of $\sim Y$ means. Be aware that the solution of $\sim Y$ does not explain why the outcome does not occur. Instead, it explains why the causal power that makes the outcome possible does not emerge (in those cases where the outcome is absent). If the solution for Y identifies causal powers,

Table 11.5   *Truth table for not-innovative regions*

Row	Human Needs	Wellbeing	Opportunity	HRST	Productive Labour	Number of Cases	~Innovative Region	Consistency
1	1	1	1	1	1	78	0	0.115385
2	0	0	0	0	0	60	1	1
3	1	1	1	1	0	16	0	0.375
4	0	0	0	0	1	14	1	0.928571
5	1	1	1	0	1	10	0	0.3
6	1	0	0	0	1	7	0	0.571429
7	1	0	0	0	0	5	1	1
8	0	0	0	1	0	5	1	1
9	0	1	1	0	0	3	1	1
10	1	0	1	0	0	2	1	1
11	1	1	1	0	0	2	1	1
12	1	1	1	1	1	2	0	0
13	0	0	1	0	1	2	0	0
14	1	1	1	0	0	1	1	1
15	0	1	0	0	1	1	1	1
16	0	0	0	1	1	1	1	1
17	0	1	0	1	1	1	1	1
18	1	0	0	1	1	1	0	0
19	0	1	1	1	1	1	0	0

Row	Human Needs	Wellbeing	Opportunity	HRST	Productive Labour	Number of Cases	~Innovative Region	Consistency
20	0	0	1	0	0	0		
21	0	1	1	0	0	0		
22	1	0	0	1	0	0		
23	0	1	0	1	0	0		
24	1	1	0	1	0	0		
25	0	0	1	1	0	0		
26	1	0	1	1	0	0		
27	0	1	1	1	0	0		
28	0	0	1	0	1	0		
29	1	0	1	0	1	0		
30	0	1	1	0	1	0		
31	1	1	0	1	1	0		
32	1	0	1	1	1	0		

the solution for ~*Y* identifies constraints – that is, what prevents causal power from emerging.

Configuration 5 in Table 11.6 (remember to assign each configuration a unique number, so do not start again with 1 for the configurations in the solution for ~*Y*) [not-HRST AND productive labour] suggests that the presence of productive labour cannot compensate for the absence of HRST; that in a not-knowledge-intensive economy, the causal power for regional innovation will not emerge from productive labour alone. Or that, in the absence of HRST, productive labour will not 'produce' enough innovations to push the region over the threshold for 'innovative region'. Configuration 6 suggests that, in the absence of 'human needs provided' and 'opportunities available', a region is not sufficiently attractive for knowledge workers to settle in large enough numbers to 'make' the region an innovative region. In other words, either being a not-knowledge-intensive region or being a not-attractive region for knowledge workers constrains the emergence of causal power for regional innovation.

Table 11.6   Solution for not-innovative region

(Intermediate Solution)	Coverage		Consistency
	Raw	Unique	
(5) ~HRST • labourprod	0.63	0.09	1.00
(6) ~needs • ~opportunity	0.72	0.18	0.99
Solution coverage	*0.81*		
Solution consistency	*0.99*		

Frequency threshold: 1; consistency threshold: 0.928; counterfactual assumption: all conditions absent

While causal powers (the analysis of *Y*) point at 'things' that must be in place if the outcome is to be possible, constraints (the analysis of ~*Y*) point at 'things' that must be removed or eliminated for the outcome to be possible. Thinking along these lines does justice to QCA's asymmetrical causality. It contributes to more sophisticated explanations of phenomena in social reality because configurations for *Y* and ~*Y* must be theorized differently.

NOTES

1. Note the • symbol is absent on the software.
2. The codes in brackets are NUTS codes for the regions.

12. Getting QCA right: a small-N example

This chapter draws together what it means to do QCA. It uses a small-N example to contrast it with the large-N example of the previous chapter and to demonstrate how qualitative (interview) data may be used in the dialogue between knowledge of cases, context and concepts. The qualitative data in this example is too thin for a proper study but still illustrates how to use this kind of data. The chapter is brief. Its purpose is not to introduce new material but to illustrate how QCA is done. The steps in this chapter provide the basic structure for QCA studies. If you can follow the deliberately brief discussions in this chapter and understand why they lead to the conclusions they do, you understand QCA. You will be able to learn from cases with QCA.

EXPLANATORY CONDITIONS AND CAUSAL POWERS

The previous chapter investigated knowledge creation in regions. This chapter explains knowledge creation in regional networks, although its purpose is to demonstrate (small-N) QCA rather than to contribute to the (regional) knowledge-creation literature. As argued, knowledge creation is a human activity that is organized in firms and their networks (Faulconbridge, 2014; Rutten, 2014). How knowledge creation is organized decides its efficacy (Nonaka, 1994). This study investigates knowledge creation in so-called regional clusters. Clusters in this context are small networks of two to five firms, mostly SMEs, in the manufacturing industry in the Dutch Eindhoven region (Romme, 2022). This region is home to high-tech giants such as Philips and ASML, but faced disastrous economic decline in the mid-1990s. In response, an EU co-funded cluster scheme was developed, which facilitated regional manufacturing SMEs to form small networks (clusters) to work on product development. These clusters would strengthen the regional economy by forging regional collaborations on innovation. From 1994 to 2006, a total of 102 cluster projects were funded. Projects lasted two years on average and most introduced their new product on the market. In 2006, I was involved in an evaluation of the cluster scheme and collected data on 41 of the clusters. Using that data, the present study investigates how knowledge creation was organized in the clusters and whether that explains cluster knowledge creation (Rutten and Oerlemans, 2009).

The (organizational) knowledge-creation literature suggests that knowledge creation requires both tight and loose control (Butler et al., 1998; Gebert, Boerner and Kearney, 2010; Nonaka, 1994). Tight control emphasizes focus and efficiency, while loose control emphasizes creativity and adaptability. Tight control aligns the knowledge-creation effort with organizational goals, while loose control allows the human agents involved in the knowledge-creation process to address unforeseen problems and pursue opportunities. Too much emphasis on tight control (error of tightness) frustrates creativity, while too much emphasis on looseness (error of looseness) weakens the efficacy of knowledge creation.

This suggests the configurational hypothesis that the causal power for knowledge creation emerges from tight control and loose control. Using two tight-control and two loose-control conditions enables the investigation of this hypothesis as well as whether tight and loose control are equally important. So, we want to know which configurations of tight-control and loose-control conditions explain successful knowledge creation in the above clusters.

The outcome of this study is knowledge creation. A cluster is considered to be a knowledge-creating cluster when all cluster firms indicated that they strengthened their skills and competences as a result of their participating in the cluster (Rutten and Oerlemans, 2009). The two explanatory conditions for tightness are formalization and focus. In a formalized cluster, knowledge creation (social interaction between engineers) follows strict rules and procedures. A focused cluster pursues clearly defined goals with clearly specified resources. The explanatory conditions for looseness are autonomy and slack. In an autonomous cluster, engineers are free to make their own decisions regarding how to achieve their goals and spend resources. A slack cluster allows engineers access to additional resources if they so require (Nohria and Gulati, 1997).

EVENTS STUDIED AS CASES

The 41 clusters (cases), or knowledge-creating events, on which data are available are not a homogeneous group. Some clusters include large firms as well as SMEs. As knowledge-creation dynamics may be different in SMEs-only clusters compared with mixed-firm-size clusters, exclusively SMEs-only clusters were defined as cases. The threshold for being an SME is having no more than 100 full-time equivalent (FTE) employees, which is the Dutch definition of SMEs. In other words, SMEs-only cluster is a scope condition of this study. But there are additional scope conditions. All firms are manufacturing firms and all are located in a high-tech region. This region (Eindhoven region) is characterized by strong social capital in its manufacturing industry (Rutten and Boekema, 2007). Finally, all firms are at least moderately innovative, or they would not have qualified for the cluster scheme. The findings of this study may thus be generalized to small networks of (at least) moderately knowledge-intensive manufacturing SMEs in high-tech regions with high levels of social capital. Think of such networks in the Munich, Grenoble and Bologna regions, to name but a few European examples (Romme, 2022; Rutten and Oerlemans, 2009).

Finally, cases were eliminated from the case population on the grounds of missing data. Obviously, one cannot learn from cases on which one has no or incomplete data. At least 75 per cent of a cluster's firms must have participated in the evaluation, with no missing data for any firm on the relevant questions in the questionnaire (see Table 12.1). Missing data are much more problematic in case-based studies than in variable-based studies. They severely limit what one can learn from cases, and thus frustrate the dialogue between ideas and evidence. It is far more advisable to drop cases with missing data than to compromise the quality of this dialogue. Dropping the cases with missing data resulted in a case population of 15 clusters. It matters not whether these 15 clusters are representative of the 102 clusters overall. In fact, they are not. The 15 clusters are a case population of its own, defined by the above scope conditions with findings generalizable as indicated above. A case population of 15 is completely unproblematic for a QCA study with four explanatory conditions.

QCA is largely agnostic with regard to the kind of data one uses and how they were collected. The evaluation study collected data through structured interviews, where an interviewer talked respondents through a Likert scale questionnaire of 101 questions. Respondents could clarify some of their answers with brief (qualitative) comments. Key firm and cluster characteristics (i.e., firm size, turnover, expenditure on research and development, cluster budget and cluster lifetime) were retrieved from project files (Rutten and Oerlemans, 2009). Based on the above definitions of the conditions, two questions were selected from the questionnaire to measure each condition (except for 'autonomy', which is measured with a single question). Respondent answers to both questions were aggregated with a logical AND to establish the presence or absence of the condition for a particular firm. Table 12.1 presents all measurements.

For calibration, the verbal labels of the Likert scales (very low, low, neither low nor high, high, very high) were used rather than their numerical values. Answering my reservations to fuzzy sets in QCA (see Chapter 9), I calibrated crisp sets only. However, I also did so because different respondents may have perceived their cluster differently. This makes comparing (and aggregating) Likert scores of different respondents somewhat speculative. In such situations, categorical differences (e.g., between neither low nor high versus high and very high) are more likely to have the same meaning than gradual

Table 12.1   *Measurements*

Outcome	Knowledge creation
Concept	Knowledge created in the cluster contributed to new products or the competences to develop them
Measurement	To what extent have the technological competences of your organization improved?
	To what extent did the collaboration yield new knowledge for your organization?
Condition	Formalized cluster
Concept	Formalizing interactions between individuals to make knowledge-creating behaviour comply with organizational goals
Measurement	To what extent did communication follow formal lines?
	To what extent did the cluster work on the basis of fixed rules and procedures?
Condition	Focused cluster
Concept	Focusing knowledge-creating behaviour on organizational goals
Measurement	To what extent were the objectives [of the cluster], as specified in the collaboration agreement, sufficiently clear?
	To what extent were the expected contributions [resources allocated] of the firms clear at the start of the project?
Condition	Autonomous cluster
Concept	Allowing individuals in the product development project to make their own decisions
Measurement	To what extent did you have the opportunity to allocate resources and perform work based on your own ideas?
Condition	Slack cluster
Concept	Giving individuals in the product development project access to surplus resources
Measurement	To what extent did your organization offer help, resources and facilities to support the project?
	To what extent did you have access to the knowledge of your partners [individuals] and their organizations?

differences (e.g., between high and very high). The following protocol was used to aggregate individual respondent scores into calibrated clusters (cases):

- To be calibrated 1, all respondents in a cluster must have answered '(very) high'.
- If only one respondent (firm) answered 'neither', the cluster is still calibrated 1, except for clusters with only two firms.

- If two or more respondents answered 'neither', the cluster is calibrated 0.
- If one or more respondents answered '(very) low', the cluster is calibrated 0.
- Formalization is calibrated as 'no absence of formalization'. Respondents answering that their cluster was neither formal nor informal suggest that formalization was not-absent. This calibrates the cluster as 1 (formalized cluster). It effectively lowers the semantical threshold for formalization, to account for the fact that formalization is not usually well pronounced in small teams.

SET ANALYSIS AND SOLUTION

The analysis of necessity (Table 12.2) identified no necessary conditions for the presence of knowledge creation in a cluster. The absence of focus (~focused cluster) is necessary for the absence of knowledge creation in a cluster. This suggests that, in the absence of a clear commitment to knowledge-creation goals, it is not possible for clusters to successfully create new knowledge.

Table 12.2   Necessary condition analysis

	Knowledge-creating Cluster		~Knowledge-creating Cluster	
	Consistency	Coverage	Consistency	Coverage
Focused cluster	0.82	1.00	0.00	0.00
Formalized cluster	0.55	0.67	0.75	0.33
Autonomous cluster	0.82	0.90	0.25	0.10
Slack cluster	0.82	0.90	0.25	0.10
~Focused cluster	0.18	0.33	1.00	0.67
~Formalized cluster	0.46	0.83	0.25	0.17
~Autonomous cluster	0.18	0.40	0.75	0.60
~Slack cluster	0.18	0.40	0.75	0.60

Table 12.3 shows the truth table for 'knowledge-creating cluster'. The first three rows are contradictory rows that must be resolved. In Row 1, only Cluster 22 is a not-knowledge-creating cluster, because one of its firms scored 'very low' on the question: 'To what extent have the technological competences of your organization improved?' However, elsewhere in the questionnaire, the same firm answered 'very high' on the question of whether it learnt-by-doing from participating in the cluster. This suggests that the firm did create new knowledge and that Cluster 22 may be recalibrated into a knowledge-creating cluster. This resolves the contradiction, and Row 1 is now sufficient for the outcome.

Row 2 features the absence of both loose-control conditions. Surprisingly, Cluster 11 is a knowledge-creating cluster. Archival data showed that the R&D intensity of the firms in Cluster 11 is low. R&D intensity expresses a firm's expenditure on research and development as a percentage of its turnover. The R&D intensities for the three firms in Cluster 11 are 1.3 per cent, N/A and 5.0 per cent – which is low. This suggests that Cluster 11's firms learnt new knowledge owing to their limited knowledge base rather than through exclusively tight control of their knowledge-creating process. Consequently, Row 2 is not sufficient. In Row 3, Cluster 16 is a not-knowledge-creating cluster, even though the row combines the presence of tight and loose control – suggesting that knowledge creation is possible. Archival data show that the project costs for Cluster 16 are low compared to other cluster projects. This suggests that the project was not particularly complicated and that, therefore, Cluster 16's firms did not learn new knowledge. Hence, Row 3 may be declared sufficient for the outcome. That Cluster 16 is a 'negative' case is unrelated to the explanatory conditions.

Having thus resolved the contradictory rows, we can set the remaining truth table parameters. As this is a small-N study, the frequency threshold is 1. As for directional assumptions, for all conditions their presence contributes to the emerging of causal power for knowledge creation. This produces a solution of three configurations. Doing the same for the analysis of not-knowledge-creation produces a solution of two configurations (see Figure 12.1).

INTERPRETING CAUSAL CLAIMS

All three configurations in the solution for 'knowledge creation' combine one tight and one loose control condition. This corroborates the configurational argument that knowledge creation requires both. The first two configurations in Figure 12.1 (Ia and Ib) suggest mandated self-control (on the part of the engineers doing the knowledge creation). The presence of 'focus' suggests that the cluster firms mandated their engineers to develop a new product. They set a goal for the engineers and allocated the necessary resources. Combined with 'autonomy' (Configuration Ia), engineers may use these resources at their own discretion. Combined with 'slack' (Configuration Ib), engineers are free to access additional resources when needed. Configuration II suggests regulated self-control, because here tight control comes from 'formalization' regulating engineer communication. 'Autonomy', again, suggests that engineers pursued product development at their own discretion. The solution for knowledge-creating cluster thus is summarized as:

$$[\text{focused} \bullet (\text{autonomous} + \text{slack})] + [\text{formalized} \bullet \text{autonomous}] \qquad (12.1)$$

Table 12.3   Truth table for knowledge-creating cluster

Row	Focused Cluster	Formalized Cluster	Autonomous Cluster	Slack Cluster	Number of Cases	Outcome	Confirming Cases	Contradictory Cases
1	1	1	1	1	4 (27%)	1	7; 12; 20	22
2	0	1	0	0	2 (40%)	0	5	11
3	1	0	0	1	2 (53%)	1	19	16
4	1	0	1	1	2 (67%)	1	2; 18	
5	0	0	1	0	1 (73%)	0	14	
6	0	1	0	1	1 (80%)	0	24	
7	1	0	1	0	1 (87%)	1	25	
8	0	1	1	0	1 (93%)	1	31	
9	0	1	1	1	1 (100%)	1	4	
10	0	0	0	0				
11	1	0	0	0				
12	1	1	0	0				
13	1	1	1	0				
14	0	0	0	1				
15	0	0	1	1				
16	1	1	0	1				

(intermediate solution)	knowledge creating clusters			~knowledge creating clusters	
	mandated self-control		regulated self-control	loss of direction	error of looseness
	Configuration Ia	Configuration Ib	Configuration II	Configuration III	Configuration IV
focused cluster	●	●		⊗	⊗
formalized cluster			●		⊗
autonomous cluster	●		●	⊗	
slack cluster		●			⊗
cases	2; 7; 12; 18; 20; 22; 25	4; 7; 12; 20; 22; 31	2; 7; 12; 16; 18; 19; 20; 22	5; 11; 24	14
raw coverage	0,64	0,55	0,73	0,75	0,25
unique coverage	0,09	0,18	0,18	0,75	0,25
consistency	1,00	1,00	1,00	1,00	1,00
solution coverage	1,00			1,00	
solution consistency	1,00			1,00	

● condition present   ⊗ condition absent   [BLANK] condition logically redundant

Figure 12.1   Solution table

At this point, it is useful to look at the complex solution. It has the following four configurations:

focused • autonomous • ~formalized   (12.2)

~focused • autonomous • formalized   (12.3)

focused • ~formalized • slack   (12.4)

focused • autonomous • slack   (12.5)

Notice how each configuration contains the presence of only one tightness condition. It is combined with the presence of two looseness conditions (Equation 12.5) or the presence of one looseness condition and the absence of a tightness condition (Equations 12.2, 12.3 and 12.4). This suggests that, while tightness and looseness are both necessary for knowledge creation, the emphasis is on looseness; that 'errors of tightness' are easily made.

The solution for not-knowledge-creating firms suggests that the causal power for knowledge creation is constrained in the absence of focus and autonomy (Configuration III in Figure 12.1) and in the absence of focus, formalization and slack (Configuration IV). Configuration IV suggests an 'error of looseness' because no tight control is present. Configuration III suggests a loss of direction. Direction does not follow from 'focus', nor can engineers choose their own direction as they have no autonomy.

Qualitative data are available for Cluster [case] 7 (knowledge-creating cluster) and Clusters 5 and 24 (not-knowledge-creating clusters) (you will need such data for all cases in a small-N study). Cluster 7 is covered by Configurations Ia, Ib and II, meaning the outcome is 'overdetermined' and that, in this example, Cluster 7 can be used to interpret all 'knowledge-creation' configurations (you will want a unique cluster [case] in each configuration to interpret the configuration into a causal explanation in a real study). In Cluster 7, 'focus' followed from clear agreements and a clear division of labour that allowed engineers to draw on their respective key competences. 'Formalization', though present, was not strongly developed. Only one person, the cluster manager, was in charge of the formal aspects of managing the cluster and he did not interfere in the knowledge-creation process itself. Engineers had considerable discretion ('autonomy') carrying out their tasks. 'Slack' followed from the high priority that firms attributed to the knowledge creation in their cluster. That is, tight governance ('focus' and 'formalization') legitimized the engineers to spend their time on the project and allowed them decision-making discretion and the use of slack resources. Tight governance thus set the top-down framework within which the alignment of engineer knowledge creation and organizational goals developed bottom-up. This suggests that the causal power of knowledge creation emerges from setting a framework (i.e., tight governance) at the start of the project, which allowed engineers to control their knowledge creation in a loose way during the project. That is, the emergence of causal power for knowledge creation is contingent on tight control being exercised first. Clusters 5 and 24 ('~knowledge-creating clusters') corroborate this explanation. In both clusters, agreements made at the start of the project were underspecified ('~focus') because firms underestimated the complexity of their projects. This required cluster coordinators to intervene repeatedly in the knowledge-creation process, which explains the lack of 'autonomy' that engineers experienced. Lack of 'focus' also reduced slack ('~slack') because firms did not appreciate the relevance of surplus resources. The absence of 'focus' thus led to a completely different – viz., negative – dynamic in these clusters. Because tight control was not exercised at the start of the project, knowledge creation lacked direction, requiring cluster coordinator interventions (exercising tight control) throughout the project. This frustrated engineers but failed to align knowledge creation with organizational goals, resulting in knowledge that was technologically too specific to be useful for the firms ('~knowledge creation').

The didactical point of the above discussion is to demonstrate what it means to 'go back' to the cases. In a real study, you will want to go back to more cases and corroborate the interpreted explanation with (conceptual) evidence from the literature (Furnari et al., 2021).

This suggests that the causal power for knowledge creation emerges from exercising tight and loose control, but only when tight control is exercised at the start of the project. This may be done through 'focus' (specifying objectives and resources) and 'formalization' (aligning organizational goals and knowledge creation through procedures). The evidence further suggests that exercising tight control during the project is counterproductive. Finally, while tight and loose control are both necessary but only jointly sufficient for knowledge creation in clusters, the emphasis must be on looseness.

GOING THROUGH ITERATIONS

QCA researchers find themselves going back and forth between the above steps all the time. Learning from cases is not a one-shot process. Dialoguing knowledge of cases, context and concepts leads to new insights throughout the research process and, more often than not, requires researchers to retrace their steps and redo parts of the analysis. For example, I not only changed the outcome from '0' to '1' in Rows 2 and 3, I also recalibrated Cluster 11 (Row 2) to a not-knowledge-creating cluster and recalibrated Cluster 22 (Row 1) and Cluster 16 (Row 3) to knowledge-creating clusters. Merely changing the outcome for these rows produces the following additional configuration in the solution: [formalized • ~slack]. But this configuration makes no sense at all. There is no reason that this configuration would make it possible for clusters to create knowledge. So I had to recalibrate and redo the analyses. The solution coverage evidenced that this additional configuration offers no additional explanation – because without it the solution coverage remained 1.00.

In sum, QCA has clearly defined steps, but how often one returns to each step, and in which particular order, is very much contingent on the research at hand. Learning from cases is an iterative process. Discussing a QCA study in a research paper, it is helpful to show at least some of the iterations – to show how one arrived at one's conclusions through learning from cases.

13. Capturing the logic and practice of QCA

Every method makes (implicit) assumptions on the nature of social reality, causality and our ability to know both. That is, every method philosophizes. Every method (implicitly) assumes a metaphysical position on what social reality is like, how we can know it, and, consequently, how we can make causal inferences and how they should be theorized into meaningful causal claims. In other words, there is a strong connection between philosophy, method and theorizing – and researchers need to understand this connection (Archer, 1995, pp. 16–17).

CAPTURING QCA'S LOGIC

Under the influence of correlational (variable-based) methods and their (neo-) positivist pedigree, the default metaphysical position of many social scientists is that of the unified empirical reality (see Chapter 1) (Abbott, 1988, 1998). This position rests on a number of assumptions:

- *Scientific realism.* Social reality is not merely a social construction. Once constructed, it exists (partially, at least) independent of the human agents populating it and of the social scientists studying it (Bhaskar [1975] 2008, p. 17).
- *Epistemic realism.* The concepts and definitions that social scientists use have a direct relationship with phenomena in social reality and (consequently) can be defined and measured more or less objectively (Bhaskar [1975] 2008, p. 18; Lawson, 2005). Empirical observations more or less accurately capture what social reality is like (Lakoff, 1987, pp. 203–5).
- *Ontological determinism.* If left to themselves, the same cause will always 'produce' the same outcome. That is, on an ontological level, there is a constant conjunction between cause and outcome. In a controlled environment (an experiment), this constant conjunction will manifest itself empirically (Beach and Pedersen, 2016, pp. 19–24).
- *Probabilistic causation.* The constant conjunction between cause and outcome will manifest itself in a probabilistic way in social reality. Because of the randomness in how social reality 'works', causes increase

the likelihood of the outcome. Observed empirical regularities (e.g., co-variation between independent and dependent variables) are validated against probabilistic criteria (e.g., statistical significance) (Goertz and Mahoney, 2012a, pp. 41–7; Lawson, 2005).

- *Variable-based theorizing.* Empirical regularities are theorized into causal effects using variable (correlational) language – for example, the higher the level of X, the higher the likelihood of Y (Goertz and Mahoney, 2012a, pp. 76–8).

The problems connected to the unified empirical reality have been abundantly discussed in Abbott (1988, 1992, 1998) and Bhaskar (1986; [1975] 2008; [1979] 2015) among others. Critical realists accept only the first assumption but flatly reject the next four (Archer, 1995, pp. 23–6; Gorski, 2018; Lawson, 2005). Instead, critical realists assume epistemic relativism. We cannot know social reality but through the lens of our theory- and value-laden concepts (Bhaskar [1975] 2008, p. 249). Nor do our concepts neatly map on phenomena in social reality. Concepts are products of our human minds and what we see in social reality is filtered by how our human minds allow us to see (social) reality (Lakoff, 1987, pp. 68–71). Consequently, empirical regularities are not so much observed but are a function of the concepts and measurement we use to see social reality. Seeing through the lens of different concepts produces different empirical regularities. This is why calibration matters. It makes concepts and their definitions explicit and gives meaning to what we see relative to these definitions (Ragin, 2000, p. 162). Furthermore, critical realists commit to an emergent view of social reality. Social reality is about becoming, not about being (Archer, 1995, pp. 135–7; Gerrits and Pagliarin, 2021). Because of this, every event (case) is a unique time- and place-contingent 'assemblage' of characteristics, context and human agents (Delanda, 2016). This position pulls the rug from under ontological determinism and, instead, suggests causality as a possibility; as the potential of a cause to 'produce' the outcome (Groff, 2013, pp. 76–7; 2016).

Causality, then, is the 'power to do' of human agents. They may exercise a causal power, but as other causal powers are also at work (because social reality is an open system), and because each event (case) is unique, there is no reason that (ontologically) the same cause should always produce the same outcome (Archer, 1995, pp. 54–5; Bhaskar [1975] 2008, p. 107). Causality as 'the power to do' of human agents also rejects probabilistic causation, because human agency is intentional and because (consequently) the interaction of the causal powers 'at work' is not a stochastic process (Decoteau, 2018). Interacting causal powers 'produce' a finite range of possible outcomes. Which of these outcomes will be actualized is not the result of probabilities (or randomness in social reality) but of possibilities. This is why social reality is limitedly diverse – because of how causal powers interact, some outcomes are more obvious (more possible), while others are actualized rarely, if ever.

Finally, QCA's notion of causality (statements of sufficiency and necessity) are of a very different nature than the causal effects of correlational (variable-based) methods (Goertz and Mahoney, 2012a, pp. 41–2; Ragin, 2008, pp. 111–12), which means that causal claims must be theorized (verbalized) differently. In sum, the connection between philosophy, method and theorizing is radically different in QCA versus correlational methods.

APPLYING QCA'S LOGIC

Ragin never committed QCA to a particular metaphysical position. However, his emphasis on calibration as giving meaning to data and on dialoguing knowledge of cases, context and concepts dovetails with the above critical realist position. Critical realism and its notion of causality as a power have been amply explained in Chapters 1 and 3. How to dialogue knowledge of cases, context and concepts has been demonstrated throughout this book, particularly in Chapters 11 and 12. The remainder of this chapter develops a heuristic to consistently apply critical realism throughout a QCA study. Revisiting Figure 1.1, the chapter identifies the phases of a QCA study and explains how researchers address them (see Figure 13.1).

Phase 1: Causal Powers and Constraints

QCA identifies causal powers that, when exercised, make it possible for human agents to achieve ('produce') the outcome. Causal powers are 'captured' in QCA as configurations (Boolean expressions) (see Chapter 3). QCA also identifies constraints; characteristics that, when present, compromise or prevent the emergence of causal power. Causal powers (and constraints) are real (ontological realism); they reside in the domain of the Real and exist independent of the human agents exercising them. QCA studies aim to identify causal powers (and constraints) and explain why or how they make the outcome possible. However, causal powers (the domain of the Real) cannot be directly observed; researchers can only see their consequences in the domain of the Actual (Bhaskar [1975] 2008, pp. 13–15). In this phase, researchers develop configurational research questions, based on their (conceptual and substantive) knowledge of which (explanatory) conditions contribute to the emergence of causal power to 'produce' the outcome of interest.

Phase 2: Events Studied as Cases

The domain of the Real is not directly observable because what we see is contingent on the (theory- and value-laden) concepts and measurements that we use to look at social reality (epistemic relativism). What we see are events, 'things' that happen in the domain of the Actual. Events are the outcome of multiple causal powers being 'at work' simultaneously. We cannot isolate the role of one causal power from the others because events are holistic and because social reality is an open system. We can study events as cases (as wholes). However, cases (events) are fluid; they often do not have clear beginnings and endings; they do not have clear boundaries to include and exclude human agents, organizations, geographical and social spaces, and so on. This is why casing is important. Dialoguing knowledge of cases (events), context and concepts, researchers must answer the questions: what is a case, and what is it a case of? (Ragin, 1992, 2009). That is, casing sets the boundaries (scope conditions) of events and turns them into analytically relevant cases.

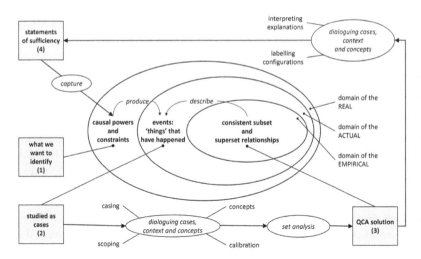

Figure 13.1   QCA going through the three domains of reality

Casing requires defining and redefining the concepts (i.e., explanatory, outcome, scope and confounding conditions) and measurements used to describe the case (event). The 'correct' definition depends on context, and arriving at the correct definition follows from dialoguing cases, context and concepts. Once we have the correct definition of a concept (i.e., what is an innovative region) and how a region's degree of innovation can be measured, we need to decide when a case is an instance of the concept (i.e., how do we know an innovative region when we see one) (Rubinson et al., 2019; Rutten and Rubinson, 2022). This is calibration. Calibration, too, is a dialogue. Trying to calibrate a case as being a member of the set of, for example, innovative regions (as having a degree of membership in the set of innovative regions) may lead a researcher to reconsider the definition of the concept (the set) and its measurement (Ragin, 2000, p. 171). Once the dialoguing has resulted in satisfactory casing, concepts and calibration, a researcher can proceed with the set analysis. They use QCA software to find consistent superset and subset relationships. Set analysis is not a one-shot process. It is a dialogue that may lead researchers to revise their casing, scoping, concepts and calibrations (Ragin, 2008, p. 82). QCA is an abductive method that deliberately blurs the distinction between the theoretical and empirical moments of a study.

Phase 3: The Solution

Given the role of dialoguing, it is clear that QCA's solution is not merely an empirical observation. Instead, it is a theory- and value-laden interpretation of reality (Ragin [1987] 2014, p. 17). Set relationships (the solution) belong to the domain of the Empirical; however, it is a different kind of empiricism than the unified empirical reality of correlational methods (Abbott, 1988, 1992, 1998). QCA's solution is a partial and perspectival description of social reality (the domain of the Actual). It must not be mistaken for causal statements or con-clusive empirical evidence (Rohlfing and Schneider, 2018). That is, in critical realism, the domain of the Empirical embraces the epistemic relativity of our (empirical) knowledge of social reality (the domain of the Actual). To get from the solution to causal claims requires another round of dialoguing.

Phase 4: Causal Claims

Researchers must explain why or how each configuration in the solution 'produces' the outcome. Again, a configuration 'captures' a causal power. Researchers must develop a plausible argument why or how exercising this power makes it possible for human agents to achieve the outcome (Ragin, 2000, p. 22). The connection to human agency is critical. Social reality (events in the domain of the Actual) do not just happen; they are not effects of blind or random forces but the consequence of (intentional) human agency (Archer, 1995, pp. 9, 15; Groff, 2013, p. 81; 2016, 2019). Events happen because human agents exercise causal powers. The causal explanation must be plausible in the light of knowledge of cases, context and concepts. This is what interpreting configurations entails and it requires researchers to go back to the cases (Ragin, 2008, pp. 125–7). The dialoguing in Phase 2 requires researchers to go back to the cases to interpret case-level knowledge into cross-case patterns – viz., truth table rows. Calibration assigns cases to a truth table row, and case-level knowledge of each case suggests that it belongs in this row. Case-level knowledge of each case in a row also informs whether the causal power that the row 'captures' (i.e., the configuration) plausibly makes the outcome possible. This is how researchers develop singular causal evidence into general causal claims on the level of truth table rows. Applying the QCA algorithm to the truth table in Phase 3 produces the solution, but this is a mathematical exercise that largely abstracts from case-level knowledge. The configurations in the solution are usually more parsimonious than the truth table rows. Going back to the cases, researchers must make it plausible that the more parsimonious configurations of the solution also 'capture' a causal power that makes the outcome possible. That is, Phase 4 is about reconnecting Boolean expressions (cross-case patterns – i.e., general causal evidence) to case-level knowledge (i.e., singular causal evidence) (Ragin [1987] 2014, pp. 164–71). This produces the plausible explanation of why or how each configuration in the solution explains the outcome. In fact, these explanations are configurational (mid-range) theories corroborated by case-level knowledge (Furnari et al., 2021). They theorize (explain) why or how the configuration (the causal power) 'produces' the outcome. Which is a two-step process – viz. (1) theorizing why or how causal power emerges from the explanatory conditions of the configuration; and (2) theorizing why or how, exercising this causal power makes it possible for human agents to achieve the outcome. Researchers must capture the meaning of each configuration (the nature of the causal power it describes) with an appropriate label (Rubinson et al., 2019). This is what makes the causal claim – that is, what makes it plausible that the solution captures causal powers that exist in the domain of the Real and that have manifested themselves in events in the domain of the Actual.

Finally, researchers formalize their causal claims in statements of necessity and sufficiency – that is, in QCA's causal language.

CONCLUSION

I started this book emphasizing the case-based logic of QCA as advocated by Charles Ragin. The logic of dialoguing knowledge of cases, context and concepts to interpret Boolean expressions into causal claims. This logic originated from and is most easily applied in small-N QCA studies, but is by no means impossible in large-N studies. However, recent years have seen a distinct move towards large-N applications of QCA where researchers have little or no recourse to cases. Instead, such studies rely heavily (sometimes exclusively) on QCA's parameters of fit and infer causal claims from the robustness of cross-case patterns. Ragin clearly rejects such practices, arguing that substantive interpretation (the dialogue) is critical for making causal claims in QCA (and case-based methods more generally). Rooting QCA in critical realism legitimizes Ragin's interpretive approach on ontological and epistemological grounds. Following the critical realist position on ontological realism and epistemic relativism, dialoguing knowledge of cases, context and concepts is the only way to get from Boolean expression (configurations, cross-case patterns) to plausible causal claims. In this logic, reducing QCA to a mathematical (algorithmic) exercise reduces it to an exclusively descriptive tool. This chapter outlined how there is a very strong connection between philosophy, method and theorizing. Researchers cannot not philosophize because (implicitly) every method assumes certain metaphysical positions. What counts as good practice, what counts as a valid inference, are contingent on the ontological and epistemological assumptions underlying a method. How to theorize empirical findings into causal claims is strongly informed by how these findings are arrived at.

In sum, QCA as a method 'negotiates' critical realism's three domains of reality in a systematic way (see Figure 13.1). Boolean expressions (set relationships) in the domain of the Empirical, interpreted from cases (i.e., events that happened in the domain of the Actual) capture causal powers that 'reside' in the domain of the Real. Researchers begin by postulating causal powers in the domain of the Real that have 'produced' events (in the domain of the Actual), which they study as cases. Drawing from empirical, contextual and conceptual knowledge, substantive interpretation (judgemental rationality) dialogues events into cases (casing) and calibrates them into sets. The truth table dialogues Boolean expressions describing single cases into Boolean expressions describing cross-case patterns. Substantive interpretation then dialogues these Boolean expressions into possibilistic causal claims about causal powers – and we have gone full circle, back to the domain of the Real. Although Ragin never committed QCA to any particular metaphysical position, his work has a clearly recognizable critical realist signature. Ragin's emphasis on substantive interpretation and his distinguishing between Boolean expressions and causal claims, commits to ontological realism paired with epistemic relativism. Casing and calibration is another commitment to ontological realism and dialoguing knowledge of cases, context and concepts confesses to judgemental rationality. From this, it follows that QCA's parameters of fit only distinguish between cross-case patterns that may and may not be interpreted into causal claims. Higher consistencies, PRI values, and so on, never make for better causal claims. Suggesting QCA's parameters of fit as mostly descriptive, rather than as evidencing the robustness of a constant conjunction between cause and outcome, is what makes QCA a qualitative method. A method where the validity of causal claims is a function of their substantive plausibility, rather than of empirical robustness. A method where case-level (singular) causal evidence trumps cross-case (general) causal evidence, which requires researchers to dialogue case-level and cross-case causal evidence. A method built around learning from cases.

References

Abbott, A. (1988). Transcending general linear reality. *Sociological Theory*, **6**(2), 169–86.

Abbott, A. (1992). From causes to events: notes on narrative positivism. *Sociological Methods & Research*, **20**(4), 428–55.

Abbott, A. (1998). The causal devolution. *Sociological Methods & Research*, **27**(2), 148–81.

Álamos-Concha, P., V. Pattyn and B. Rihoux et al. (2022). Conservative solutions for progress: on solution types when combing QCA with in-depth process tracing. *Quality & Quantity*, **56**(4), 1996–7.

Amrhein, V., S. Greenland and B. McShane (2019). Retire statistical significance. *Nature*, **257**(7748), 305–7.

Annoni, P. and L. Dijkstra (2017). The EU regional SPI: a measure of social progress in the EU regions [Methodological paper]. European Commission. Accessed 6 May 2024 at https://ec.europa.eu/regional_policy/information-sources/maps/social-progress/2016_en.

Archer, M. (1995). *Realist social theory: the morphogenetic approach*. Cambridge, UK: Cambridge University Press.

Asheim, B. and L. Coenen (2005). Knowledge bases and regional innovation systems: comparing Nordic clusters. *Research Policy*, **34**(8), 1173–90.

Baumgartner, M. (2015). Parsimony and causality. *Quality & Quantity*, **49**(2), 839–56.

Baumgartner, M. and A. Thiem (2020). Often trusted but never (properly) tested: evaluating Qualitative Comparative Analysis. *Sociological Methods & Research*, **49**(2), 279–311.

Beach, D. and R. Pedersen (2016). *Causal case study methods: foundations and guidelines for comparing, matching and tracing*. Ann Arbor, MI: University of Michigan Press.

Beach, D. and R. Pedersen (2018). Selecting appropriate cases when tracing causal mechanisms. *Sociological Methods & Research*, **47**(4), 837–71.

Bennat, T. (2021). High innovativeness of SMEs and the configuration of learning-by-doing, learning-by-using, learning-by-interacting, and learning-by-science: a regional comparison applying fuzzy set qualitative comparative analysis. *Journal of the Knowledge Economy*, **13**(2), 1666–91.

Bhaskar, R. (1986). *Scientific realism and human emancipation*. London: Verso.

Bhaskar, R. ([1975] 2008). *A realist theory of science*. London: Verso.

Bhaskar, R. ([1979] 2015). *The possibility of naturalism: a philosophical critique of the contemporary human sciences*. London: Verso.

Brady, H. (2010). Doing good and doing better: how far does the quantitative template get us? In H. Brady and D. Collier (eds), *Rethinking social inquiry: diverse tools, shared standards*. Lanham, MD: Rowman & Littlefield, pp. 67–82.

Butler, R., D. Price, P. Coates and R. Pike (1998). Organizing for innovation: tight or loose control. *Long Range Planning*, **31**(5), 775–82.

Byrne, D. (2005). Complexity, configurations and cases. *Theory, Culture & Society*, **22**(5), 95–111.

Collier, D., H. Brady and J. Seawright (2010). Sources of leverage in causal inference: toward an alternative view of methodology. In H. Brady and D. Collier (eds), *Rethinking social inquiry: diverse tools, shared standards*. Lanham, MD: Rowman & Littlefield, pp. 161–99.

Decoteau, C. (2018). Conjunctures and assemblages: approaches to multicausal explanation in the human sciences. In T. Rutzou and G. Steinmetz (eds), *Critical realism, history, and philosophy in the social sciences*. Bingley: Emerald, pp. 89–118.

Delanda, M. (2016). *Assemblage theory*. Edinburgh: Edinburgh University Press.

Duşa, A. (2022). Critical tension: sufficiency and parsimony in QCA. *Sociological Methods & Research*, **51**(2), 541–65.

Eisenhardt, K. (2021). What is the Eisenhardt method, really? *Strategic Organization*, **19**(1), 147–60.

Elder-Vass, D. (2005). Emergence and the critical realist account of cause. *Journal of Critical Realism*, **4**(2), 315–38.

Elder-Vass, D. (2010). *The causal power of social structures: emergence, structure and agency*. Cambridge, UK: Cambridge University Press.

European Commission (2016). *European Regional Innovation Scoreboard 2016*. Accessed 8 May 2024 at https://data.europa.eu/doi/10.2873/84730.

European Commission (2017). *European Regional Innovation Scoreboard 2017*. Accessed 8 May 2024 at https://data.europa.eu/doi/10.2873/593800.

Faulconbridge, J. (2014). Putting the individual in context: paths, capitals and topologies of learning. *Prometheus: Critical Studies in Innovation*, **32**(1), 75–82.

Finn, V. (2022). A qualitative assessment of QCA: method stretching in large-N studies and temporality. *Quality & Quantity*, **56**(5), 3815–30.

Fiss, P. (2011). Building better causal theories: a fuzzy set approach to typologies in organization research. *Academy of Management Journal*, **54**(2), 393–420.

Florida, R. (2002). *The rise of the creative class, and how it's transforming work, leisure, community and everyday life*. New York: Basic Books.

Florida, R., P. Adler and C. Mellander (2017). The city as innovation machine. *Regional Studies*, **51**(1), 86–96.

Furnari, S., D. Crilly and V. Misangyi et al. (2021). Capturing causal complexity: heuristics for configurational theorizing. *Academy of Management Review*, **46**(4), 778–99.

Gebert, D., S. Boerner and E. Kearney (2010). Fostering team innovation: why is it important to combine opposing action strategies? *Organization Science*, **21**(3), 593–608.

Gerrits, L. and S. Pagliarin (2021). Social and causal complexity in Qualitative Comparative Analysis (QCA): strategies to account for emergence. *International Journal of Social Research Methodology*, **24**(4), 501–14.

Gerrits, L. and S. Verweij (2016). Qualitative Comparative Analysis as a method for evaluating complex cases: an overview of literature and stepwise guide with empirical application. *Zeitschrift für Evaluation*, **15**(1), 7–22.

Gioia, D., K. Corley and A. Hamilton (2013). Seeking qualitative rigor in inductive research: notes on the Gioia methodology. *Organizational Research Methods*, **16**(1), 15–31.

Goertz, G. (2017). *Multimethod research, causal mechanisms, and case studies: an integrated approach*. Princeton, NJ: Princeton University Press.

Goertz, G. (2020). *Social science concepts and measurements*. Princeton, NJ: Princeton University Press.

Goertz, G. and J. Mahoney (2012a). *A tale of two cultures: qualitative and quantitative research in the social sciences*. Princeton, NJ: Princeton University Press.

Goertz, G. and J. Mahoney (2012b). Concepts and measurements: ontology and epistemology. *Social Science Information*, **51**(2), 205–16.

Gorski, P. (2018). After positivism: critical realism and historical sociology. In T. Rutzou and G. Steinmetz (eds), *Critical realism, history, and philosophy in the social sciences*. Bingley: Emerald, pp. 23–46.

Greckhamer, T., S. Furnari, P. Fiss and R. Aguilera (2018). Studying configurations with qualitative comparative analysis: best practices in strategy and organization research. *Strategic Organization*, **16**(4), 482–95.

Greckhamer, T., V. Misangyi and P. Fiss (2013). The two QCAs: from a small-N to a large-N set-theoretic approach. In P. Fiss, B. Cambré and A. Marx (eds), *Configurational theory and methods in organizational research*. Bingley: Emerald, pp. 49–76.

Grillitsch, M., M. Sotarauta and B. Asheim et al. (2023). Agency and economic change in regions: identifying routes to new path development using qualitative comparative analysis. *Regional Studies*, **57**(8), 145368.

Groff, R. (2013). *Ontology revisited: metaphysics in social and political philosophy*. London: Routledge.

Groff, R. (2016). Causal mechanisms and the philosophy of causation. *Journal for the Theory of Social Behaviour*, **47**(3), 286–305.

Groff, R. (2019). Sublating the free will problematic: powers, agency and causal determination. *Synthese*, **196**(1), 179–200.

Haesebrouck, T. and E. Thomann (2022). Introduction: causation, inferences, and solution types in configurational comparative methods. *Quality & Quantity*, **56**(4), 1867–88.

Hassink, R. and C. Klaerding (2012). The end of the learning region as we knew it: towards learning in space. *Regional Studies*, **46**(8), 1055–66.

Hedström, P. and P. Ylikoski (2010). Causal mechanisms in the social sciences. *Annual Review of Sociology*, **36**(1), 49–67.

Howells, J. (2012). The geography of knowledge: never so close but never so far apart. *Journal of Economic Geography*, **12**(5), 1003–20.

King, G., R. Keohane and S. Verba (1994). *Designing social inquiry: scientific inference in qualitative research*. Princeton, NJ: Princeton University Press.

Lagendijk, A. (2006). Learning from conceptual flow in regional studies: framing present debates, unbracketing past debates. *Regional Studies*, **40**(4), 385–99.

Lakoff, G. (1973). Hedges: a study in meaning criteria and the logic of fuzzy concepts. *Journal of Philosophical Logic*, **2**(4), 458–508.

Lakoff, G. (1987). *Women, fire and dangerous things: what categories reveal about the mind*. Chicago, IL: University of Chicago Press.

Lakoff, G. (2014). Set-theory and fuzzy sets: their relationship to natural language – an interview with George Lakoff. *Qualitative & Multi-Method Research*, **12**(1), 9–14.

Lawson, T. (2005). Economics and critical realism: a perspective on modern economics. In G. Steinmetz (ed.), *The politics of method in the human sciences: positivism and its epistemological others*. Durham, NC: Duke University Press, pp. 366–92.

Lucas, S. and A. Szatrowski (2014). Qualitative comparative analysis in critical perspective. *Sociological Methodology*, **44**(1), 1–79.

Mackie, J. (1965). Causes and conditions. *American Philosophical Quarterly*, **2**(4), 245–64.

Mahoney, J. (2001). Beyond correlational analysis: recent innovations in theory and method (essay). *Sociological Forum*, **16**(3), 575–93.

Mahoney, J. (2008). Toward a unified theory of causality. *Comparative Political Studies*, **41**(4/5), 412–36.

Mahoney, J. and L. Acosta (2022). A regularity theory of causality for the social sciences. *Quality & Quantity*, **56**(4), 1889–911.

Mahoney, J. and R. Barrenechea (2019). The logic of counterfactual analysis in case-study explanation. *The British Journal of Sociology*, **70**(1), 306–38.

Mahoney, J. and G. Goertz (2006). A tale of two cultures: contrasting quantitative and qualitative research. *Political Analysis*, **14**(3), 227–49.

Marx, A., B. Cambré and B. Rihoux (2013). Crisp-set Qualitative Comparative Analysis in organizational studies. In P. Fiss, B. Cambré and A. Marx (eds), *Configurational theory and methods in organizational research*. Bingley: Emerald, pp. 23–48.

Mello, P. (2021). *Qualitative comparative analysis: an introduction to research design and application*. Washington, DC: Georgetown University Press.

Morgan, K. (1997). The learning region: institutions, innovation and regional renewal. *Regional Studies*, **31**(5), 491–503.

Morgan, K. (2004). The exaggerated death of geography: learning, proximity and territorial innovation systems. *Journal of Economic Geography*, **4**(1), 3–21.

Nohria, N. and R. Gulati (1997). What is the optimum amount of slack? A study of the relationship between slack and innovation in multinational firms. *European Management Journal*, **15**(6), 603–11.

Nonaka, I. (1994). A dynamic theory of organizational knowledge creation. *Organization Science*, **5**(1), 14–37.

Oana, I. and C. Schneider (2024). A robustness test protocol for applied QCA: theory and R software application. *Sociological Methods & Research*, **53**(1), 57–88.

Oana, I., C. Schneider and E. Thomann (2021). *Qualitative comparative analysis using R: a beginner's guide*. Cambridge, UK: Cambridge University Press.

Pagliarin, S., S. La Mendola and B. Vis (2023). The 'qualitative' in qualitative comparative analysis (QCA): research moves, case-intimacy, and face-to-face interviews. *Quality & Quantity*, **57**(1), 458–507.

Pappas, I. and A. Woodside (2021). Fuzzy-set Qualitative Comparative Analysis (fsQCA): guidelines for research practice in information systems. *International Journal of Information Management*, **58**, 102310.

Porpora, D. (2018). Critical realism as a relational sociology. In F. Dépelteau (ed.), *The Palgrave handbook of relational sociology*. London: Palgrave Macmillan, pp. 413–29.

Pula, B. (2021). The logico-formalist turn in comparative and case study methods: a critical realist critique. *International Journal of Social Research Methodology*, **24**(6), 739–51.

Punstein, A. and J. Glückler (2020). In the mood for learning? How thought collectives of designers and co-engineers create innovations. *Journal of Economic Geography*, **20**(2), 543–70.

Ragin, C. ([1987] 2014). *The comparative method: moving beyond qualitative and quantitative strategies*. Oakland, CA: University of California Press.

Ragin, C. (1992). 'Casing' and the process of social inquiry. In C. Ragin and H. Becker (eds), *What is a case? Exploring the foundations of social inquiry*. Cambridge, UK: Cambridge University Press, pp. 217–26.

Ragin, C. (2000). *Fuzzy-set social science*. Chicago, IL: University of Chicago Press.

Ragin, C. (2008). *Redesigning social inquiry: fuzzy sets and beyond*. Chicago, IL: University of Chicago Press.

Ragin, C. (2009). Reflections on casing and case-oriented research. In D. Byrne and C. Ragin (eds), *The SAGE handbook of case-based methods*. London: SAGE, pp. 522–34.

Ragin, C. (2014). Comment: Lucas and Szatrowski in critical perspective. *Sociological Methodology*, **44**(1), 80–94.

Ragin, C. (2023). *Analytical induction for social research*. Oakland, CA: University of California Press.

Ragin, C., S. Davey and A. Corcaci (2023). *fsQCA 4.1* [Software program]. Accessed 20 April 2024 at https://compasss.org/software/.

Ragin, C. and P. Fiss (2017). *Intersectional inequality: race, class, test scores and poverty*. Chicago, IL: University of Chicago Press.

Rohlfing, I. (2018). Power and false negatives in Qualitative Comparative Analysis: foundations, simulation and estimation for empirical studies. *Political Analysis*, **26**(1), 72–89.

Rohlfing, I. and C. Schneider (2018). A unifying framework for causal analysis in set-theoretic multimethod research. *Sociological Methods & Research*, **47**(1), 37–63.

Rohlfing, I. and C. Zuber (2021). Check your truth conditions! Clarifying the relationship between theories of causation and social science methods for causal inference. *Sociological Methods & Research*, **50**(4), 1623–59.

Romme, A. (2022). Against all odds: how Eindhoven emerged as a deeptech ecosystem. *Systems*, **10**(4), 119.

Rubinson, C., L. Gerrits, R. Rutten and T. Greckhamer (2019). Avoiding common errors in QCA: a short guide for new practitioners. Accessed 3 May 2024 at Compasss.org/wp-content/uploads/2019/07/Common_Errors_in_QCA.pdf.

Russo, I. and I. Confente (2019). From dataset to qualitative comparative analysis – challenges and tricky points: a research note on contrarian case analysis and data calibration. *Australasian Marketing Journal*, **27**(1), 129–35.

Rutten, R. (2014). Learning in socio-spatial context: an individual perspective. *Prometheus: Critical Studies in Innovation*, **32**(1), 67–74.

Rutten, R. (2017). Beyond proximities: the socio-spatial dynamics of knowledge creation. *Progress in Human Geography*, **41**(2), 159–77.

Rutten, R. (2019). Openness values and regional innovation: a set-analysis. *Journal of Economic Geography*, **19**(6), 1211–32.

Rutten, R. (2020). Comparing causal logics: a configurational analysis of proximities using simulated data. *Zeitschrift für Wirtschafstgeographie*, **64**(3), 134–48.

Rutten, R. (2022). Applying and assessing large-N QCA: causality and robustness from a critical realist perspective. *Sociological Methods & Research*, **51**(3), 1211–43.

Rutten, R. (2023). Uncertainty, possibility and causal power in QCA. *Sociological Methods & Research*, **52**(4), 1707–36.

Rutten, R. and F. Boekema (2007). Regional social capital: embeddedness, innovation networks and regional economic development. *Technological Forecasting and Social Change*, **74**(9), 1834–46.

Rutten, R. and L. Oerlemans (2009). Temporary inter-organisational collaboration as a driver of regional innovation: an evaluation. *International Journal of Innovation and Regional Development*, **1**(3), 211–34.

Rutten, R. and C. Rubinson (2022). A vocabulary for QCA. Accessed 2 May 2024 at Compasss.org/wp-content/uploads/2023/02/vocabulary.pdf.

Schneider, C. and C. Wagemann (2012). *Set-theoretic methods for the social sciences: a guide to Qualitative Comparative Analysis*. Cambridge, UK: Cambridge University Press.

Shearmur, R. (2011). Innovation, regions and proximity: from neo-regionalism to spatial analysis. *Regional Studies*, **45**(9), 1225–43.

Shearmur, R. (2012). Are cities the font of innovation? A critical review of the literature on cities and innovation. *Cities*, **29**(Supplement), S9–S18.

Skaaning, S. (2011). Assessing the robustness of crisp and fuzzy-set QCA results. *Sociological Methods & Research*, **40**(2), 391–408.

Smithson, J. and J. Verkuilen (2006). *Fuzzy set theory applications in the social sciences*. Thousand Oaks, CA: SAGE.

Smithson, M. (1987). *Fuzzy set analysis for behavioral and social sciences*. New York: Springer.

Thomann, E. and M. Maggetti (2020). Designing research with qualitative comparative analysis (QCA): approaches, challenges, tools. *Sociological Methods & Research*, **49**(2), 356–86.

Vaisey, S. (2010). QCA 3.0: The 'Ragin revolution' continues. *Social Forces*, **88**(40), 1934–6.

Wasserstein, R., A. Schirm and N. Lazar (2019). Moving to a world beyond '$p < 0.05$'. *The American Statistician*, **73**(S1), 1–19.

Zadeh, L. (1965). Fuzzy sets. *Information and Control*, **8**(3), 338–53.

Zadeh, L. (1972). A fuzzy-set theoretic interpretation of linguistic hedges. *Journal of Cybernetics*, **2**(3), 4–34.

Appendix: resources

SOFTWARE

Set analysis, such as truth table minimization and the analysis of necessity, must be performed with software. The two principal software packages currently in use are the fsQCA software from Charles Ragin himself and the R package developed by Adrian Dușa. Both packages can be downloaded free of charge from the compasss.org website (https://compasss.org/software/). Working with drop-down menus makes Ragin's fsQCA software very easy to use. The R package for QCA has automated many more functions but may be intimidating for users unfamiliar with the R environment. Both software packages are available for Windows and iMac. They have an equal status within the QCA community, perform the same calculations, and produce the exact same results. The fsQCA software comes with a easy-to-read manual. This software is a bit picky in that it only reads '.CSV' files, demands that the first column in the spreadsheet always lists the cases, and only reads letters and numbers. Deviating from these rules causes the software to crash. So far, I have always worked with the fsQCA software. The most up-to-date self-study guide for R is the handbook *Qualitative Comparative Analysis Using R: A Beginner's Guide*, written by Iona Oana, Carsten Schneider and Eva Thomann (Cambridge University Press, 2021).

COMPASSS.ORG

COMPASSS (http://www.compasss.org) is the international, interdisciplinary research network of methodologists and practitioners of systematic cross-case comparative analysis, including QCA. Founded in 2003 by Benoît Rihoux (UC Louvain), COMPASSS is now directed by Claude Rubinson (University of Houston-Downtown). Check this website for updates on forthcoming QCA conferences, workshops and training, subscribe to its newsletter, and browse its various resources, including tutorials, research memos, bibliographies and archive of working papers.

FURTHER READING

For this section, I have borrowed from the 'suggestions for further reading' from my note 'A vocabulary for QCA' (2022), which I co-authored with Claude Rubinson.

This book gives a solid introduction to QCA, but there is so much more to read. For a good understanding of QCA, case-based methods in general and the critical realist philosophy that I draw from, I warmly recommend the following books and papers. And they are merely the tip of the iceberg of good QCA works available.

QCA Essentials

Ragin, C. ([1987] 2014). *The comparative method: moving beyond qualitative and quantitative strategies*. Oakland, CA: University of California Press.
Ragin, C. (2000). *Fuzzy-set social science*. Chicago, IL: University of Chicago Press.
Ragin, C. (2008). *Redesigning social inquiry: fuzzy sets and beyond*. Chicago, IL: University of Chicago Press.

QCA Quick References

Rubinson, C., L. Gerrits, R. Rutten and T. Greckhamer (2019). Avoiding common errors in QCA: a short guide for new practitioners. Accessed 3 May 2024 at Compasss.org/wp-content/uploads/2019/07/Common_Errors_in_QCA.pdf.
Rutten, R. and C. Rubinson (2022). A vocabulary for QCA. Accessed 2 May 2024 at Compasss.org/wp-content/uploads/2023/02/vocabulary.pdf.

Other QCA Handbooks

Duşa, A. (2019). *QCA with R: a comprehensive resource*. Cham: Springer.
Mello, P. (2021). *Qualitative comparative analysis: an introduction to research design and application*. Washington, DC: Georgetown University Press.
Oana, I., C. Schneider and E. Thomann (2021). *Qualitative comparative analysis using R: a beginner's guide*. Cambridge, UK: Cambridge University Press.
Schneider, C. and C. Wagemann (2012). *Set-theoretic methods for the social sciences: a guide to Qualitative Comparative Analysis*. Cambridge, UK: Cambridge University Press.

Set-theoretical Versus Correlational Methods

Goertz, G. and J. Mahoney (2012). *A tale of two cultures: qualitative and quantitative research in the social sciences*. Princeton, NJ: Princeton University Press.
Mahoney, J. and G. Goertz (2006). A tale of two cultures: contrasting quantitative and qualitative research. *Political Analysis*, **14**(3), 227–49.

Rutten, R. (2020). Comparing causal logics: a configurational analysis of proximities using simulated data. *Zeitschrift für Wirtschafstgeographie*, **64**(3), 134–48.

Designing Research with QCA

Goertz, G. (2017). *Multimethod research, causal mechanisms, and case studies: an integrated approach*. Princeton, NJ: Princeton University Press.

Thomann, E. and M. Maggetti (2020). Designing research with qualitative comparative analysis (QCA): approaches, challenges, tools. *Sociological Methods & Research*, **49**(2), 356–86.

Concepts and Measurements

Goertz, G. (2020). *Social science concepts and measurements*. Princeton, NJ: Princeton University Press.

Goertz, G. and J. Mahoney (2012). Concepts and measurements: ontology and epistemology. *Social Science Information*, **51**(2), 205–16.

Robustness

Oana, I. and C. Schneider (2024). A robustness test protocol for applied QCA: theory and R software application. *Sociological Methods & Research*, **53**(1), 57–88.

Rutten, R. (2022). Applying and assessing large-N QCA: causality and robustness from a critical realist perspective. *Sociological Methods & Research*, **51**(3), 1211–43.

Skaaning, S. (2011). Assessing the robustness of crisp and fuzzy-set QCA results. *Sociological Methods & Research*, **40**(2), 391–408.

Presenting QCA

Rubinson, C. (2019). Presenting qualitative comparative analysis: notation, tabular layout, and visualization. *Methodological Innovations*, **12**(2), 1–22.

Critical Realism

Collier, A. (1994). *An introduction to Roy Bhaskar's philosophy*. London: Verso.

Elder-Vass, D. (2010). *The causal power of social structures: emergence, structure and agency*. Cambridge, UK: Cambridge University Press.

Groff, R. (2016). Causal mechanisms and the philosophy of causation. *Journal for the Theory of Social Behaviour*, **47**(3), 286–305.

Index